ANITA BLAKE
The Laughing Corpse

ANIMATOR

ANITA BLAKE, VAMPIRE HUNTER: THE LAUGHING CORPSE BOOK 1 — ANIMATOR. Contains material originally published in magazine form as ANITA BLAKE: THE LAUGHING CORPSE — ANIMATOR #1-5. First printing 2009. Hardcover ISBN# 978-0-7851-3632-3. Softcover ISBN# 978-0-7851-3527-2. Published by MARVEL PUBLISHING, INC., a subsidiary of MARVEL ENTERTAINMENT, INC. OFFICE OF PUBLICATION: 417 5th Avenue, New York, NY 10016. Copyright © 2008 and 2009 Laurell K. Hamilton. All rights reserved. Hardcover: $19.99 per copy in the U.S. (GST #R127032852). Softcover: $16.99 per copy in the U.S. (GST #R127032852). Canadian Agreement #40668537. Anita Blake: Vampire Hunter and all characters featured in this issue and the distinctive names and likenesses thereof, and all related indicia are trademarks of Laurell K. Hamilton. Marvel, Wolverine, Captain America, Thor, the Incredible Hulk, Spider-Man and the Fantastic Four, and their distinctive likenesses are TM and (c) 2009 Marvel Entertainment, Inc. and it's subsidiaries. All rights reserved. No similarity between any of the names, characters, persons, and/or institutions in this magazine with those of any living or dead person or institution is intended, and any such similarity which may exist is purely coincidental. **Printed in the U.S.A. ALAN** FINE, CEO Marvel Toys & Publishing Divisions and CMO Marvel Characters, Inc.; JIM SOKOLOWSKI, Chief Operating Officer; DAVID GABRIEL, SVP of Publishing Sales & Circulation; DAVID BOGART, SVP of Business Affairs & Talent Management; MICHAEL PASCIULLO, VP Merchandising & Communications; JIM O'KEEFE, VP of Operations & Logistics; DAN CARR, Executive Director of Publishing Technology; JUSTIN F. GABRIE, Director of Publishing & Editorial Operations; SUSAN CRESPI, Editorial Operations Manager; ALEX MORALES, Publishing Operations Manager; STAN LEE, Chairman Emeritus. For information regarding advertising in Marvel Comics or on Marvel.com, please contact Mitch Dane, Advertising Director, at mdane@marvel.com. For Marvel subscription inquiries, please call 800-217-9158.

10 9 8 7 6 5 4 3 2 1

ANITA BLAKE
The Laughing Corpse
ANIMATOR

WRITER . . . . LAURELL K. HAMILTON

ADAPTATION . . . . JESS RUFFNER-BOOTH

ART . . . . RON LIM

COLORS . . . . JOEL SEGUIN & JUNE CHUNG

LETTERS . . . . BILL TORTOLINI

ASSISTANT EDITOR . . . . JORDAN D. WHITE

EDITOR . . . . MICHAEL HORWITZ

SENIOR EDITORS . . . . MARK PANICCIA & RALPH MACCHIO

SPECIAL THANKS TO JONATHON GREEN, MELISSA MCALISTER & ANNE TREDWAY

COLLECTION EDITOR . . . . CORY LEVINE

EDITORIAL ASSISTANT . . . . ALEX STARBUCK

ASSISTANT EDITOR . . . . JOHN DENNING

EDITORS, SPECIAL PROJECTS . . . . JENNIFER GRÜNWALD & MARK D. BEAZLEY

SENIOR EDITOR, SPECIAL PROJECTS . . . . JEFF YOUNGQUIST

SENIOR VICE PRESIDENT OF SALES . . . . DAVID GABRIEL

SENIOR VICE PRESIDENT OF STRATEGIC DEVELOPMENT . . . . . RUWAN JAYATILLEKE

PRODUCTION . . . . JERRY KALINOWSKI

BOOK DESIGN . . . . SPRING HOTELING

ST. LOUIS ISN'T JUST A CITY OF THE LIVING ANYMORE. VAMPIRES AND WEREWOLVES PROWL THE BACK ALLEYS AND QUARTERS OF THIS BEAUTIFUL AND DAMNED CITY, FEARING NOTHING...NOTHING, THAT IS, EXCEPT FOR ANITA BLAKE, THE EXECUTIONER. A COURT-APPOINTED VAMPIRE EXECUTIONER, ANITA REMINDS THESE MONSTERS THAT THE LAWS OF MAN APPLY TO THE UNDEAD...

BUT ANITA ISN'T ONLY KNOWN FOR HER DEADLY TALENTS; SHE IS ALSO AN ANIMATOR, CAPABLE OF RESURRECTING THE RECENTLY DECEASED AS ZOMBIES. RECOVERING FROM A CASE INVOLVING THE PREVIOUS VAMPIRIC MASTER OF THE CITY, ANITA'S VACATION IS CUT SHORT WHEN HER MANAGER OFFERS HER WHAT MAY BE THE STRANGEST ASSIGNMENT OF HER CAREER...

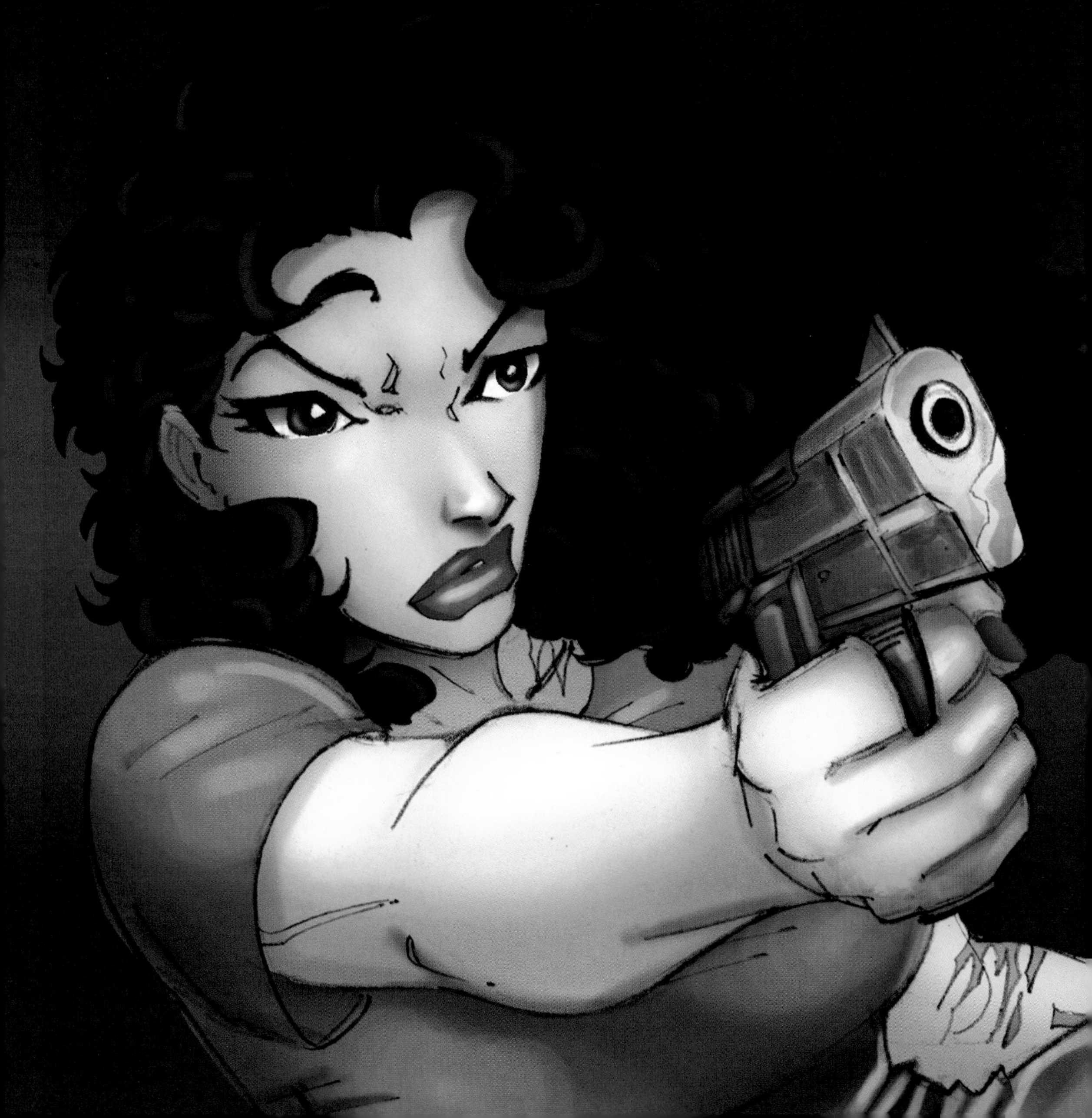

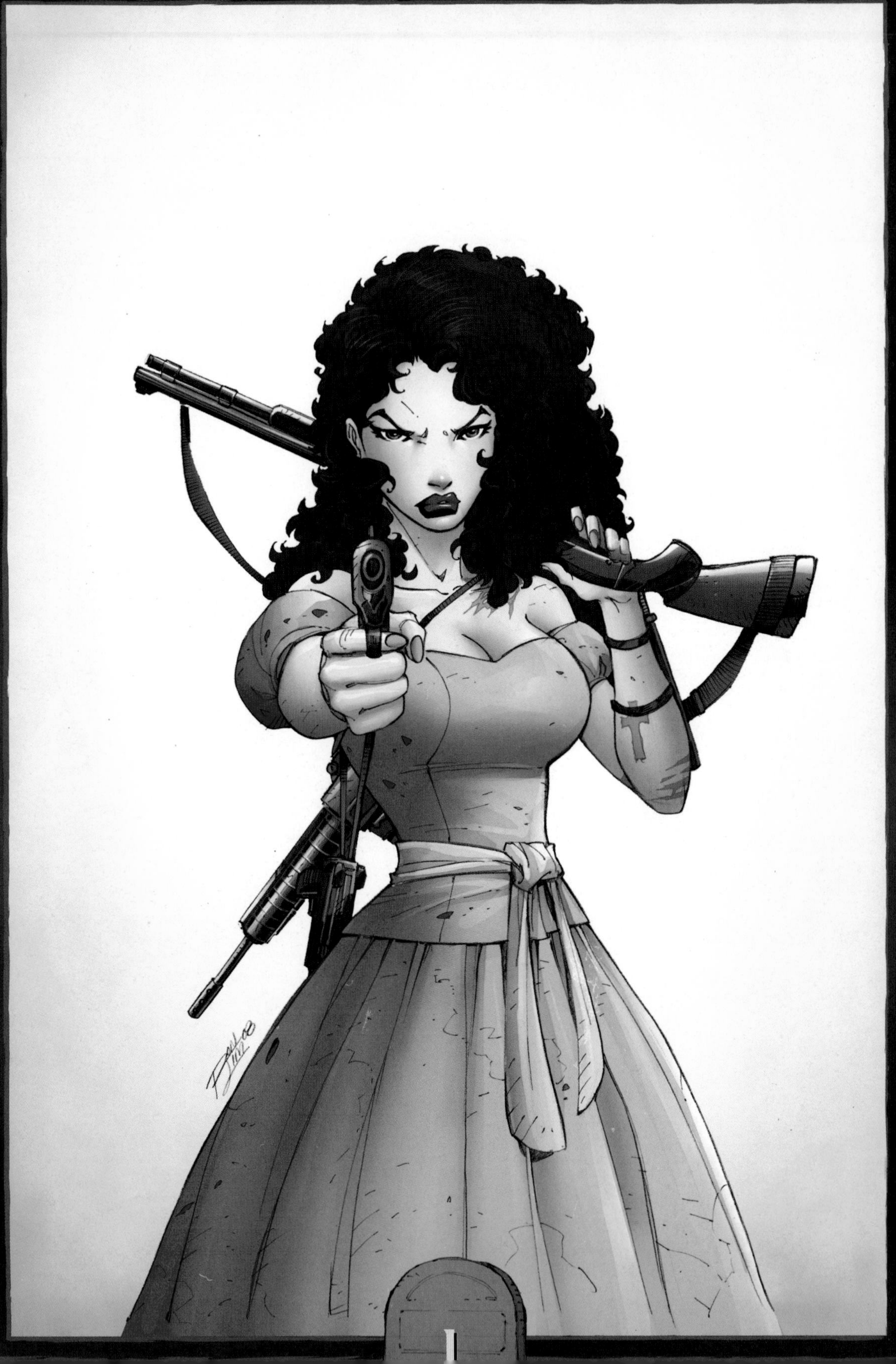
I

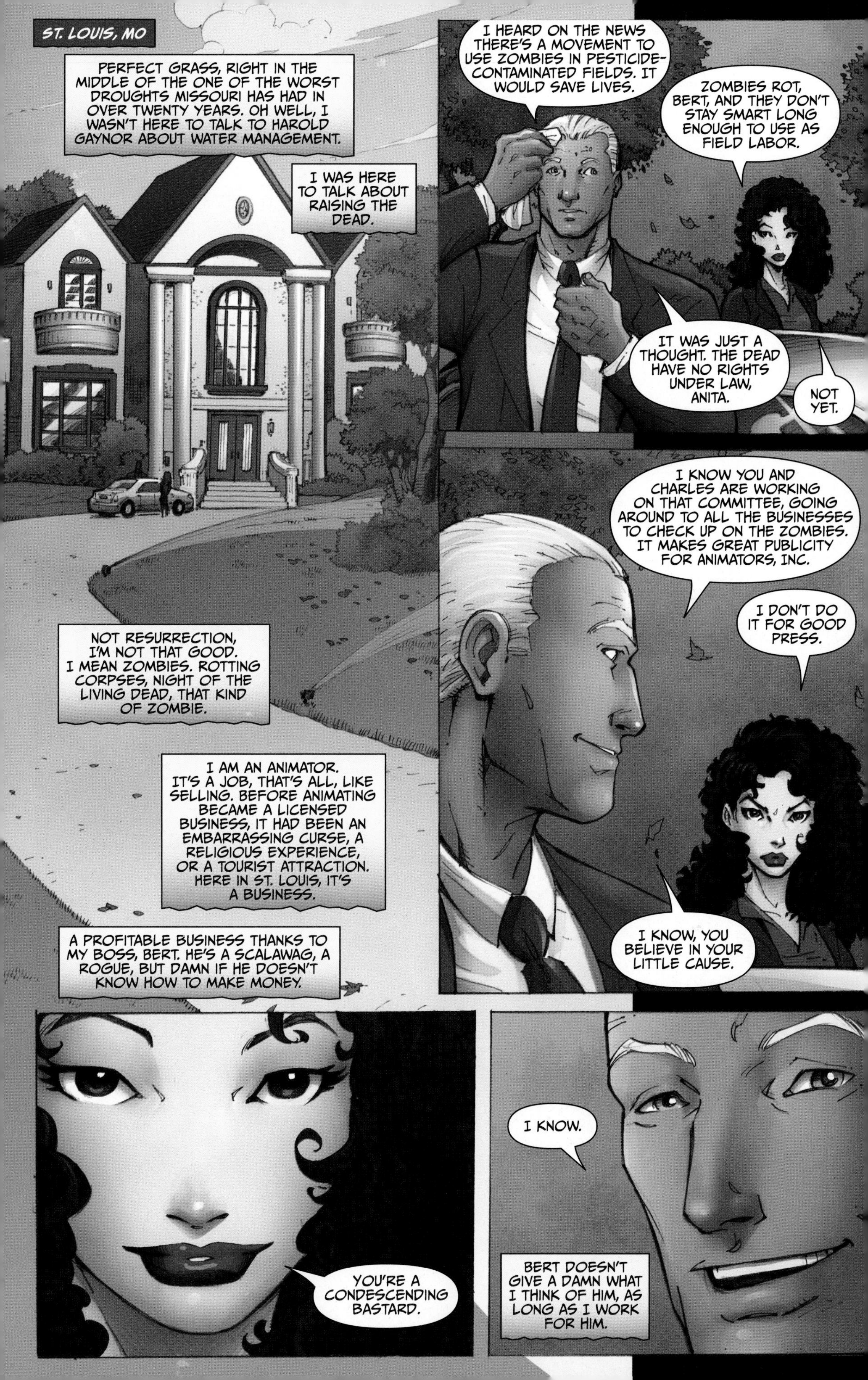
ST. LOUIS, MO
PERFECT GRASS, RIGHT IN THE MIDDLE OF THE ONE OF THE WORST DROUGHTS MISSOURI HAS HAD IN OVER TWENTY YEARS. OH WELL, I WASN'T HERE TO TALK TO HAROLD GAYNOR ABOUT WATER MANAGEMENT.
I WAS HERE TO TALK ABOUT RAISING THE DEAD.
NOT RESURRECTION, I'M NOT THAT GOOD. I MEAN ZOMBIES. ROTTING CORPSES, NIGHT OF THE LIVING DEAD, THAT KIND OF ZOMBIE.
I AM AN ANIMATOR. IT'S A JOB, THAT'S ALL, LIKE SELLING. BEFORE ANIMATING BECAME A LICENSED BUSINESS, IT HAD BEEN AN EMBARRASSING CURSE, A RELIGIOUS EXPERIENCE, OR A TOURIST ATTRACTION. HERE IN ST. LOUIS, IT'S A BUSINESS.
A PROFITABLE BUSINESS THANKS TO MY BOSS, BERT. HE'S A SCALAWAG, A ROGUE, BUT DAMN IF HE DOESN'T KNOW HOW TO MAKE MONEY.
I HEARD ON THE NEWS THERE'S A MOVEMENT TO USE ZOMBIES IN PESTICIDE-CONTAMINATED FIELDS. IT WOULD SAVE LIVES.
ZOMBIES ROT, BERT, AND THEY DON'T STAY SMART LONG ENOUGH TO USE AS FIELD LABOR.
IT WAS JUST A THOUGHT. THE DEAD HAVE NO RIGHTS UNDER LAW, ANITA.
NOT YET.
I KNOW YOU AND CHARLES ARE WORKING ON THAT COMMITTEE, GOING AROUND TO ALL THE BUSINESSES TO CHECK UP ON THE ZOMBIES. IT MAKES GREAT PUBLICITY FOR ANIMATORS, INC.
I DON'T DO IT FOR GOOD PRESS.
I KNOW, YOU BELIEVE IN YOUR LITTLE CAUSE.
YOU'RE A CONDESCENDING BASTARD.
I KNOW.
BERT DOESN'T GIVE A DAMN WHAT I THINK OF HIM, AS LONG AS I WORK FOR HIM.

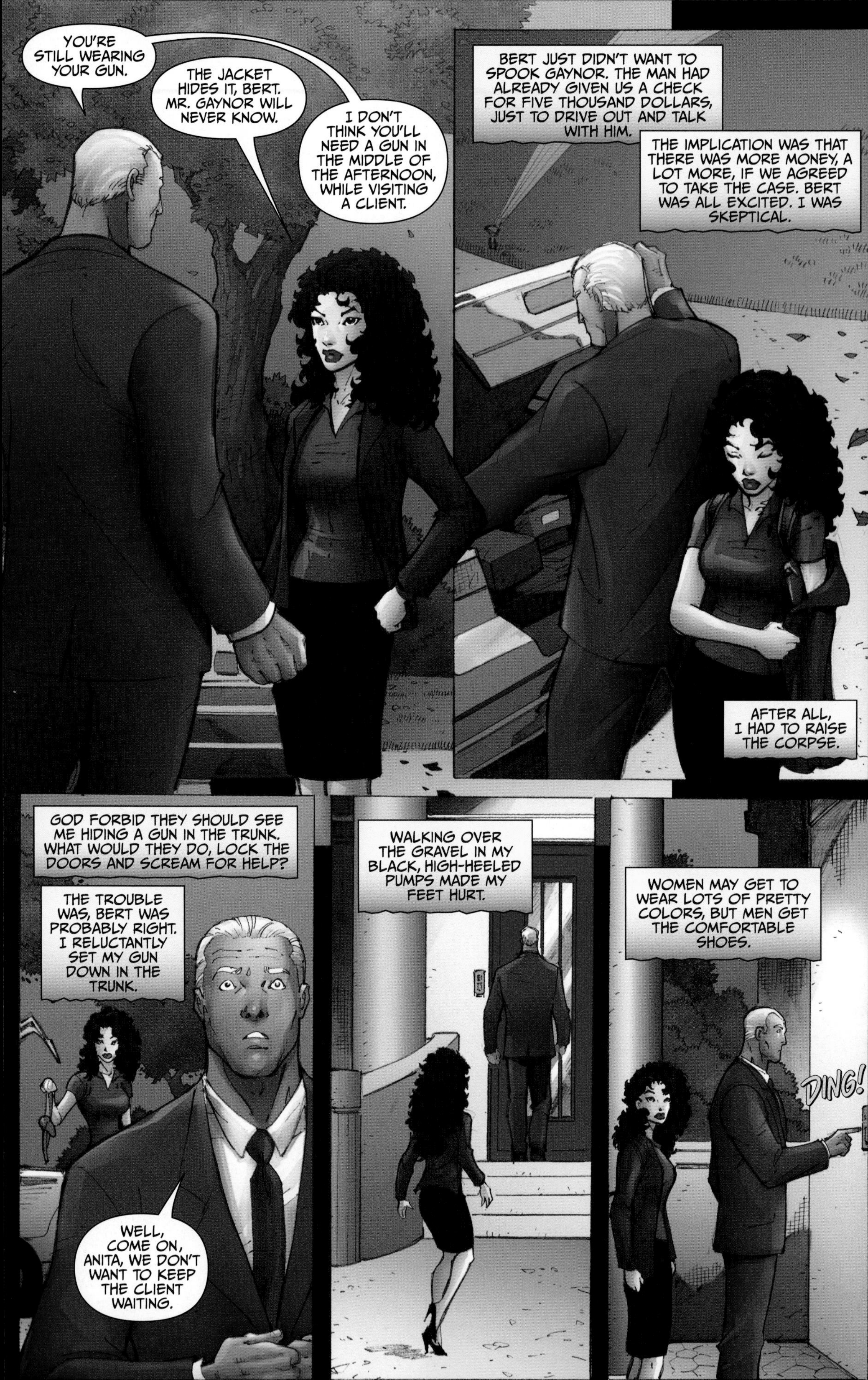
YOU'RE STILL WEARING YOUR GUN.
THE JACKET HIDES IT, BERT. MR. GAYNOR WILL NEVER KNOW.
I DON'T THINK YOU'LL NEED A GUN IN THE MIDDLE OF THE AFTERNOON, WHILE VISITING A CLIENT.
BERT JUST DIDN'T WANT TO SPOOK GAYNOR. THE MAN HAD ALREADY GIVEN US A CHECK FOR FIVE THOUSAND DOLLARS, JUST TO DRIVE OUT AND TALK WITH HIM.
THE IMPLICATION WAS THAT THERE WAS MORE MONEY, A LOT MORE, IF WE AGREED TO TAKE THE CASE. BERT WAS ALL EXCITED. I WAS SKEPTICAL.
AFTER ALL, I HAD TO RAISE THE CORPSE.
GOD FORBID THEY SHOULD SEE ME HIDING A GUN IN THE TRUNK. WHAT WOULD THEY DO, LOCK THE DOORS AND SCREAM FOR HELP?
THE TROUBLE WAS, BERT WAS PROBABLY RIGHT. I RELUCTANTLY SET MY GUN DOWN IN THE TRUNK.
WELL, COME ON, ANITA, WE DON'T WANT TO KEEP THE CLIENT WAITING.
WALKING OVER THE GRAVEL IN MY BLACK, HIGH-HEELED PUMPS MADE MY FEET HURT.
WOMEN MAY GET TO WEAR LOTS OF PRETTY COLORS, BUT MEN GET THE COMFORTABLE SHOES.
DING!

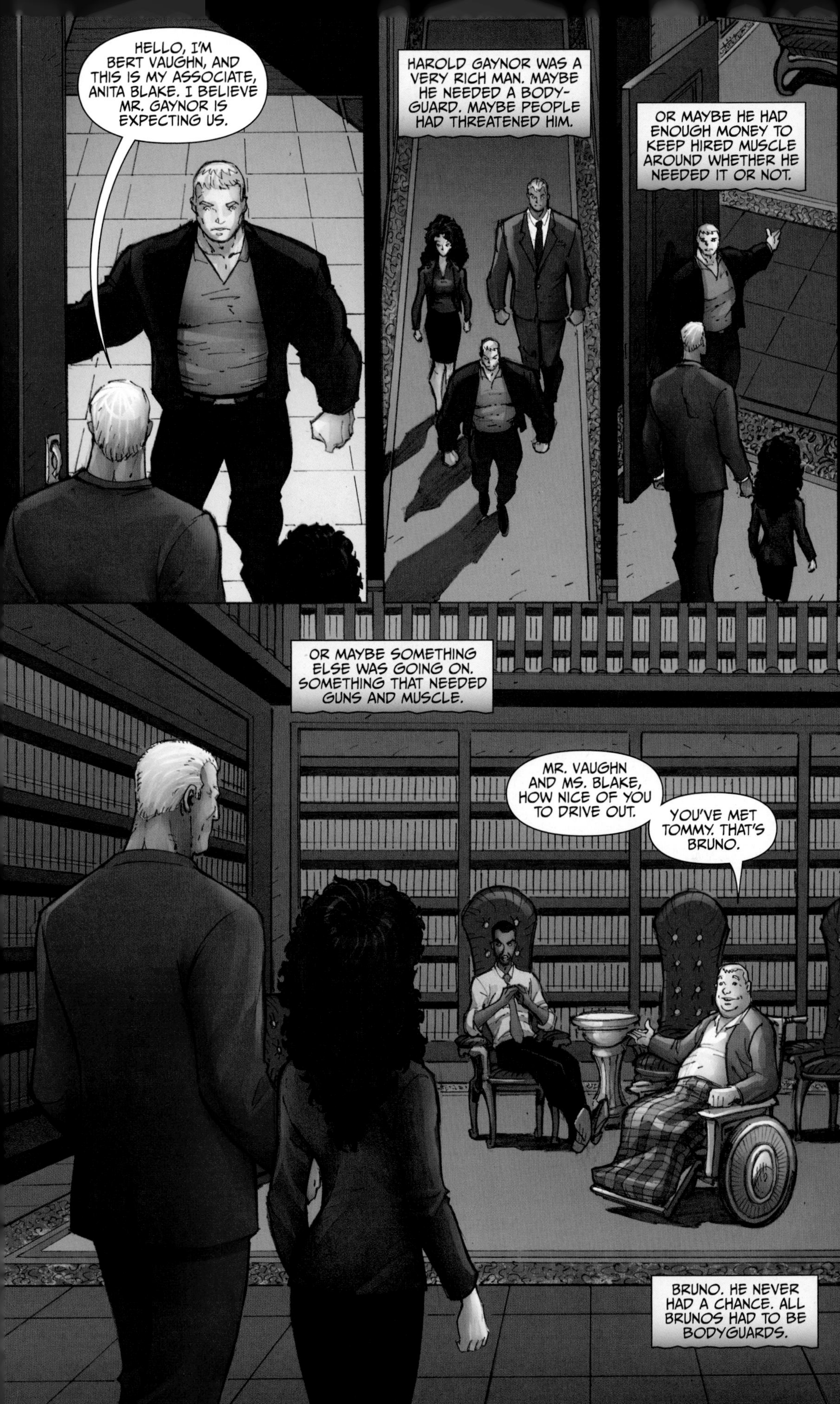
HELLO, I'M BERT VAUGHN, AND THIS IS MY ASSOCIATE, ANITA BLAKE. I BELIEVE MR. GAYNOR IS EXPECTING US.
HAROLD GAYNOR WAS A VERY RICH MAN. MAYBE HE NEEDED A BODY-GUARD. MAYBE PEOPLE HAD THREATENED HIM.
OR MAYBE HE HAD ENOUGH MONEY TO KEEP HIRED MUSCLE AROUND WHETHER HE NEEDED IT OR NOT.
OR MAYBE SOMETHING ELSE WAS GOING ON. SOMETHING THAT NEEDED GUNS AND MUSCLE.
MR. VAUGHN AND MS. BLAKE, HOW NICE OF YOU TO DRIVE OUT.
YOU'VE MET TOMMY. THAT'S BRUNO.
BRUNO. HE NEVER HAD A CHANCE. ALL BRUNOS HAD TO BE BODYGUARDS.

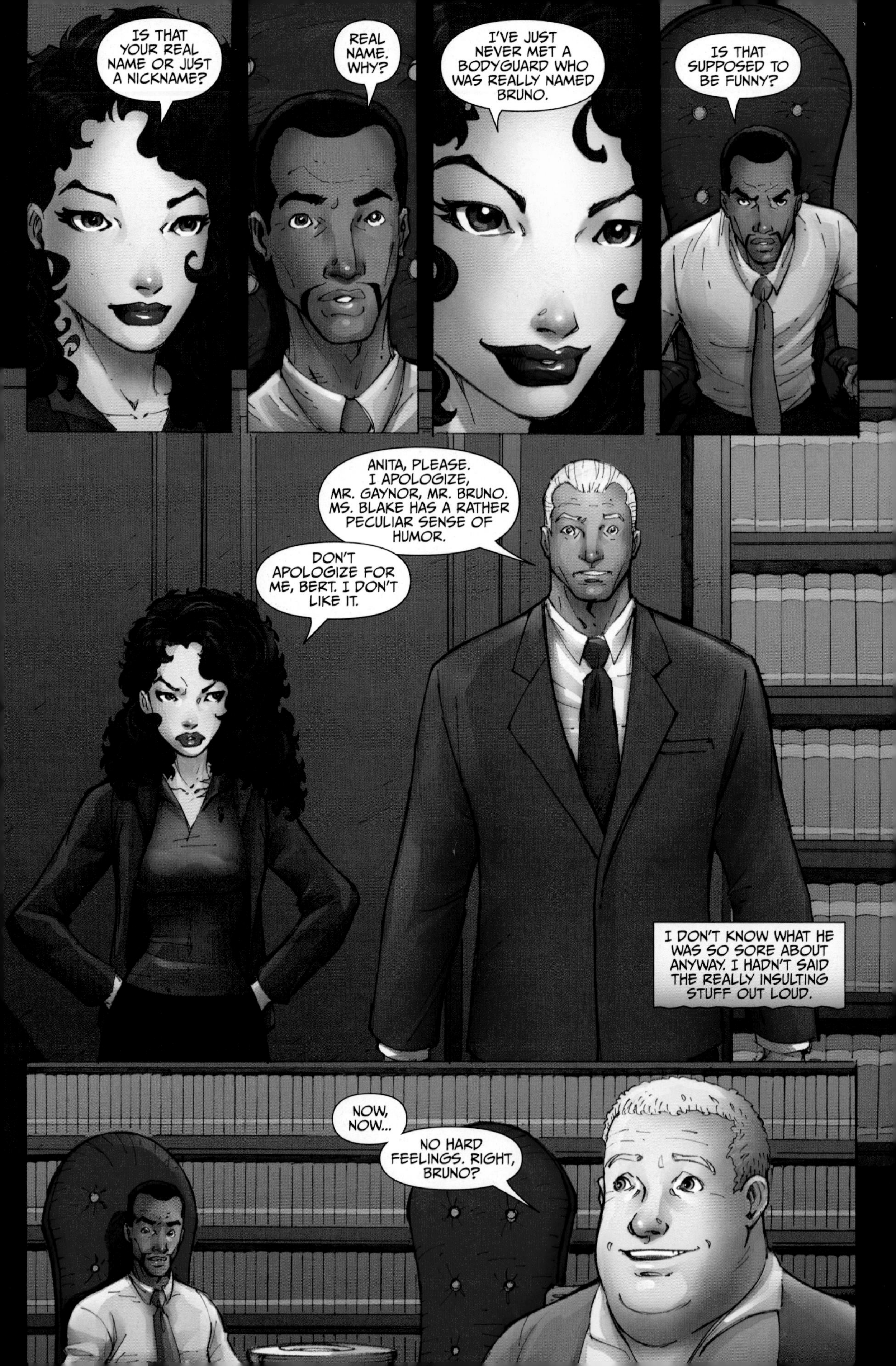
IS THAT YOUR REAL NAME OR JUST A NICKNAME?
REAL NAME. WHY?
I'VE JUST NEVER MET A BODYGUARD WHO WAS REALLY NAMED BRUNO.
IS THAT SUPPOSED TO BE FUNNY?
ANITA, PLEASE. I APOLOGIZE, MR. GAYNOR, MR. BRUNO. MS. BLAKE HAS A RATHER PECULIAR SENSE OF HUMOR.
DON'T APOLOGIZE FOR ME, BERT. I DON'T LIKE IT.
I DON'T KNOW WHAT HE WAS SO SORE ABOUT ANYWAY. I HADN'T SAID THE REALLY INSULTING STUFF OUT LOUD.
NOW, NOW...
NO HARD FEELINGS. RIGHT, BRUNO?

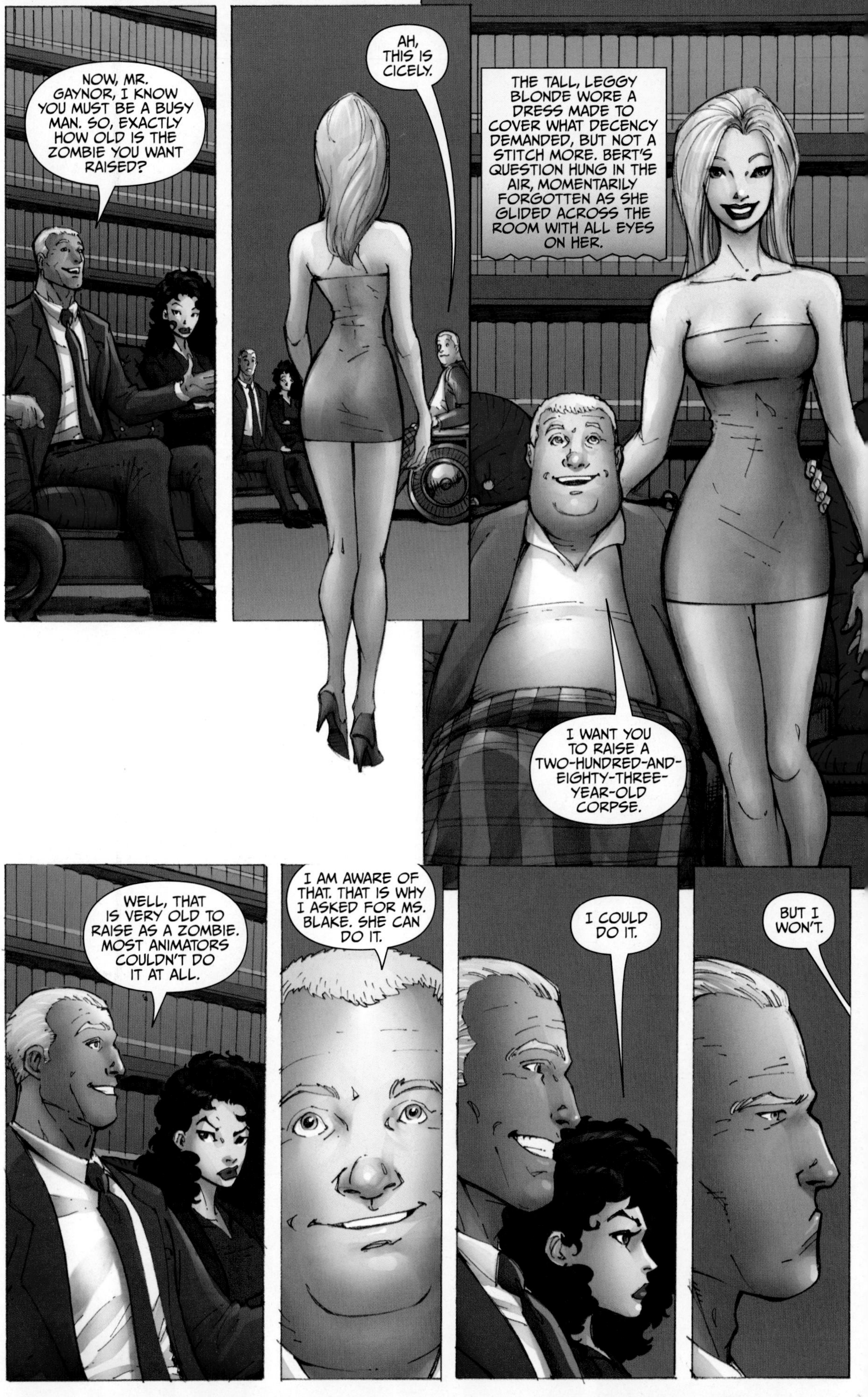
NOW, MR. GAYNOR, I KNOW YOU MUST BE A BUSY MAN. SO, EXACTLY HOW OLD IS THE ZOMBIE YOU WANT RAISED?
AH, THIS IS CICELY.
THE TALL, LEGGY BLONDE WORE A DRESS MADE TO COVER WHAT DECENCY DEMANDED, BUT NOT A STITCH MORE. BERT'S QUESTION HUNG IN THE AIR, MOMENTARILY FORGOTTEN AS SHE GLIDED ACROSS THE ROOM WITH ALL EYES ON HER.
I WANT YOU TO RAISE A TWO-HUNDRED-AND-EIGHTY-THREE-YEAR-OLD CORPSE.
WELL, THAT IS VERY OLD TO RAISE AS A ZOMBIE. MOST ANIMATORS COULDN'T DO IT AT ALL.
I AM AWARE OF THAT. THAT IS WHY I ASKED FOR MS. BLAKE. SHE CAN DO IT.
I COULD DO IT.
BUT I WON'T.

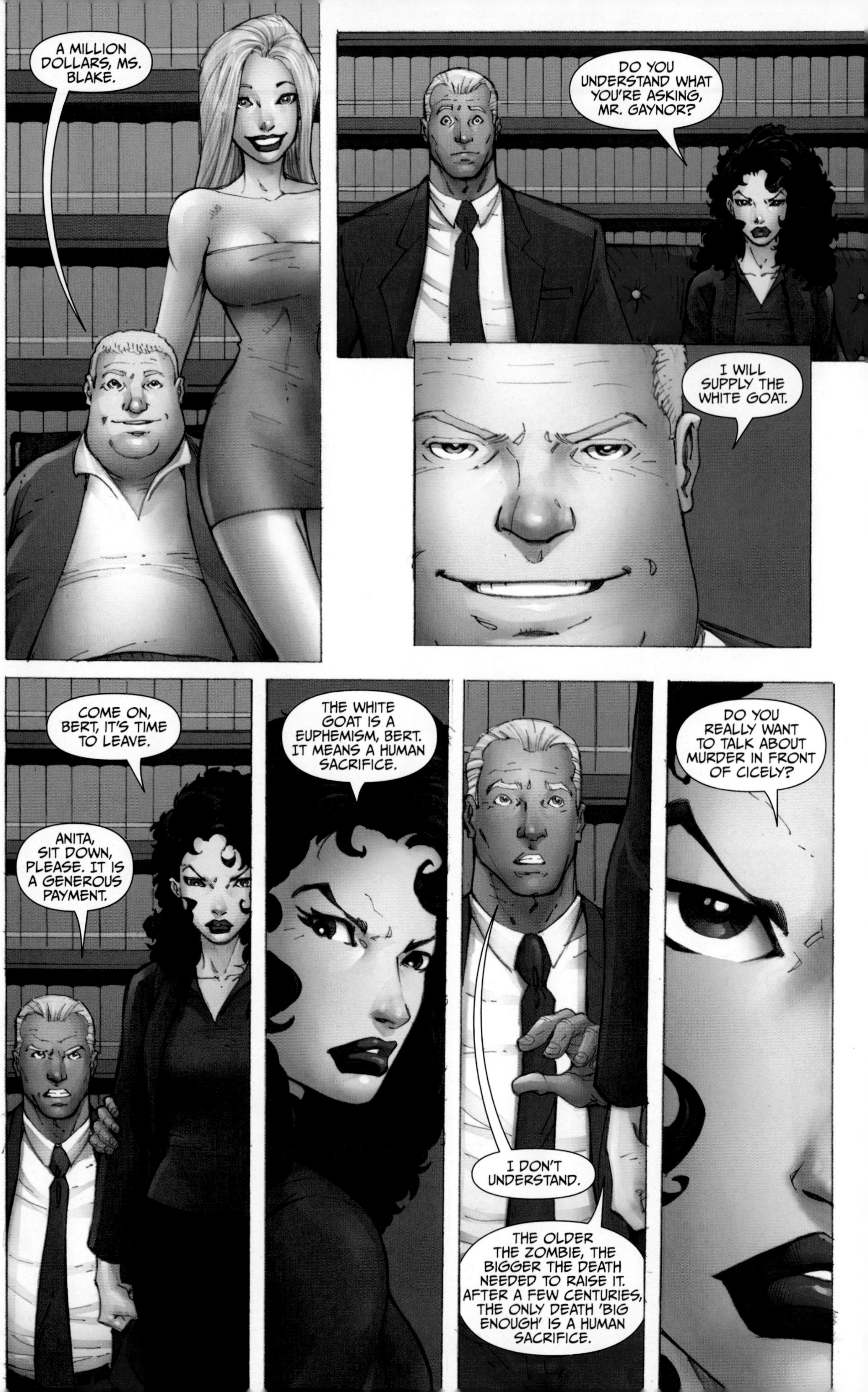
A MILLION DOLLARS, MS. BLAKE.
DO YOU UNDERSTAND WHAT YOU'RE ASKING, MR. GAYNOR?
I WILL SUPPLY THE WHITE GOAT.
COME ON, BERT, IT'S TIME TO LEAVE.
ANITA, SIT DOWN, PLEASE. IT IS A GENEROUS PAYMENT.
THE WHITE GOAT IS A EUPHEMISM, BERT. IT MEANS A HUMAN SACRIFICE.
I DON'T UNDERSTAND.
THE OLDER THE ZOMBIE, THE BIGGER THE DEATH NEEDED TO RAISE IT. AFTER A FEW CENTURIES, THE ONLY DEATH 'BIG ENOUGH' IS A HUMAN SACRIFICE.
DO YOU REALLY WANT TO TALK ABOUT MURDER IN FRONT OF CICELY?

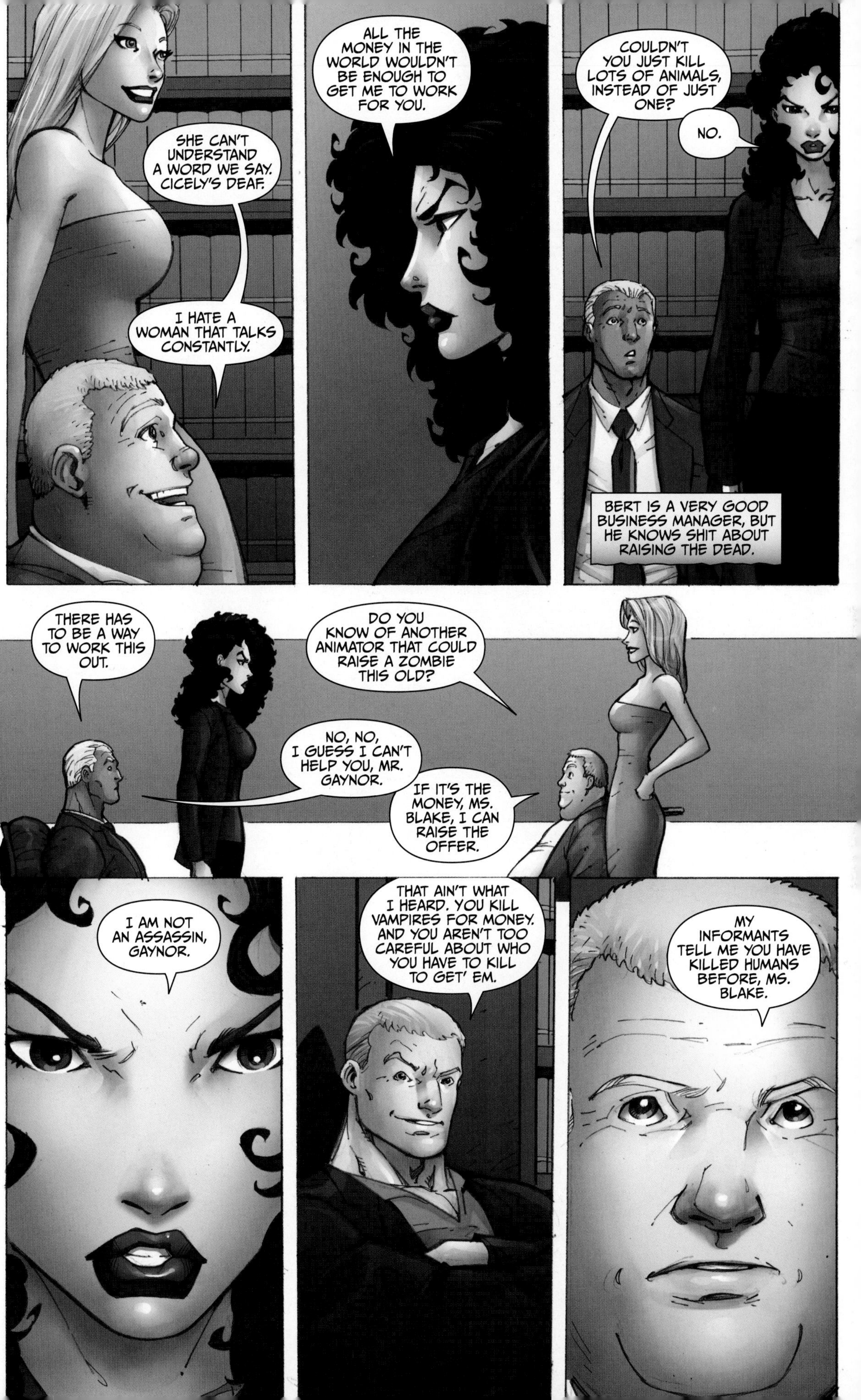
SHE CAN'T UNDERSTAND A WORD WE SAY. CICELY'S DEAF.
I HATE A WOMAN THAT TALKS CONSTANTLY.
ALL THE MONEY IN THE WORLD WOULDN'T BE ENOUGH TO GET ME TO WORK FOR YOU.
COULDN'T YOU JUST KILL LOTS OF ANIMALS, INSTEAD OF JUST ONE?
NO.
BERT IS A VERY GOOD BUSINESS MANAGER, BUT HE KNOWS SHIT ABOUT RAISING THE DEAD.
THERE HAS TO BE A WAY TO WORK THIS OUT.
DO YOU KNOW OF ANOTHER ANIMATOR THAT COULD RAISE A ZOMBIE THIS OLD?
NO, NO, I GUESS I CAN'T HELP YOU, MR. GAYNOR.
IF IT'S THE MONEY, MS. BLAKE, I CAN RAISE THE OFFER.
I AM NOT AN ASSASSIN, GAYNOR.
THAT AIN'T WHAT I HEARD. YOU KILL VAMPIRES FOR MONEY. AND YOU AREN'T TOO CAREFUL ABOUT WHO YOU HAVE TO KILL TO GET' EM.
MY INFORMANTS TELL ME YOU HAVE KILLED HUMANS BEFORE, MS. BLAKE.

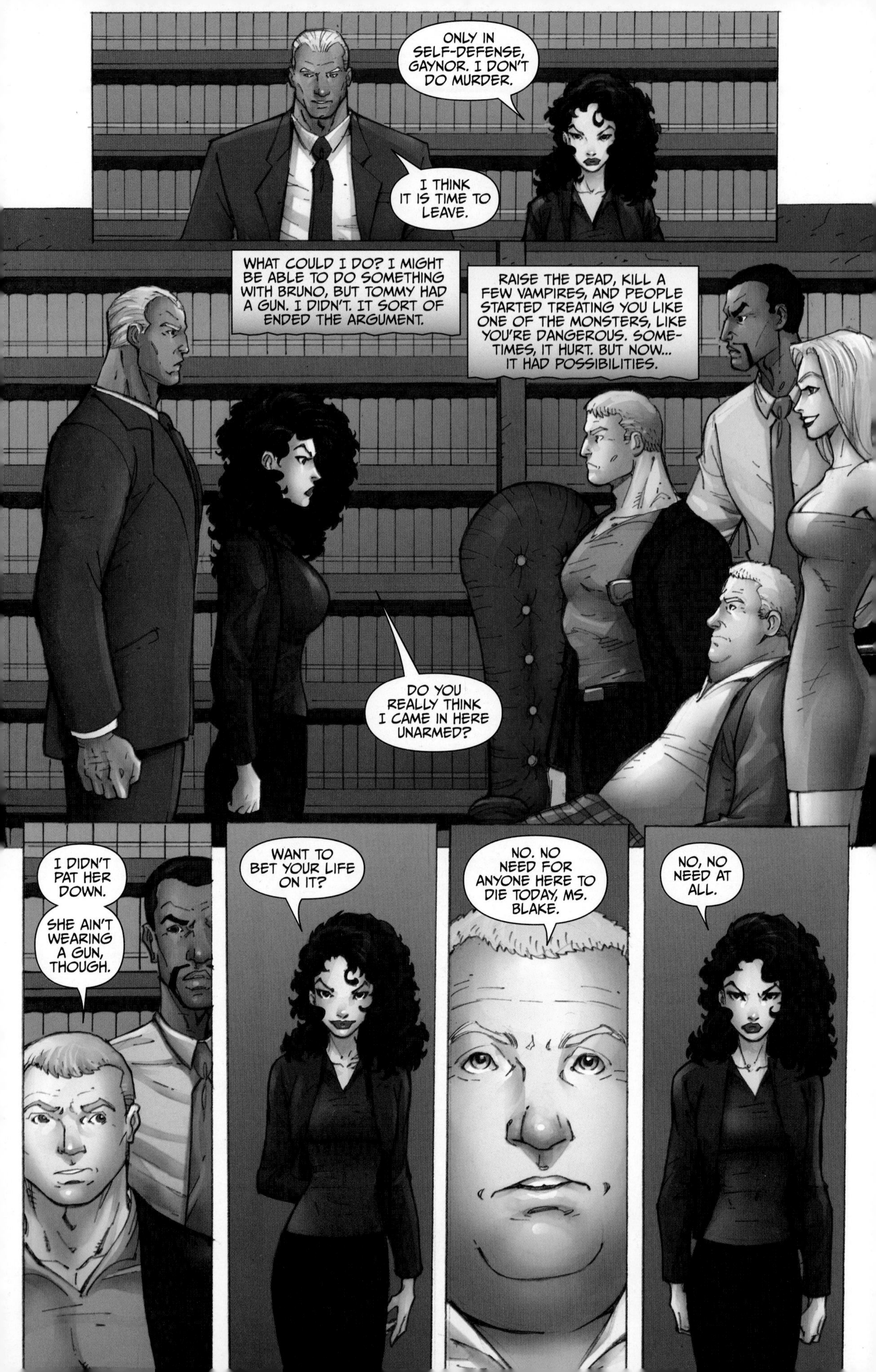

ONLY IN SELF-DEFENSE, GAYNOR. I DON'T DO MURDER.
I THINK IT IS TIME TO LEAVE.
WHAT COULD I DO? I MIGHT BE ABLE TO DO SOMETHING WITH BRUNO, BUT TOMMY HAD A GUN. I DIDN'T. IT SORT OF ENDED THE ARGUMENT.
RAISE THE DEAD, KILL A FEW VAMPIRES, AND PEOPLE STARTED TREATING YOU LIKE ONE OF THE MONSTERS, LIKE YOU'RE DANGEROUS. SOMETIMES, IT HURT. BUT NOW... IT HAD POSSIBILITIES.
DO YOU REALLY THINK I CAME IN HERE UNARMED?
I DIDN'T PAT HER DOWN.
SHE AIN'T WEARING A GUN, THOUGH.
WANT TO BET YOUR LIFE ON IT?
NO. NO NEED FOR ANYONE HERE TO DIE TODAY, MS. BLAKE.
NO, NO NEED AT ALL.

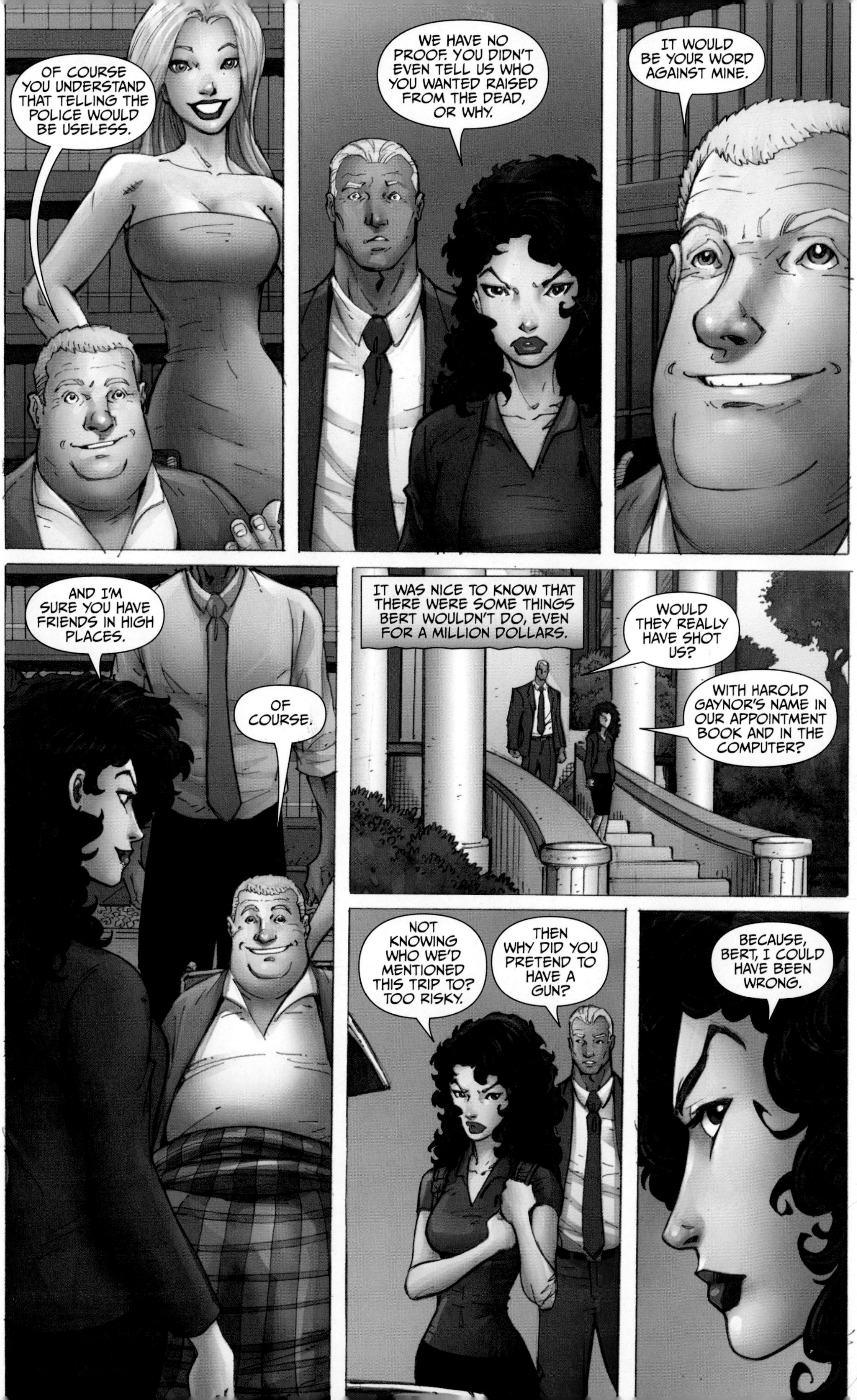
OF COURSE YOU UNDERSTAND THAT TELLING THE POLICE WOULD BE USELESS.
WE HAVE NO PROOF. YOU DIDN'T EVEN TELL US WHO YOU WANTED RAISED FROM THE DEAD, OR WHY.
IT WOULD BE YOUR WORD AGAINST MINE.
AND I'M SURE YOU HAVE FRIENDS IN HIGH PLACES.
OF COURSE.
IT WAS NICE TO KNOW THAT THERE WERE SOME THINGS BERT WOULDN'T DO, EVEN FOR A MILLION DOLLARS.
WOULD THEY REALLY HAVE SHOT US?
WITH HAROLD GAYNOR'S NAME IN OUR APPOINTMENT BOOK AND IN THE COMPUTER?
NOT KNOWING WHO WE'D MENTIONED THIS TRIP TO? TOO RISKY.
THEN WHY DID YOU PRETEND TO HAVE A GUN?
BECAUSE, BERT, I COULD HAVE BEEN WRONG.

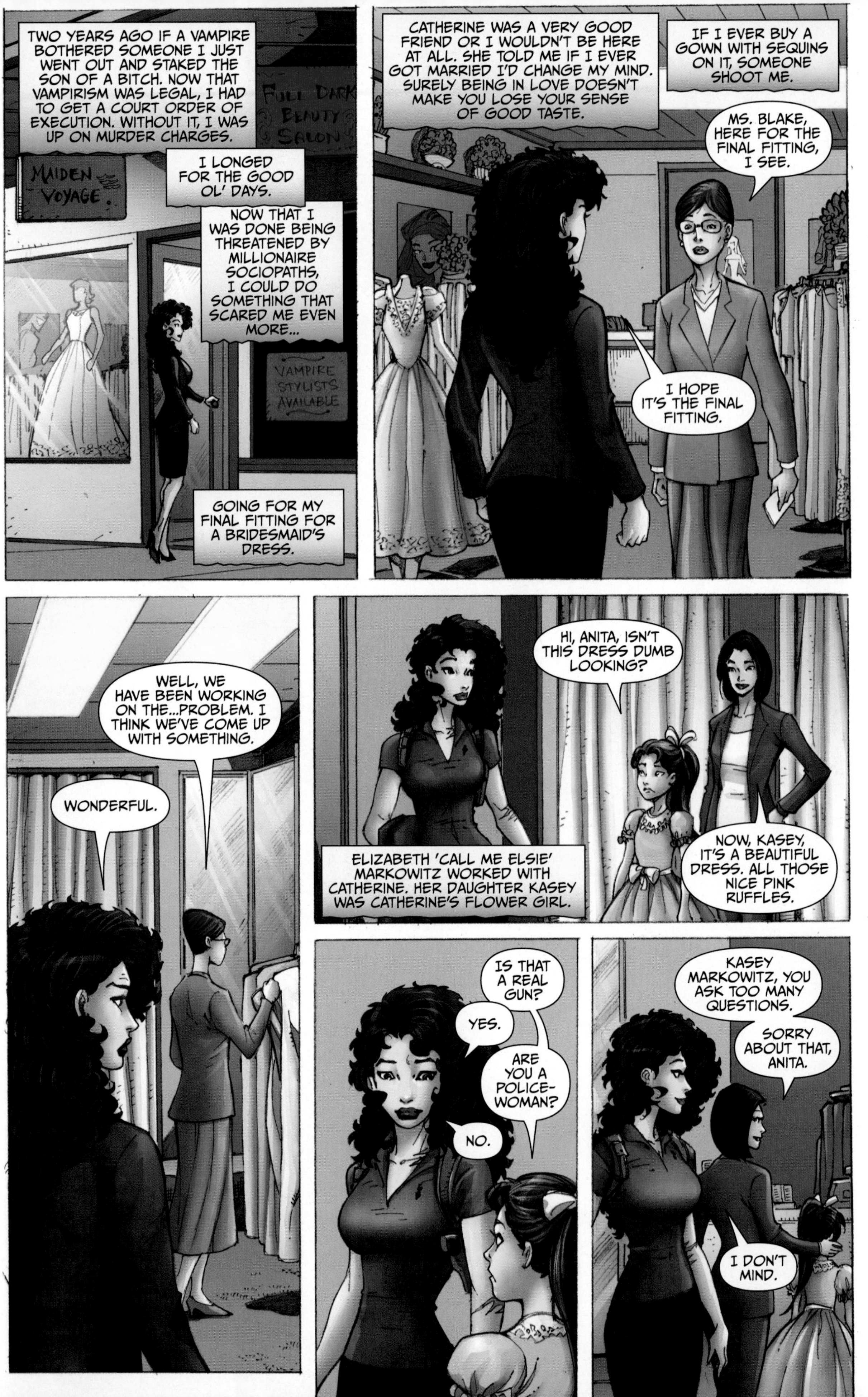
TWO YEARS AGO IF A VAMPIRE BOTHERED SOMEONE I JUST WENT OUT AND STAKED THE SON OF A BITCH. NOW THAT VAMPIRISM WAS LEGAL, I HAD TO GET A COURT ORDER OF EXECUTION. WITHOUT IT, I WAS UP ON MURDER CHARGES.
FULL DARK BEAUTY SALON
MAIDEN VOYAGE
I LONGED FOR THE GOOD OL' DAYS.
NOW THAT I WAS DONE BEING THREATENED BY MILLIONAIRE SOCIOPATHS, I COULD DO SOMETHING THAT SCARED ME EVEN MORE...
VAMPIRE STYLISTS AVAILABLE
GOING FOR MY FINAL FITTING FOR A BRIDESMAID'S DRESS.
CATHERINE WAS A VERY GOOD FRIEND OR I WOULDN'T BE HERE AT ALL. SHE TOLD ME IF I EVER GOT MARRIED I'D CHANGE MY MIND. SURELY BEING IN LOVE DOESN'T MAKE YOU LOSE YOUR SENSE OF GOOD TASTE.
IF I EVER BUY A GOWN WITH SEQUINS ON IT, SOMEONE SHOOT ME.
MS. BLAKE, HERE FOR THE FINAL FITTING, I SEE.
I HOPE IT'S THE FINAL FITTING.
WELL, WE HAVE BEEN WORKING ON THE...PROBLEM. I THINK WE'VE COME UP WITH SOMETHING.
WONDERFUL.
HI, ANITA, ISN'T THIS DRESS DUMB LOOKING?
ELIZABETH 'CALL ME ELSIE' MARKOWITZ WORKED WITH CATHERINE. HER DAUGHTER KASEY WAS CATHERINE'S FLOWER GIRL.
NOW, KASEY, IT'S A BEAUTIFUL DRESS. ALL THOSE NICE PINK RUFFLES.
IS THAT A REAL GUN?
YES.
ARE YOU A POLICE-WOMAN?
NO.
KASEY MARKOWITZ, YOU ASK TOO MANY QUESTIONS.
SORRY ABOUT THAT, ANITA.
I DON'T MIND.

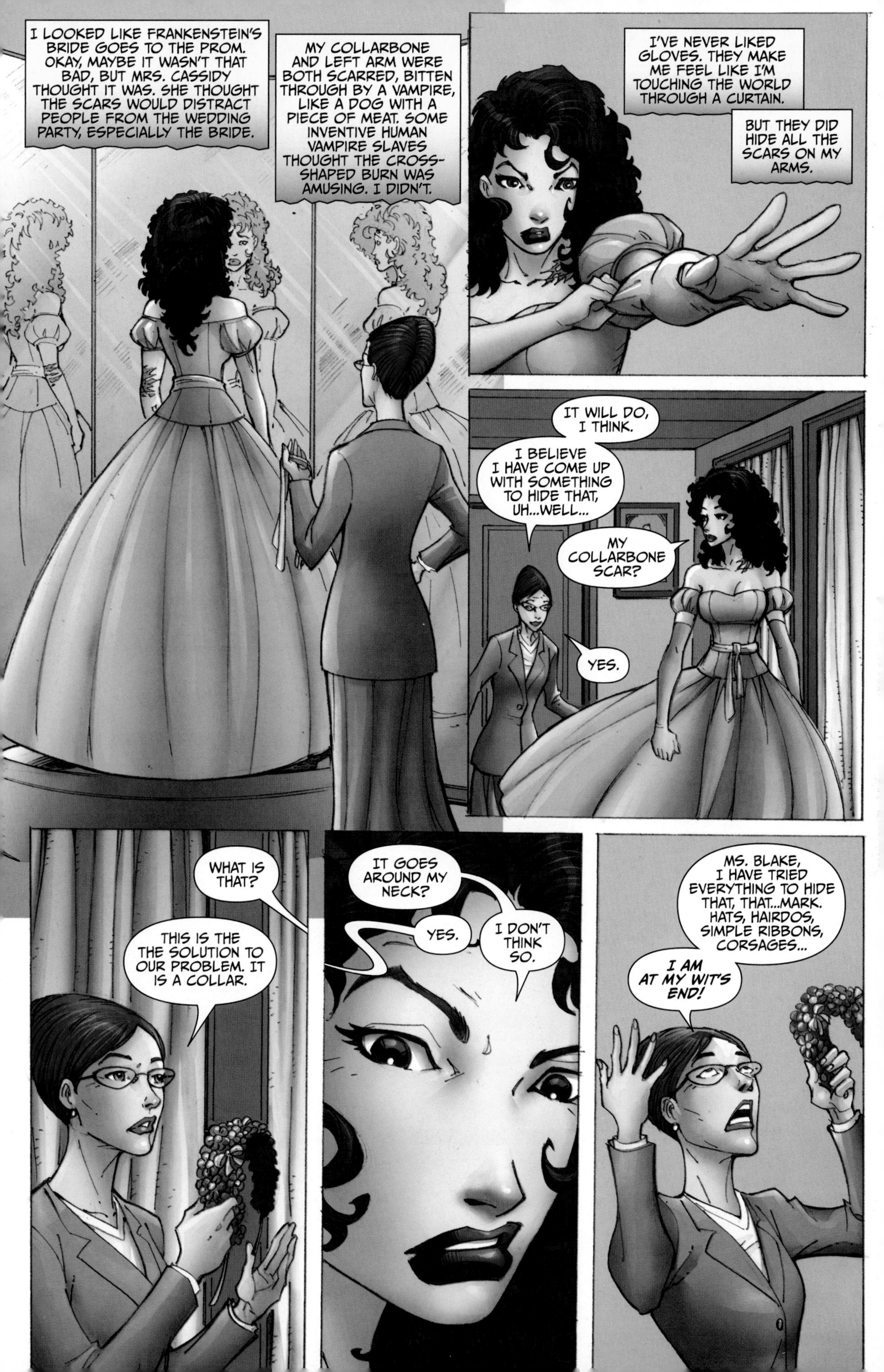
I LOOKED LIKE FRANKENSTEIN'S BRIDE GOES TO THE PROM. OKAY, MAYBE IT WASN'T THAT BAD, BUT MRS. CASSIDY THOUGHT IT WAS. SHE THOUGHT THE SCARS WOULD DISTRACT PEOPLE FROM THE WEDDING PARTY, ESPECIALLY THE BRIDE.
MY COLLARBONE AND LEFT ARM WERE BOTH SCARRED, BITTEN THROUGH BY A VAMPIRE, LIKE A DOG WITH A PIECE OF MEAT. SOME INVENTIVE HUMAN VAMPIRE SLAVES THOUGHT THE CROSS-SHAPED BURN WAS AMUSING. I DIDN'T.
I'VE NEVER LIKED GLOVES. THEY MAKE ME FEEL LIKE I'M TOUCHING THE WORLD THROUGH A CURTAIN.
BUT THEY DID HIDE ALL THE SCARS ON MY ARMS.
IT WILL DO, I THINK.
I BELIEVE I HAVE COME UP WITH SOMETHING TO HIDE THAT, UH...WELL...
MY COLLARBONE SCAR?
YES.
WHAT IS THAT?
THIS IS THE THE SOLUTION TO OUR PROBLEM. IT IS A COLLAR.
IT GOES AROUND MY NECK?
YES.
I DON'T THINK SO.
MS. BLAKE, I HAVE TRIED EVERYTHING TO HIDE THAT, THAT...MARK. HATS, HAIRDOS, SIMPLE RIBBONS, CORSAGES...
I AM AT MY WIT'S END!

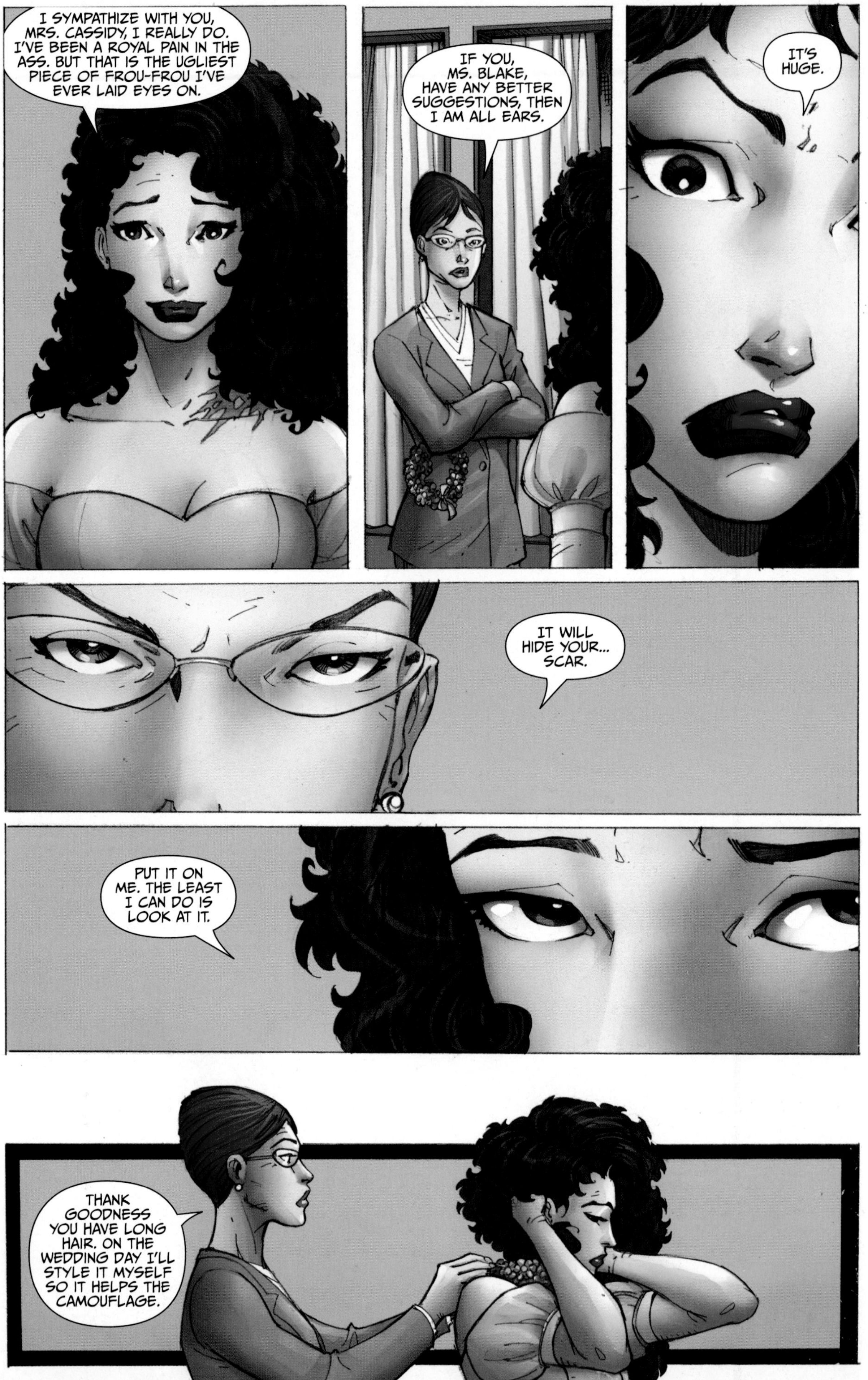
I SYMPATHIZE WITH YOU, MRS. CASSIDY, I REALLY DO. I'VE BEEN A ROYAL PAIN IN THE ASS. BUT THAT IS THE UGLIEST PIECE OF FROU-FROU I'VE EVER LAID EYES ON.
IF YOU, MS. BLAKE, HAVE ANY BETTER SUGGESTIONS, THEN I AM ALL EARS.
IT'S HUGE.
IT WILL HIDE YOUR... SCAR.
PUT IT ON ME. THE LEAST I CAN DO IS LOOK AT IT.
THANK GOODNESS YOU HAVE LONG HAIR. ON THE WEDDING DAY I'LL STYLE IT MYSELF SO IT HELPS THE CAMOUFLAGE.

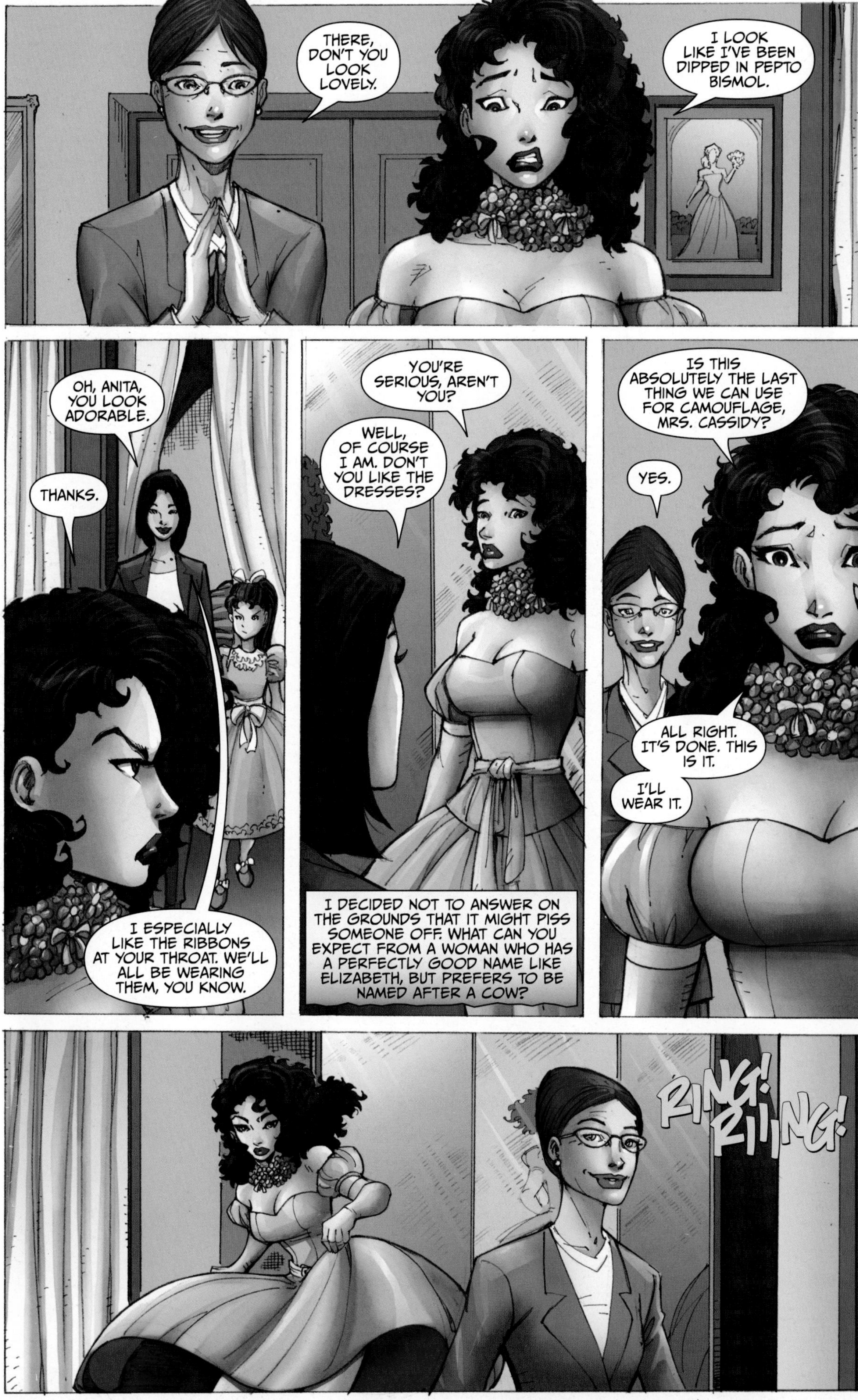
THERE, DON'T YOU LOOK LOVELY.
I LOOK LIKE I'VE BEEN DIPPED IN PEPTO BISMOL.
OH, ANITA, YOU LOOK ADORABLE.
THANKS.
I ESPECIALLY LIKE THE RIBBONS AT YOUR THROAT. WE'LL ALL BE WEARING THEM, YOU KNOW.
YOU'RE SERIOUS, AREN'T YOU?
WELL, OF COURSE I AM. DON'T YOU LIKE THE DRESSES?
I DECIDED NOT TO ANSWER ON THE GROUNDS THAT IT MIGHT PISS SOMEONE OFF. WHAT CAN YOU EXPECT FROM A WOMAN WHO HAS A PERFECTLY GOOD NAME LIKE ELIZABETH, BUT PREFERS TO BE NAMED AFTER A COW?
IS THIS ABSOLUTELY THE LAST THING WE CAN USE FOR CAMOUFLAGE, MRS. CASSIDY?
YES.
ALL RIGHT. IT'S DONE. THIS IS IT.
I'LL WEAR IT.
RING! RIIING!

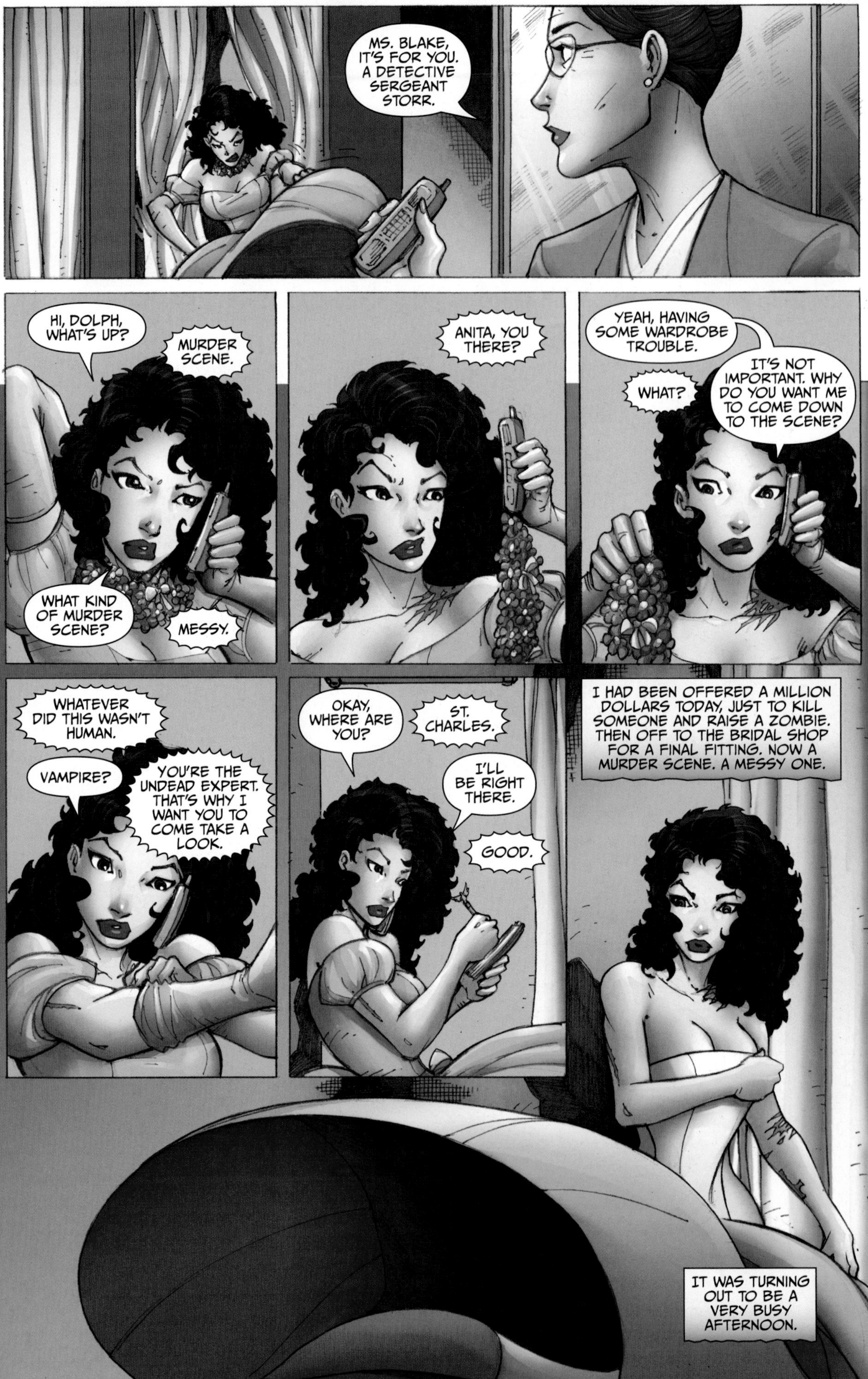
MS. BLAKE, IT'S FOR YOU. A DETECTIVE SERGEANT STORR.
HI, DOLPH, WHAT'S UP?
MURDER SCENE.
WHAT KIND OF MURDER SCENE?
MESSY.
ANITA, YOU THERE?
YEAH, HAVING SOME WARDROBE TROUBLE.
WHAT?
IT'S NOT IMPORTANT. WHY DO YOU WANT ME TO COME DOWN TO THE SCENE?
WHATEVER DID THIS WASN'T HUMAN.
VAMPIRE?
YOU'RE THE UNDEAD EXPERT. THAT'S WHY I WANT YOU TO COME TAKE A LOOK.
OKAY, WHERE ARE YOU?
ST. CHARLES.
I'LL BE RIGHT THERE.
GOOD.
I HAD BEEN OFFERED A MILLION DOLLARS TODAY, JUST TO KILL SOMEONE AND RAISE A ZOMBIE. THEN OFF TO THE BRIDAL SHOP FOR A FINAL FITTING. NOW A MURDER SCENE. A MESSY ONE.
IT WAS TURNING OUT TO BE A VERY BUSY AFTERNOON.

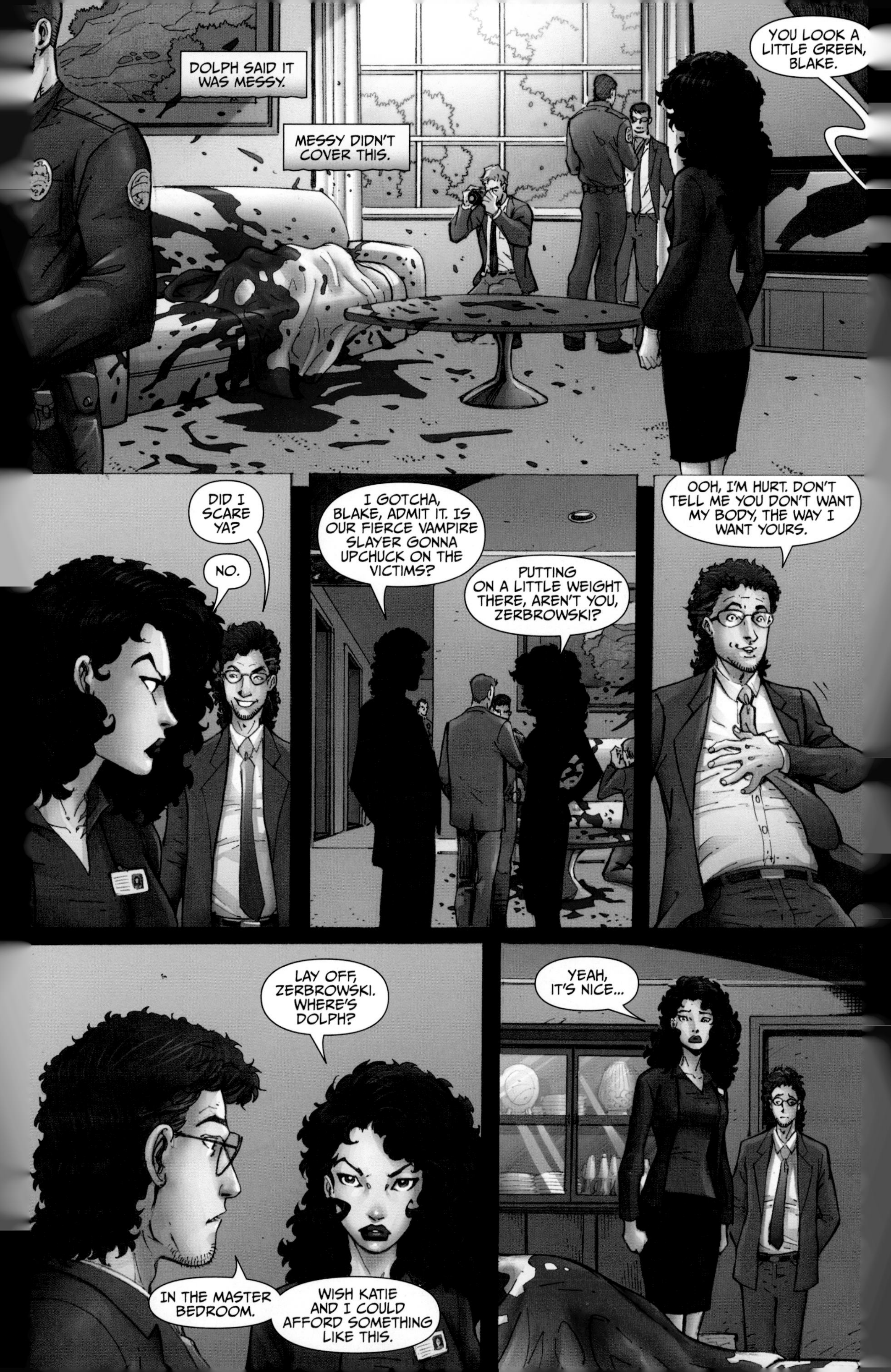

DOLPH SAID IT WAS MESSY.
MESSY DIDN'T COVER THIS.
YOU LOOK A LITTLE GREEN, BLAKE.
DID I SCARE YA?
NO.
I GOTCHA, BLAKE, ADMIT IT. IS OUR FIERCE VAMPIRE SLAYER GONNA UPCHUCK ON THE VICTIMS?
PUTTING ON A LITTLE WEIGHT THERE, AREN'T YOU, ZERBROWSKI?
OOH, I'M HURT. DON'T TELL ME YOU DON'T WANT MY BODY, THE WAY I WANT YOURS.
LAY OFF, ZERBROWSKI. WHERE'S DOLPH?
IN THE MASTER BEDROOM.
WISH KATIE AND I COULD AFFORD SOMETHING LIKE THIS.
YEAH, IT'S NICE...

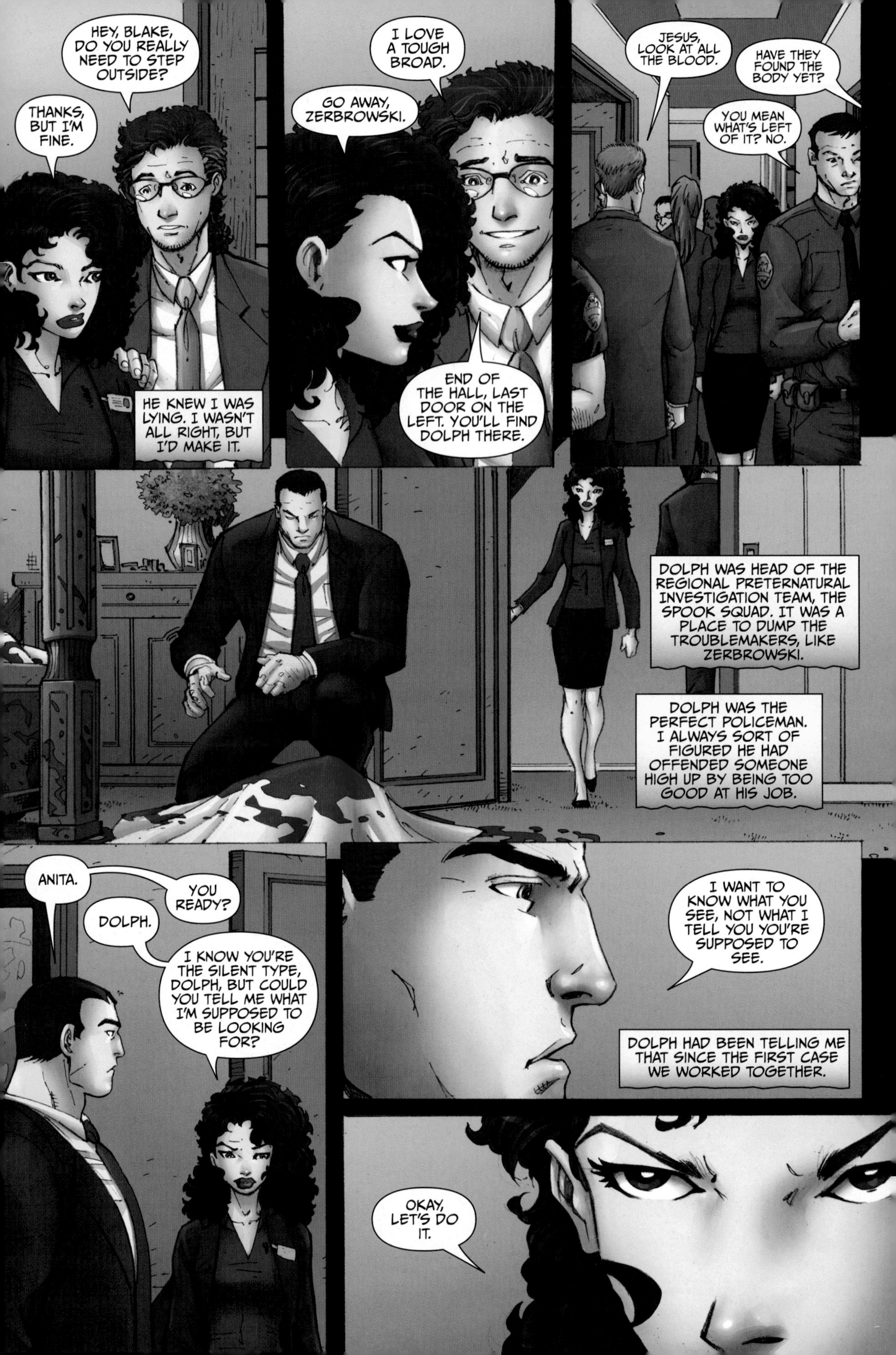
HEY, BLAKE, DO YOU REALLY NEED TO STEP OUTSIDE?
THANKS, BUT I'M FINE.
HE KNEW I WAS LYING. I WASN'T ALL RIGHT, BUT I'D MAKE IT.
I LOVE A TOUGH BROAD.
GO AWAY, ZERBROWSKI.
END OF THE HALL, LAST DOOR ON THE LEFT. YOU'LL FIND DOLPH THERE.
JESUS, LOOK AT ALL THE BLOOD.
HAVE THEY FOUND THE BODY YET?
YOU MEAN WHAT'S LEFT OF IT? NO.
DOLPH WAS HEAD OF THE REGIONAL PRETERNATURAL INVESTIGATION TEAM, THE SPOOK SQUAD. IT WAS A PLACE TO DUMP THE TROUBLEMAKERS, LIKE ZERBROWSKI.
DOLPH WAS THE PERFECT POLICEMAN. I ALWAYS SORT OF FIGURED HE HAD OFFENDED SOMEONE HIGH UP BY BEING TOO GOOD AT HIS JOB.
ANITA.
YOU READY?
DOLPH.
I KNOW YOU'RE THE SILENT TYPE, DOLPH, BUT COULD YOU TELL ME WHAT I'M SUPPOSED TO BE LOOKING FOR?
I WANT TO KNOW WHAT YOU SEE, NOT WHAT I TELL YOU YOU'RE SUPPOSED TO SEE.
DOLPH HAD BEEN TELLING ME THAT SINCE THE FIRST CASE WE WORKED TOGETHER.
OKAY, LET'S DO IT.

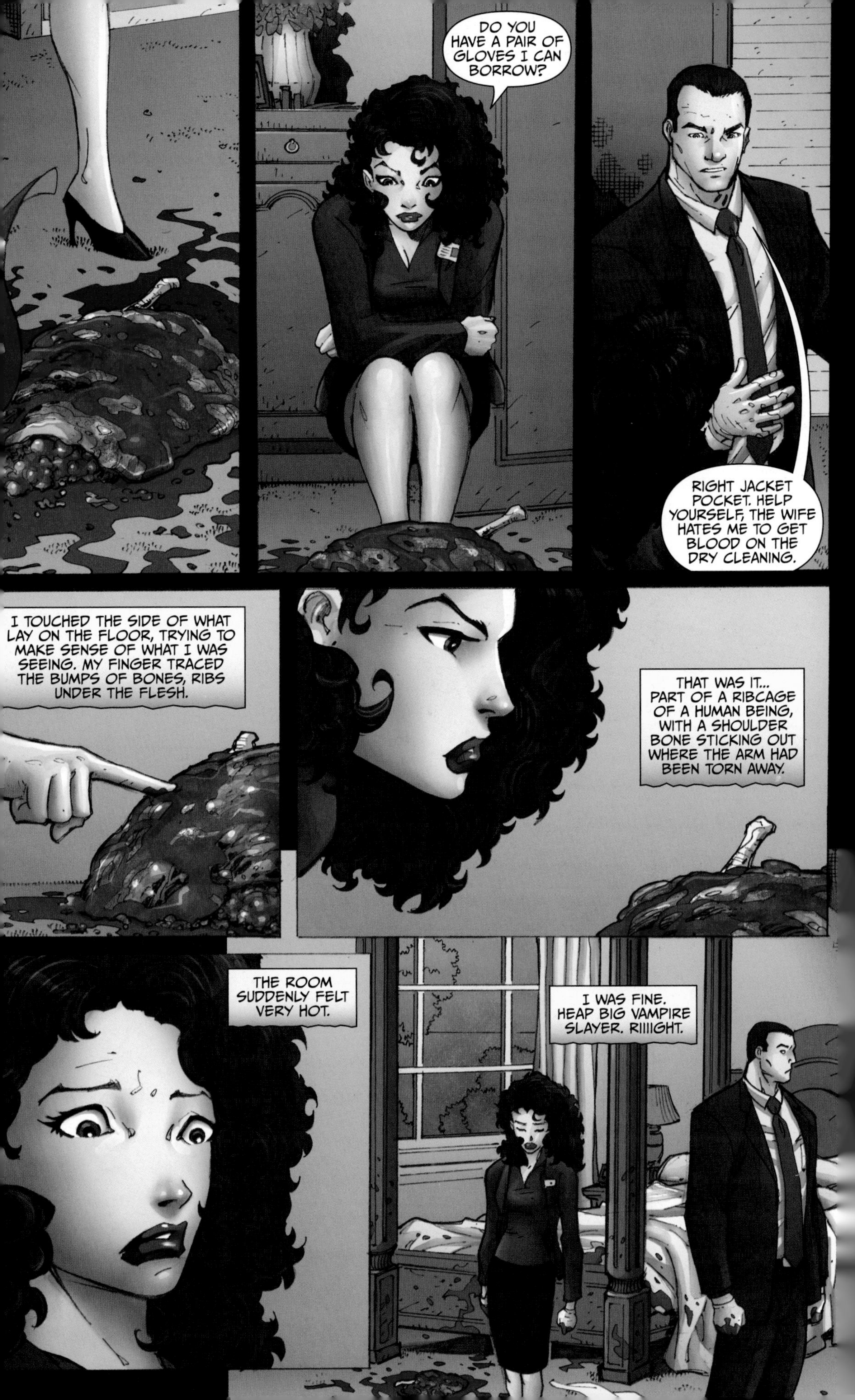
DO YOU HAVE A PAIR OF GLOVES I CAN BORROW?
RIGHT JACKET POCKET. HELP YOURSELF, THE WIFE HATES ME TO GET BLOOD ON THE DRY CLEANING.
I TOUCHED THE SIDE OF WHAT LAY ON THE FLOOR, TRYING TO MAKE SENSE OF WHAT I WAS SEEING. MY FINGER TRACED THE BUMPS OF BONES, RIBS UNDER THE FLESH.
THAT WAS IT... PART OF A RIBCAGE OF A HUMAN BEING, WITH A SHOULDER BONE STICKING OUT WHERE THE ARM HAD BEEN TORN AWAY.
THE ROOM SUDDENLY FELT VERY HOT.
I WAS FINE. HEAP BIG VAMPIRE SLAYER. RIIIIGHT.

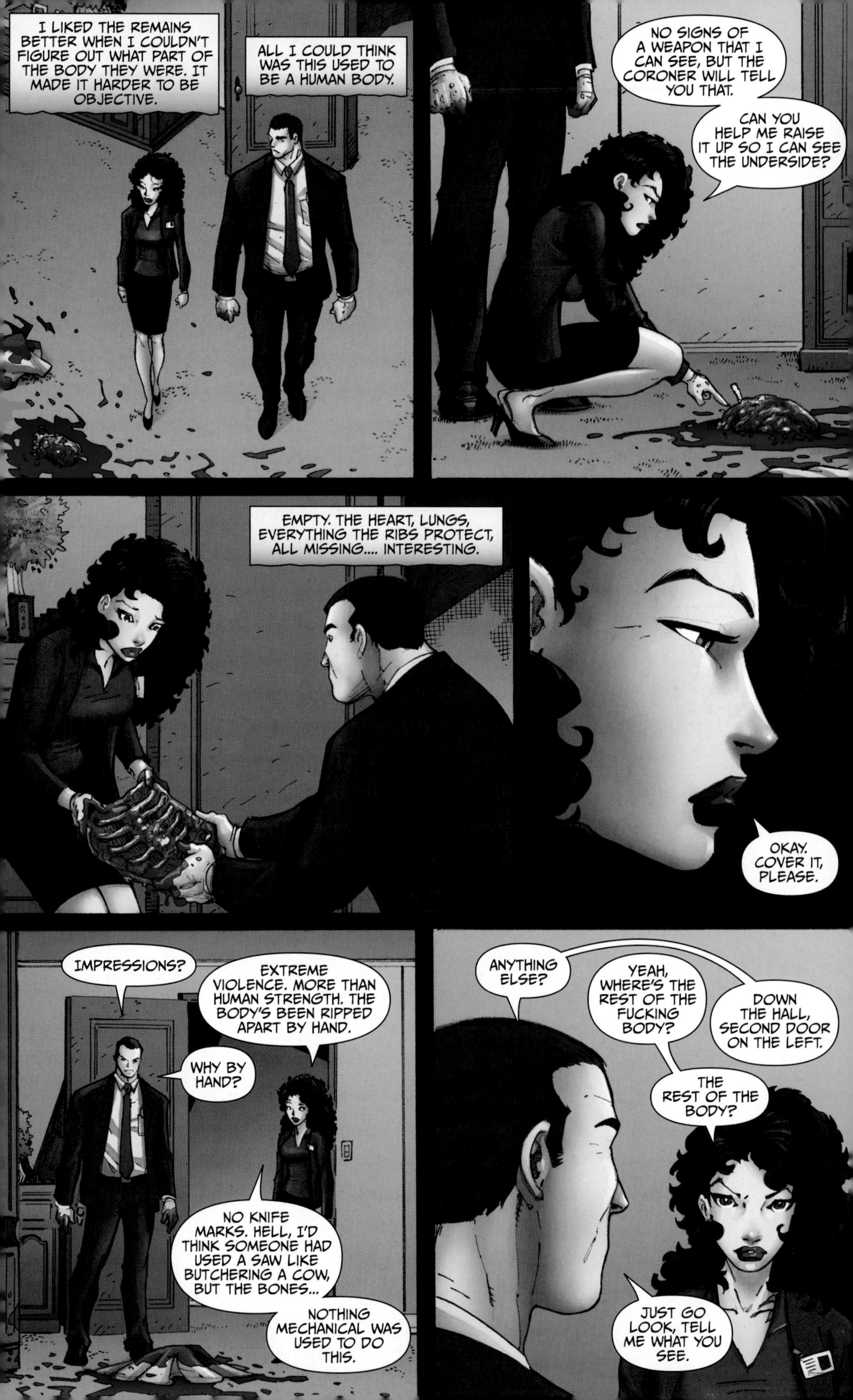
I LIKED THE REMAINS BETTER WHEN I COULDN'T FIGURE OUT WHAT PART OF THE BODY THEY WERE. IT MADE IT HARDER TO BE OBJECTIVE.
ALL I COULD THINK WAS THIS USED TO BE A HUMAN BODY.
NO SIGNS OF A WEAPON THAT I CAN SEE, BUT THE CORONER WILL TELL YOU THAT.
CAN YOU HELP ME RAISE IT UP SO I CAN SEE THE UNDERSIDE?
EMPTY. THE HEART, LUNGS, EVERYTHING THE RIBS PROTECT, ALL MISSING.... INTERESTING.
OKAY. COVER IT, PLEASE.
IMPRESSIONS?
EXTREME VIOLENCE. MORE THAN HUMAN STRENGTH. THE BODY'S BEEN RIPPED APART BY HAND.
WHY BY HAND?
NO KNIFE MARKS. HELL, I'D THINK SOMEONE HAD USED A SAW LIKE BUTCHERING A COW, BUT THE BONES...
NOTHING MECHANICAL WAS USED TO DO THIS.
ANYTHING ELSE?
YEAH, WHERE'S THE REST OF THE FUCKING BODY?
DOWN THE HALL, SECOND DOOR ON THE LEFT.
THE REST OF THE BODY?
JUST GO LOOK, TELL ME WHAT YOU SEE.

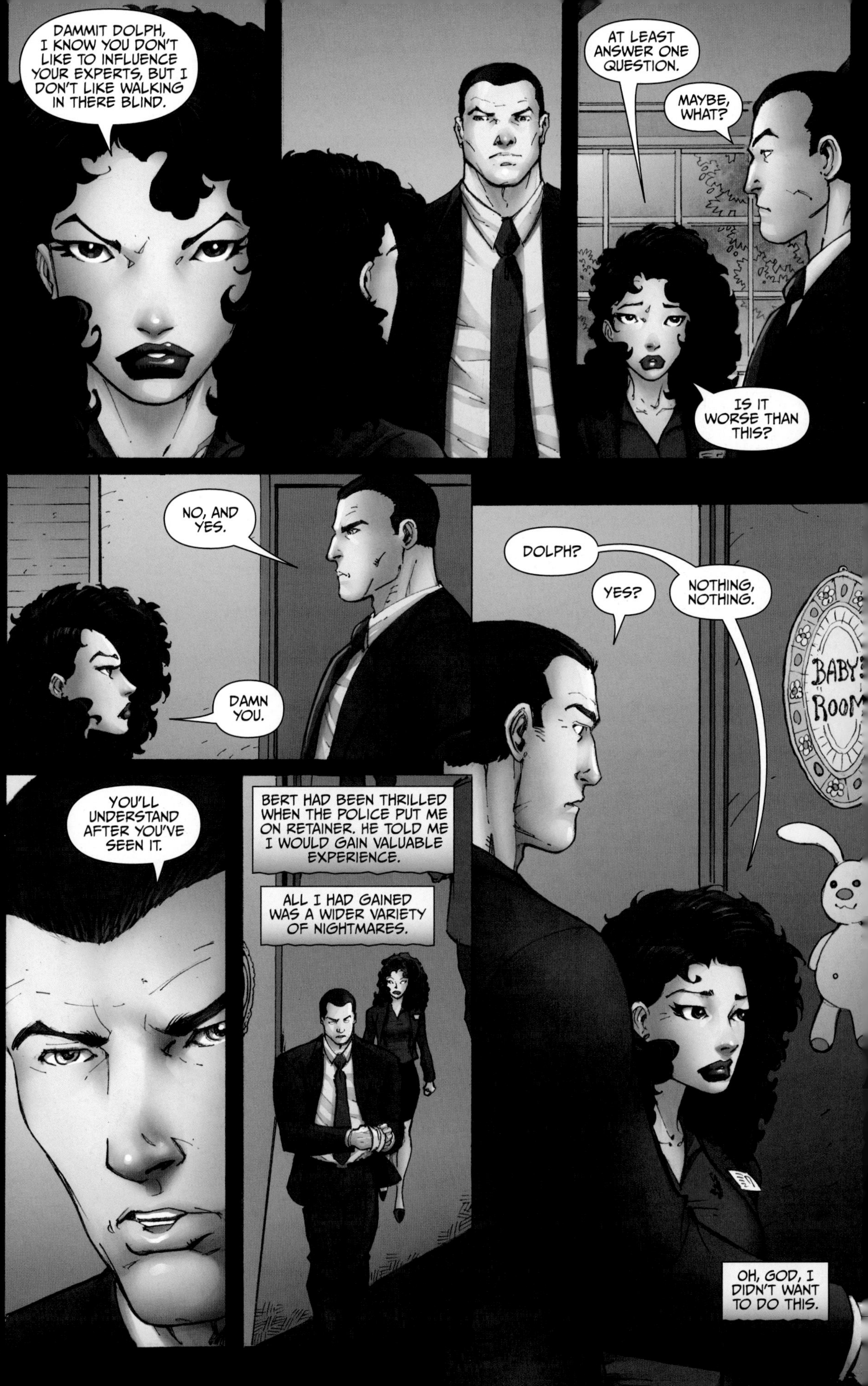

DAMMIT DOLPH, I KNOW YOU DON'T LIKE TO INFLUENCE YOUR EXPERTS, BUT I DON'T LIKE WALKING IN THERE BLIND.
AT LEAST ANSWER ONE QUESTION.
MAYBE, WHAT?
IS IT WORSE THAN THIS?
NO, AND YES.
DAMN YOU.
DOLPH?
YES?
NOTHING, NOTHING.
BABY'S ROOM
YOU'LL UNDERSTAND AFTER YOU'VE SEEN IT.
BERT HAD BEEN THRILLED WHEN THE POLICE PUT ME ON RETAINER. HE TOLD ME I WOULD GAIN VALUABLE EXPERIENCE.
ALL I HAD GAINED WAS A WIDER VARIETY OF NIGHTMARES.
OH, GOD, I DIDN'T WANT TO DO THIS.

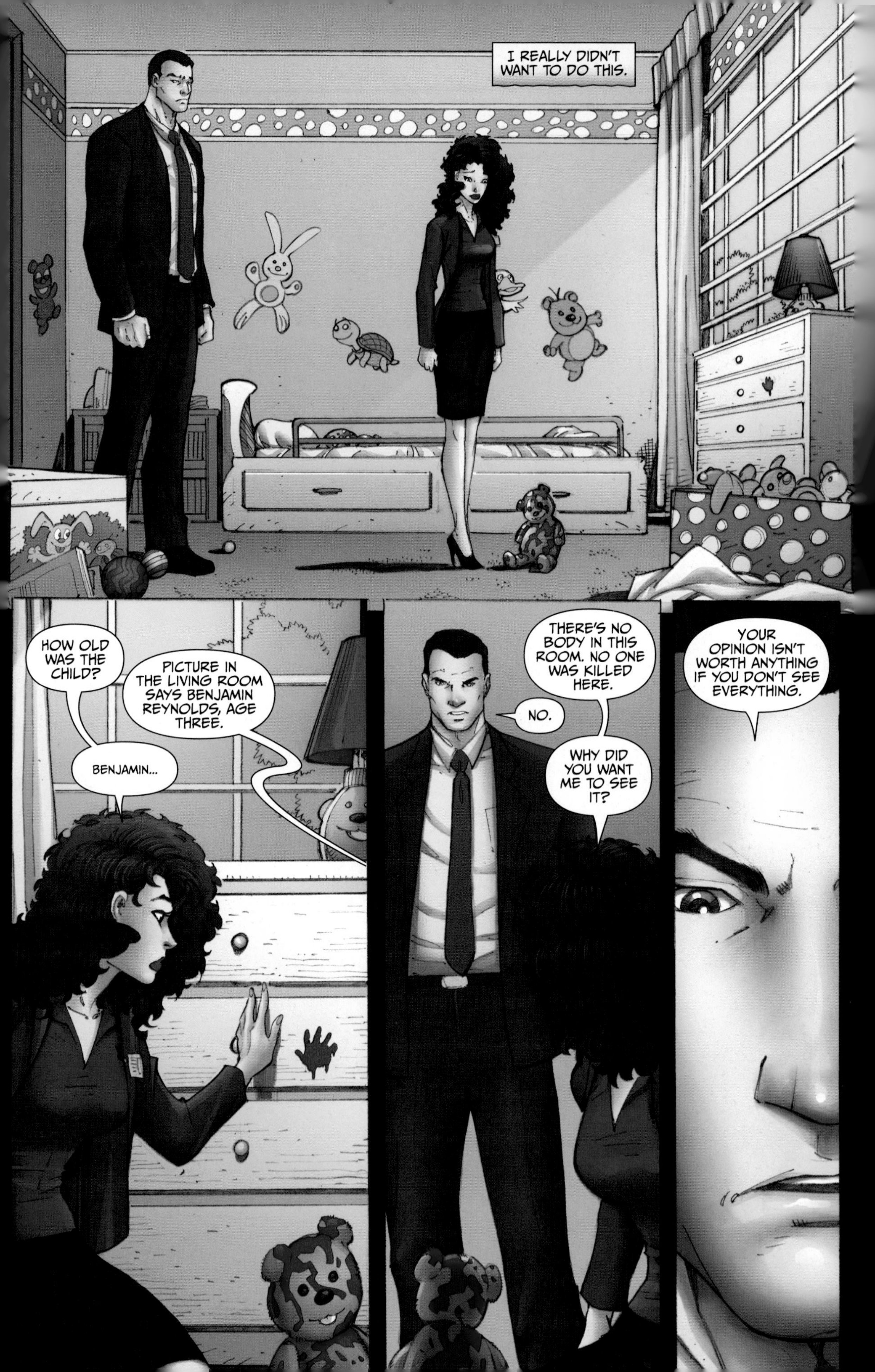
I REALLY DIDN'T WANT TO DO THIS.
HOW OLD WAS THE CHILD?
PICTURE IN THE LIVING ROOM SAYS BENJAMIN REYNOLDS, AGE THREE.
BENJAMIN...
NO.
THERE'S NO BODY IN THIS ROOM. NO ONE WAS KILLED HERE.
WHY DID YOU WANT ME TO SEE IT?
YOUR OPINION ISN'T WORTH ANYTHING IF YOU DON'T SEE EVERYTHING.

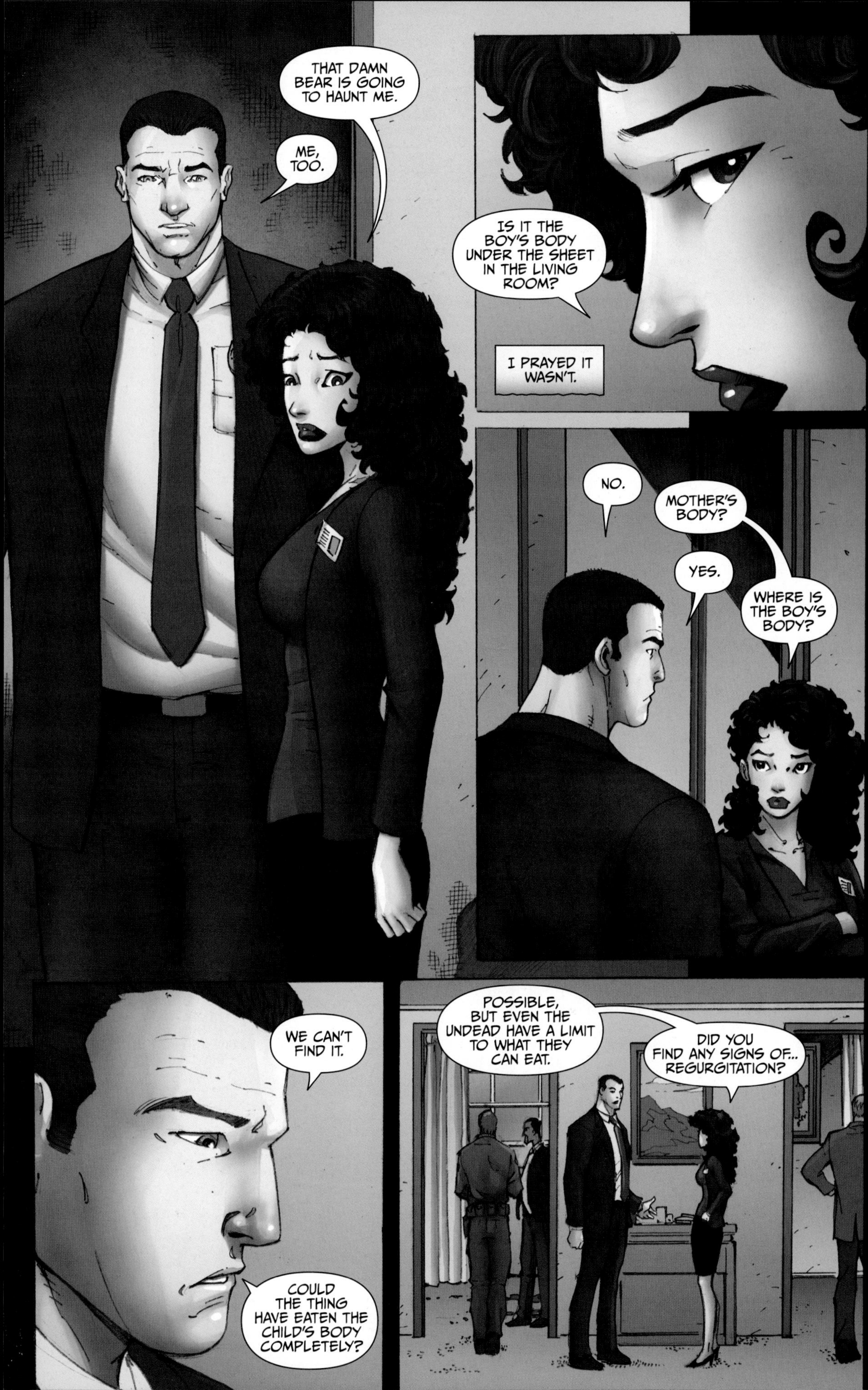
THAT DAMN BEAR IS GOING TO HAUNT ME.
ME, TOO.
IS IT THE BOY'S BODY UNDER THE SHEET IN THE LIVING ROOM?
I PRAYED IT WASN'T.
NO.
MOTHER'S BODY?
YES.
WHERE IS THE BOY'S BODY?
WE CAN'T FIND IT.
COULD THE THING HAVE EATEN THE CHILD'S BODY COMPLETELY?
POSSIBLE, BUT EVEN THE UNDEAD HAVE A LIMIT TO WHAT THEY CAN EAT.
DID YOU FIND ANY SIGNS OF... REGURGITATION?

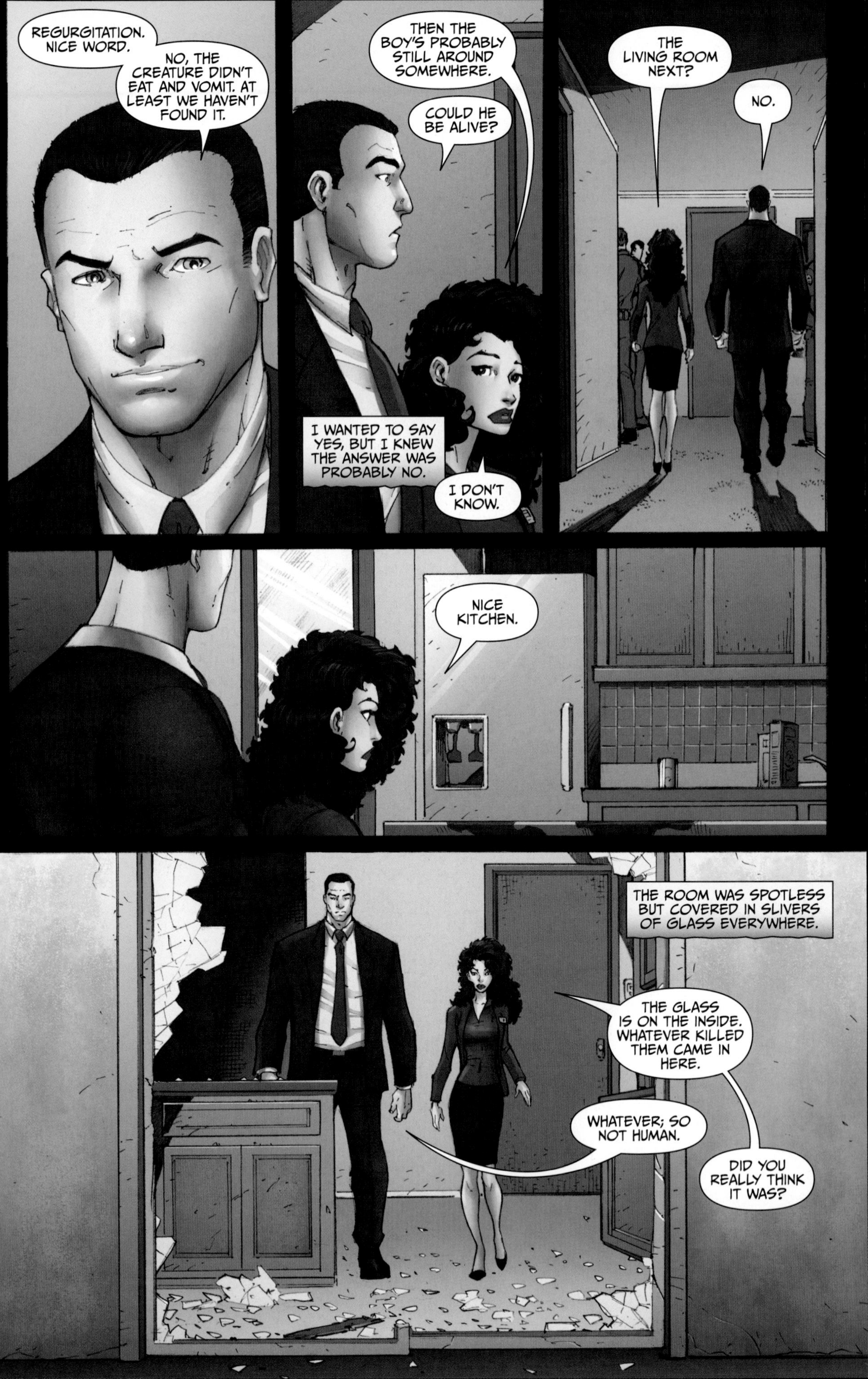
REGURGITATION. NICE WORD.
NO, THE CREATURE DIDN'T EAT AND VOMIT. AT LEAST WE HAVEN'T FOUND IT.
THEN THE BOY'S PROBABLY STILL AROUND SOMEWHERE.
COULD HE BE ALIVE?
I WANTED TO SAY YES, BUT I KNEW THE ANSWER WAS PROBABLY NO.
I DON'T KNOW.
THE LIVING ROOM NEXT?
NO.
NICE KITCHEN.
THE ROOM WAS SPOTLESS BUT COVERED IN SLIVERS OF GLASS EVERYWHERE.
THE GLASS IS ON THE INSIDE. WHATEVER KILLED THEM CAME IN HERE.
WHATEVER; SO NOT HUMAN.
DID YOU REALLY THINK IT WAS?

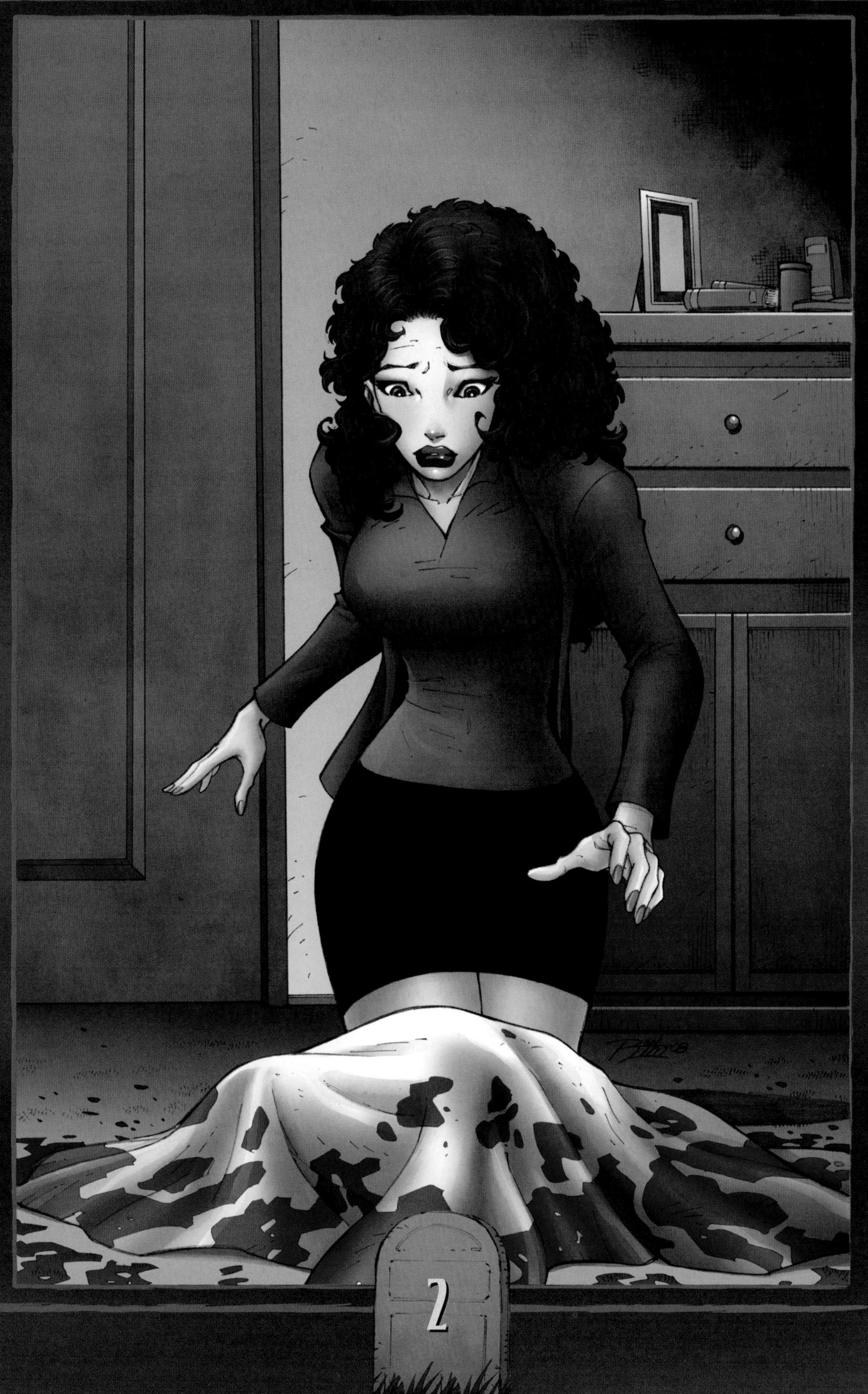
2

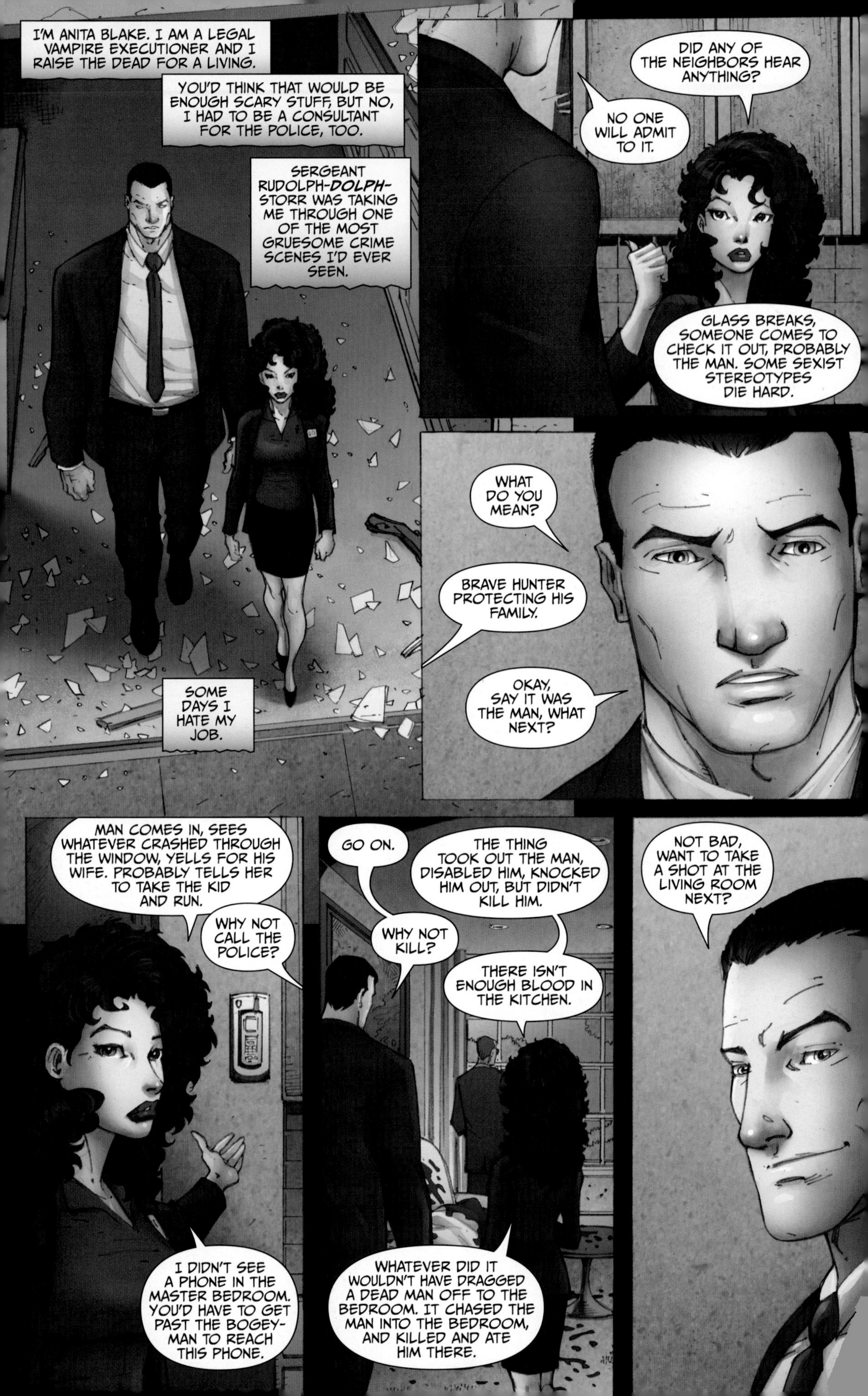
I'M ANITA BLAKE. I AM A LEGAL VAMPIRE EXECUTIONER AND I RAISE THE DEAD FOR A LIVING.
YOU'D THINK THAT WOULD BE ENOUGH SCARY STUFF, BUT NO, I HAD TO BE A CONSULTANT FOR THE POLICE, TOO.
SERGEANT RUDOLPH-DOLPH-STORR WAS TAKING ME THROUGH ONE OF THE MOST GRUESOME CRIME SCENES I'D EVER SEEN.
SOME DAYS I HATE MY JOB.
DID ANY OF THE NEIGHBORS HEAR ANYTHING?
NO ONE WILL ADMIT TO IT.
GLASS BREAKS, SOMEONE COMES TO CHECK IT OUT, PROBABLY THE MAN. SOME SEXIST STEREOTYPES DIE HARD.
WHAT DO YOU MEAN?
BRAVE HUNTER PROTECTING HIS FAMILY.
OKAY, SAY IT WAS THE MAN, WHAT NEXT?
MAN COMES IN, SEES WHATEVER CRASHED THROUGH THE WINDOW, YELLS FOR HIS WIFE. PROBABLY TELLS HER TO TAKE THE KID AND RUN.
WHY NOT CALL THE POLICE?
I DIDN'T SEE A PHONE IN THE MASTER BEDROOM. YOU'D HAVE TO GET PAST THE BOGEY-MAN TO REACH THIS PHONE.
GO ON.
THE THING TOOK OUT THE MAN, DISABLED HIM, KNOCKED HIM OUT, BUT DIDN'T KILL HIM.
WHY NOT KILL?
THERE ISN'T ENOUGH BLOOD IN THE KITCHEN.
WHATEVER DID IT WOULDN'T HAVE DRAGGED A DEAD MAN OFF TO THE BEDROOM. IT CHASED THE MAN INTO THE BEDROOM, AND KILLED AND ATE HIM THERE.
NOT BAD, WANT TO TAKE A SHOT AT THE LIVING ROOM NEXT?

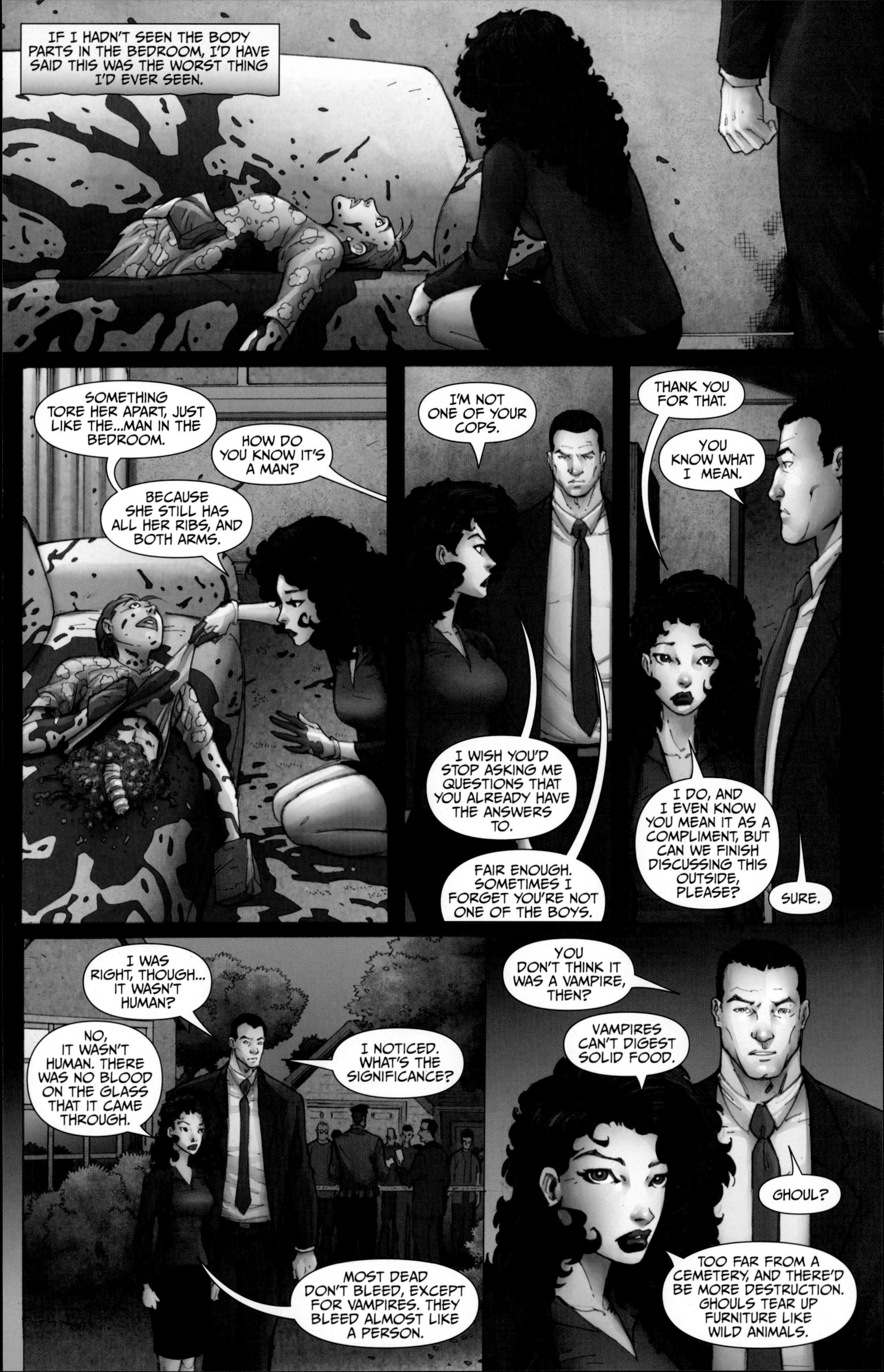
IF I HADN'T SEEN THE BODY PARTS IN THE BEDROOM, I'D HAVE SAID THIS WAS THE WORST THING I'D EVER SEEN.
SOMETHING TORE HER APART, JUST LIKE THE...MAN IN THE BEDROOM.
HOW DO YOU KNOW IT'S A MAN?
BECAUSE SHE STILL HAS ALL HER RIBS, AND BOTH ARMS.
I'M NOT ONE OF YOUR COPS.
I WISH YOU'D STOP ASKING ME QUESTIONS THAT YOU ALREADY HAVE THE ANSWERS TO.
FAIR ENOUGH. SOMETIMES I FORGET YOU'RE NOT ONE OF THE BOYS.
THANK YOU FOR THAT.
YOU KNOW WHAT I MEAN.
I DO, AND I EVEN KNOW YOU MEAN IT AS A COMPLIMENT, BUT CAN WE FINISH DISCUSSING THIS OUTSIDE, PLEASE?
SURE.
I WAS RIGHT, THOUGH... IT WASN'T HUMAN?
NO, IT WASN'T HUMAN. THERE WAS NO BLOOD ON THE GLASS THAT IT CAME THROUGH.
I NOTICED. WHAT'S THE SIGNIFICANCE?
MOST DEAD DON'T BLEED, EXCEPT FOR VAMPIRES. THEY BLEED ALMOST LIKE A PERSON.
YOU DON'T THINK IT WAS A VAMPIRE, THEN?
VAMPIRES CAN'T DIGEST SOLID FOOD.
GHOUL?
TOO FAR FROM A CEMETERY, AND THERE'D BE MORE DESTRUCTION. GHOULS TEAR UP FURNITURE LIKE WILD ANIMALS.

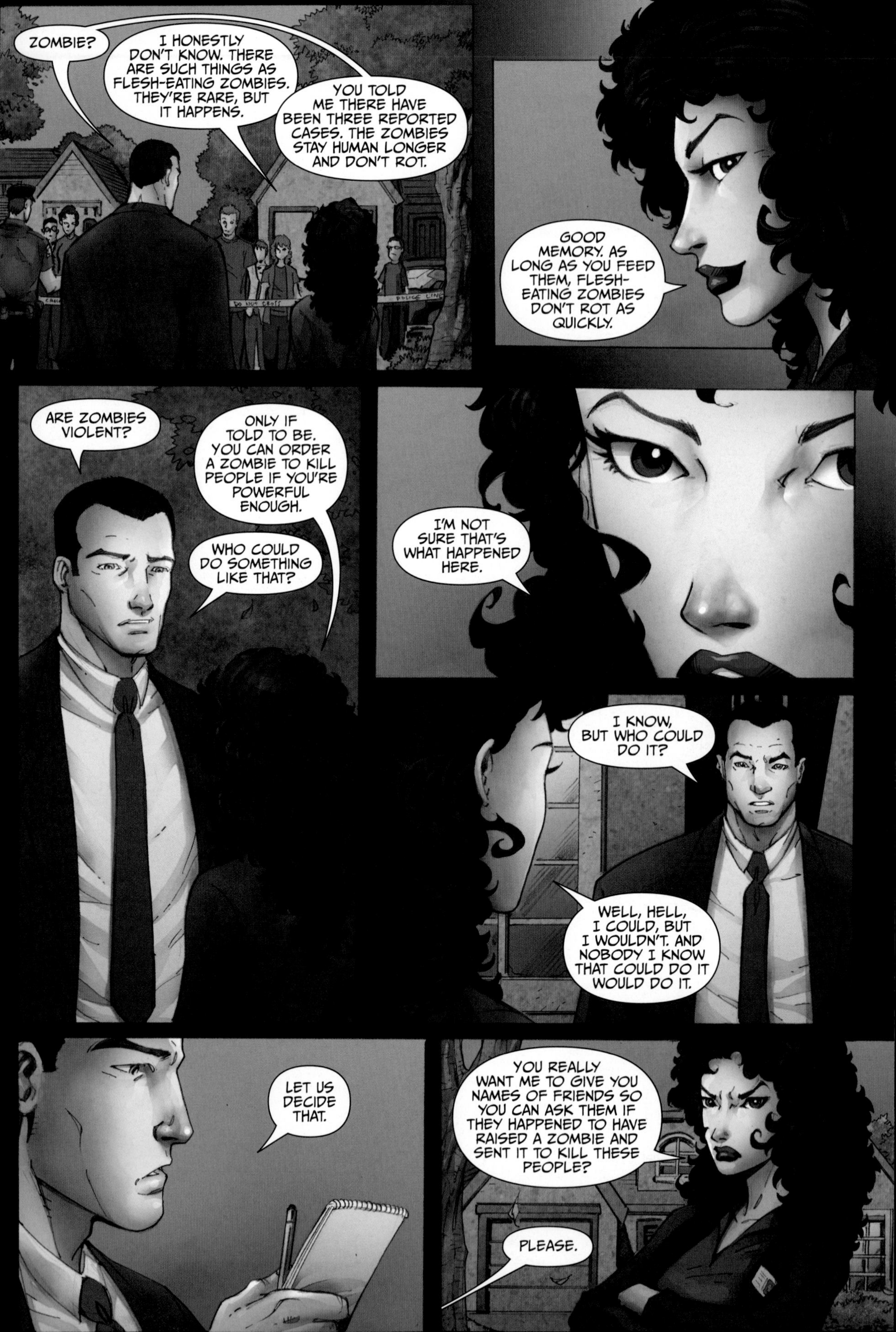
ZOMBIE?
I HONESTLY DON'T KNOW. THERE ARE SUCH THINGS AS FLESH-EATING ZOMBIES. THEY'RE RARE, BUT IT HAPPENS.
YOU TOLD ME THERE HAVE BEEN THREE REPORTED CASES. THE ZOMBIES STAY HUMAN LONGER AND DON'T ROT.
GOOD MEMORY. AS LONG AS YOU FEED THEM, FLESH-EATING ZOMBIES DON'T ROT AS QUICKLY.
ARE ZOMBIES VIOLENT?
ONLY IF TOLD TO BE. YOU CAN ORDER A ZOMBIE TO KILL PEOPLE IF YOU'RE POWERFUL ENOUGH.
WHO COULD DO SOMETHING LIKE THAT?
I'M NOT SURE THAT'S WHAT HAPPENED HERE.
I KNOW, BUT WHO COULD DO IT?
WELL, HELL, I COULD, BUT I WOULDN'T. AND NOBODY I KNOW THAT COULD DO IT WOULD DO IT.
LET US DECIDE THAT.
YOU REALLY WANT ME TO GIVE YOU NAMES OF FRIENDS SO YOU CAN ASK THEM IF THEY HAPPENED TO HAVE RAISED A ZOMBIE AND SENT IT TO KILL THESE PEOPLE?
PLEASE.

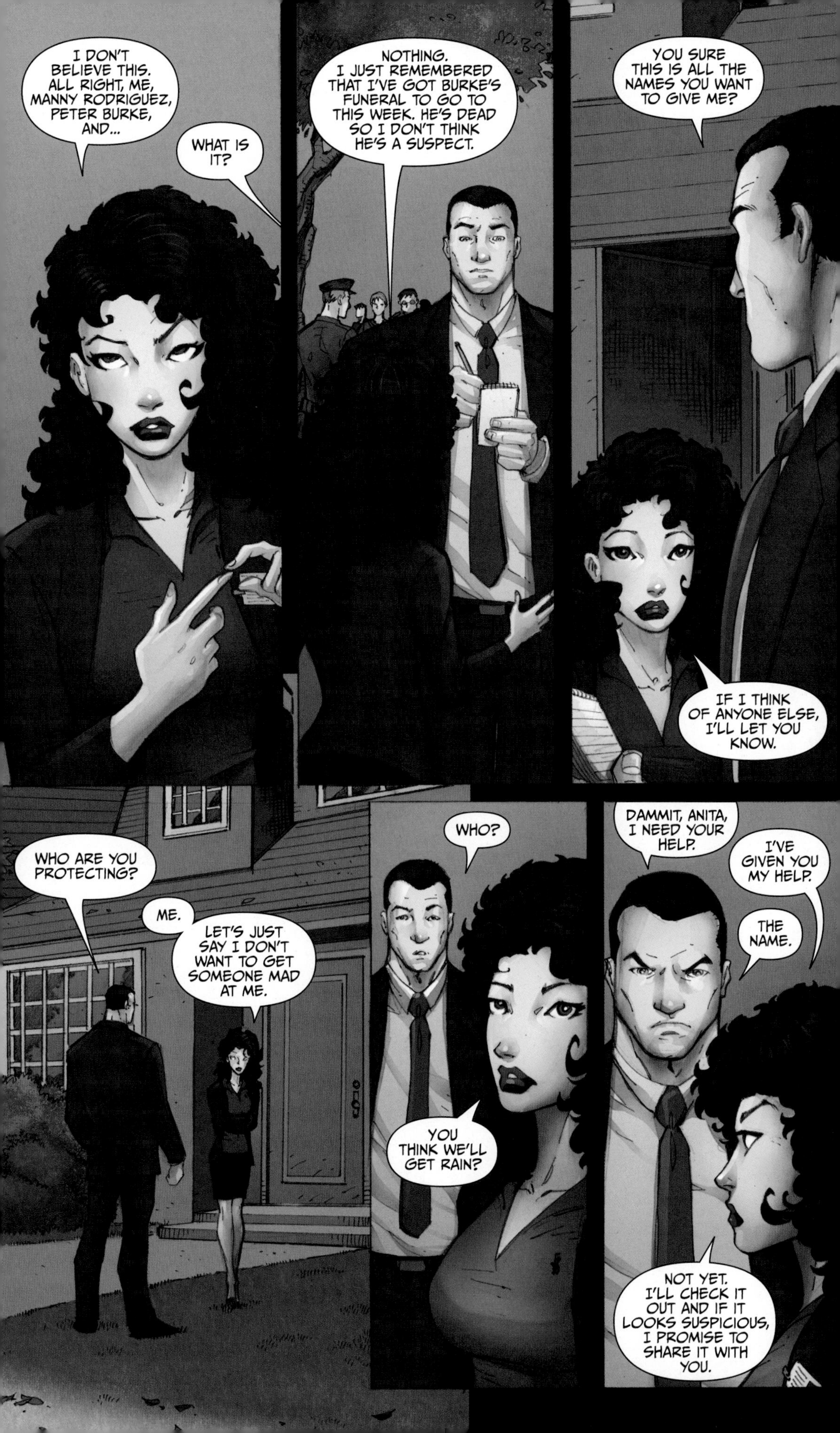
I DON'T BELIEVE THIS. ALL RIGHT, ME, MANNY RODRIGUEZ, PETER BURKE, AND...
WHAT IS IT?
NOTHING. I JUST REMEMBERED THAT I'VE GOT BURKE'S FUNERAL TO GO TO THIS WEEK. HE'S DEAD SO I DON'T THINK HE'S A SUSPECT.
YOU SURE THIS IS ALL THE NAMES YOU WANT TO GIVE ME?
IF I THINK OF ANYONE ELSE, I'LL LET YOU KNOW.
WHO ARE YOU PROTECTING?
ME.
LET'S JUST SAY I DON'T WANT TO GET SOMEONE MAD AT ME.
WHO?
YOU THINK WE'LL GET RAIN?
DAMMIT, ANITA, I NEED YOUR HELP.
I'VE GIVEN YOU MY HELP.
THE NAME.
NOT YET. I'LL CHECK IT OUT AND IF IT LOOKS SUSPICIOUS, I PROMISE TO SHARE IT WITH YOU.

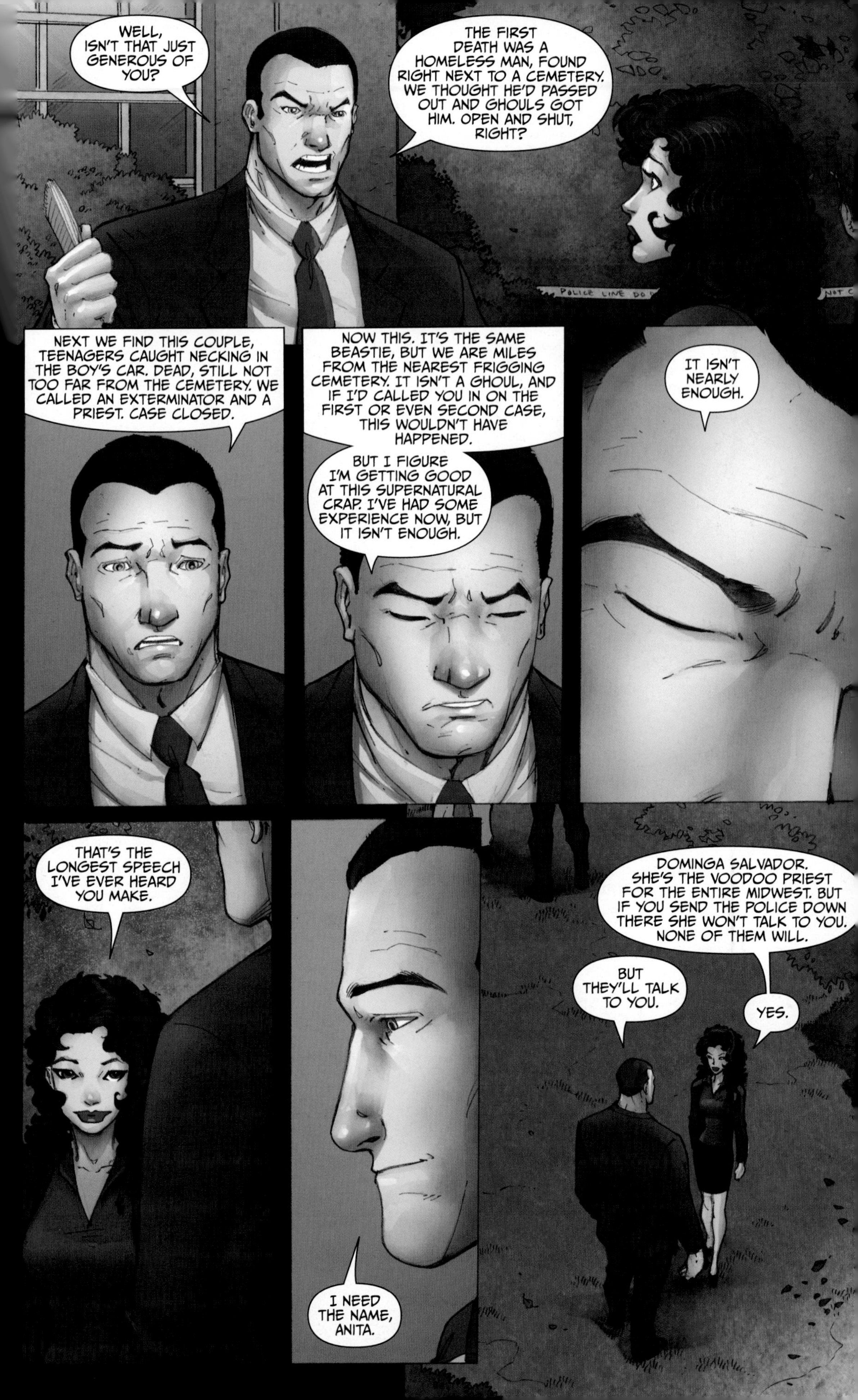
WELL, ISN'T THAT JUST GENEROUS OF YOU?
THE FIRST DEATH WAS A HOMELESS MAN, FOUND RIGHT NEXT TO A CEMETERY. WE THOUGHT HE'D PASSED OUT AND GHOULS GOT HIM. OPEN AND SHUT, RIGHT?
POLICE LINE DO
NOT C
NEXT WE FIND THIS COUPLE, TEENAGERS CAUGHT NECKING IN THE BOY'S CAR. DEAD, STILL NOT TOO FAR FROM THE CEMETERY. WE CALLED AN EXTERMINATOR AND A PRIEST. CASE CLOSED.
NOW THIS. IT'S THE SAME BEASTIE, BUT WE ARE MILES FROM THE NEAREST FRIGGING CEMETERY. IT ISN'T A GHOUL, AND IF I'D CALLED YOU IN ON THE FIRST OR EVEN SECOND CASE, THIS WOULDN'T HAVE HAPPENED.
BUT I FIGURE I'M GETTING GOOD AT THIS SUPERNATURAL CRAP. I'VE HAD SOME EXPERIENCE NOW, BUT IT ISN'T ENOUGH.
IT ISN'T NEARLY ENOUGH.
THAT'S THE LONGEST SPEECH I'VE EVER HEARD YOU MAKE.
I NEED THE NAME, ANITA.
DOMINGA SALVADOR. SHE'S THE VOODOO PRIEST FOR THE ENTIRE MIDWEST. BUT IF YOU SEND THE POLICE DOWN THERE SHE WON'T TALK TO YOU. NONE OF THEM WILL.
BUT THEY'LL TALK TO YOU.
YES.

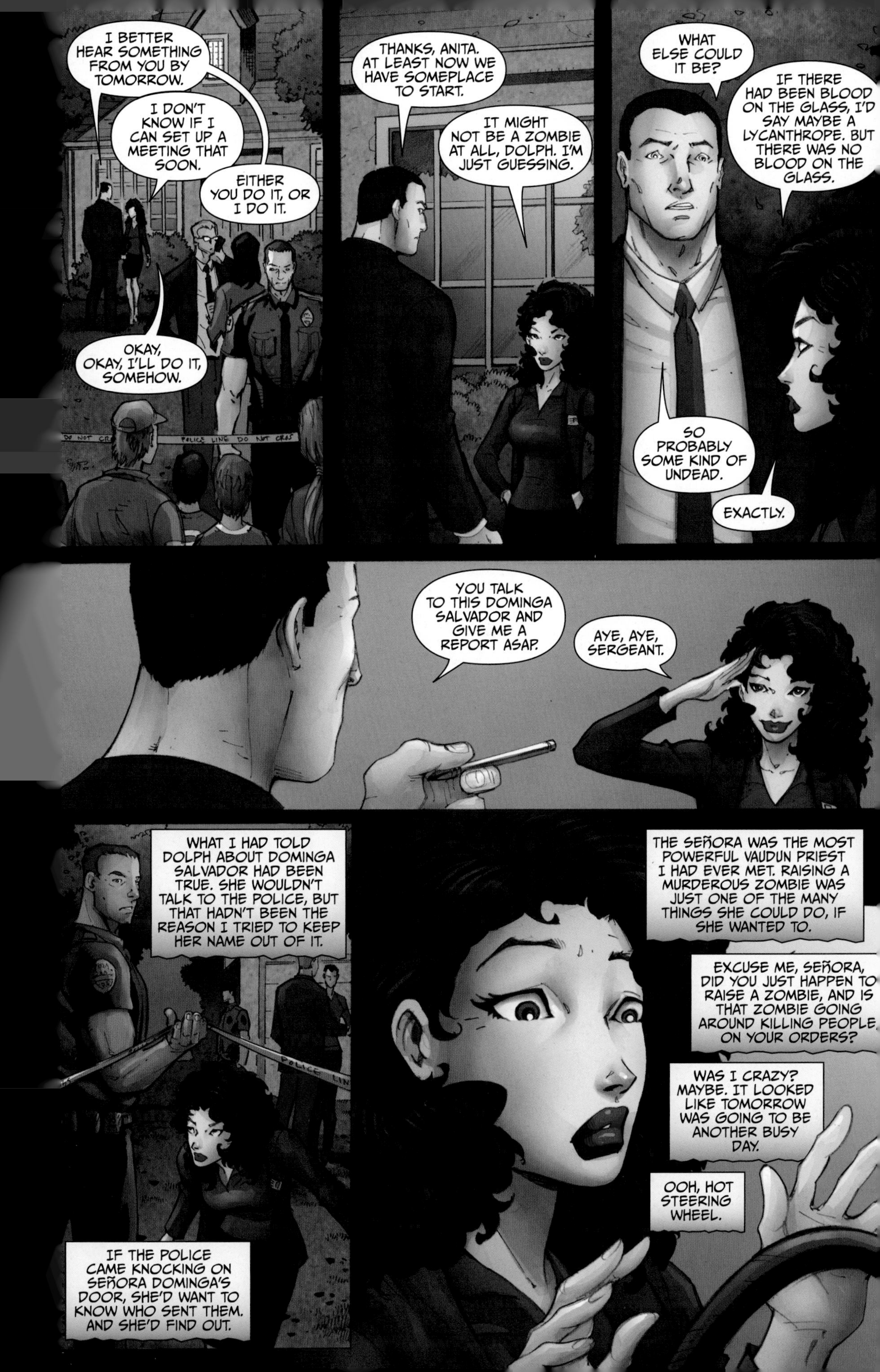
I BETTER HEAR SOMETHING FROM YOU BY TOMORROW.
I DON'T KNOW IF I CAN SET UP A MEETING THAT SOON.
EITHER YOU DO IT, OR I DO IT.
OKAY, OKAY, I'LL DO IT, SOMEHOW.
POLICE LINE DO NOT CROSS
THANKS, ANITA. AT LEAST NOW WE HAVE SOMEPLACE TO START.
IT MIGHT NOT BE A ZOMBIE AT ALL, DOLPH. I'M JUST GUESSING.
WHAT ELSE COULD IT BE?
IF THERE HAD BEEN BLOOD ON THE GLASS, I'D SAY MAYBE A LYCANTHROPE. BUT THERE WAS NO BLOOD ON THE GLASS.
SO PROBABLY SOME KIND OF UNDEAD.
EXACTLY.
YOU TALK TO THIS DOMINGA SALVADOR AND GIVE ME A REPORT ASAP.
AYE, AYE, SERGEANT.
WHAT I HAD TOLD DOLPH ABOUT DOMINGA SALVADOR HAD BEEN TRUE. SHE WOULDN'T TALK TO THE POLICE, BUT THAT HADN'T BEEN THE REASON I TRIED TO KEEP HER NAME OUT OF IT.
IF THE POLICE CAME KNOCKING ON SEÑORA DOMINGA'S DOOR, SHE'D WANT TO KNOW WHO SENT THEM. AND SHE'D FIND OUT.
THE SEÑORA WAS THE MOST POWERFUL VAUDUN PRIEST I HAD EVER MET. RAISING A MURDEROUS ZOMBIE WAS JUST ONE OF THE MANY THINGS SHE COULD DO, IF SHE WANTED TO.
EXCUSE ME, SEÑORA, DID YOU JUST HAPPEN TO RAISE A ZOMBIE, AND IS THAT ZOMBIE GOING AROUND KILLING PEOPLE ON YOUR ORDERS?
WAS I CRAZY? MAYBE. IT LOOKED LIKE TOMORROW WAS GOING TO BE ANOTHER BUSY DAY.
OOH, HOT STEERING WHEEL.

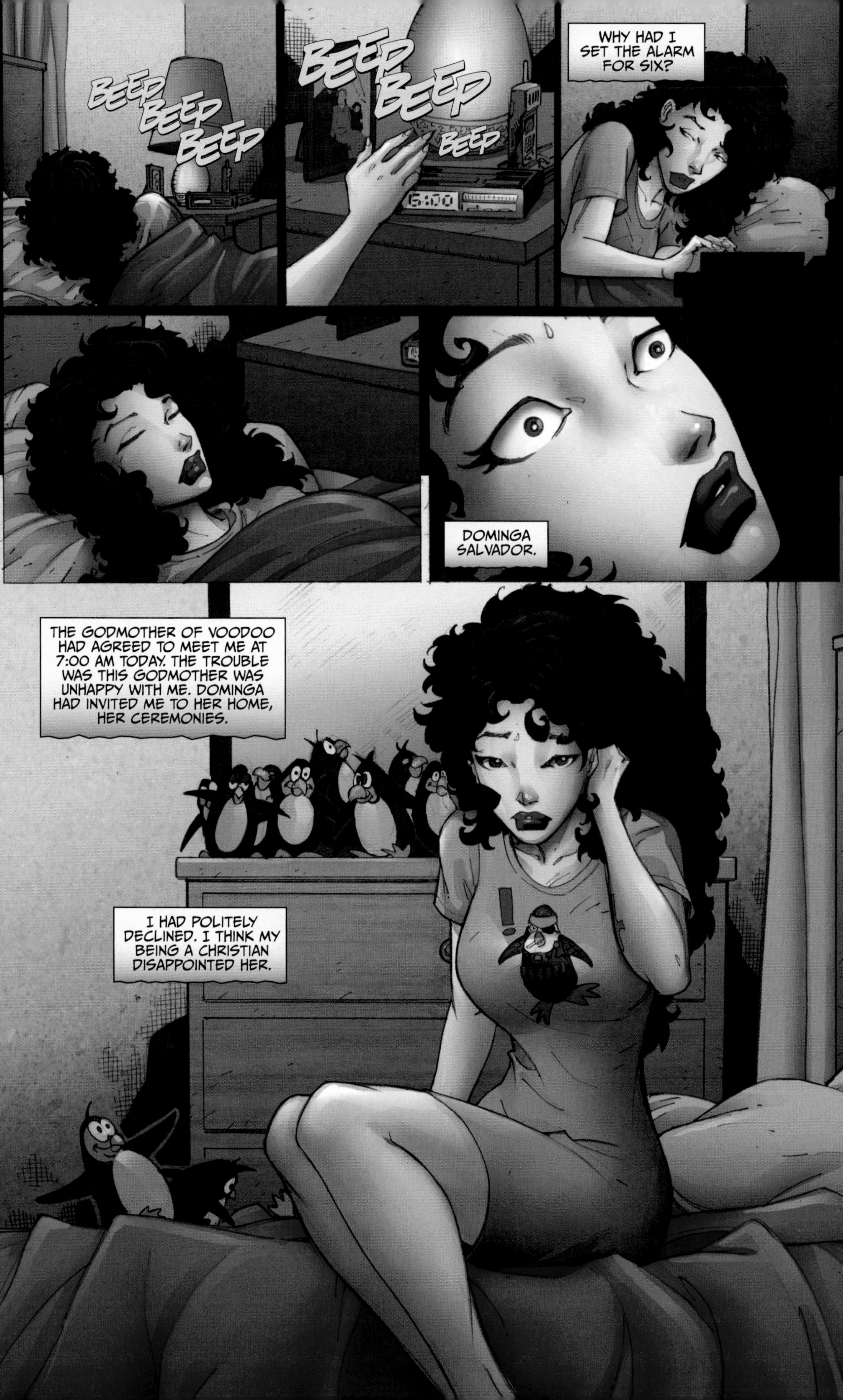
BEEP BEEP BEEP
BEEP BEEP BEEP
6:00
WHY HAD I SET THE ALARM FOR SIX?
DOMINGA SALVADOR.
THE GODMOTHER OF VOODOO HAD AGREED TO MEET ME AT 7:00 AM TODAY. THE TROUBLE WAS THIS GODMOTHER WAS UNHAPPY WITH ME. DOMINGA HAD INVITED ME TO HER HOME, HER CEREMONIES.
I HAD POLITELY DECLINED. I THINK MY BEING A CHRISTIAN DISAPPOINTED HER.

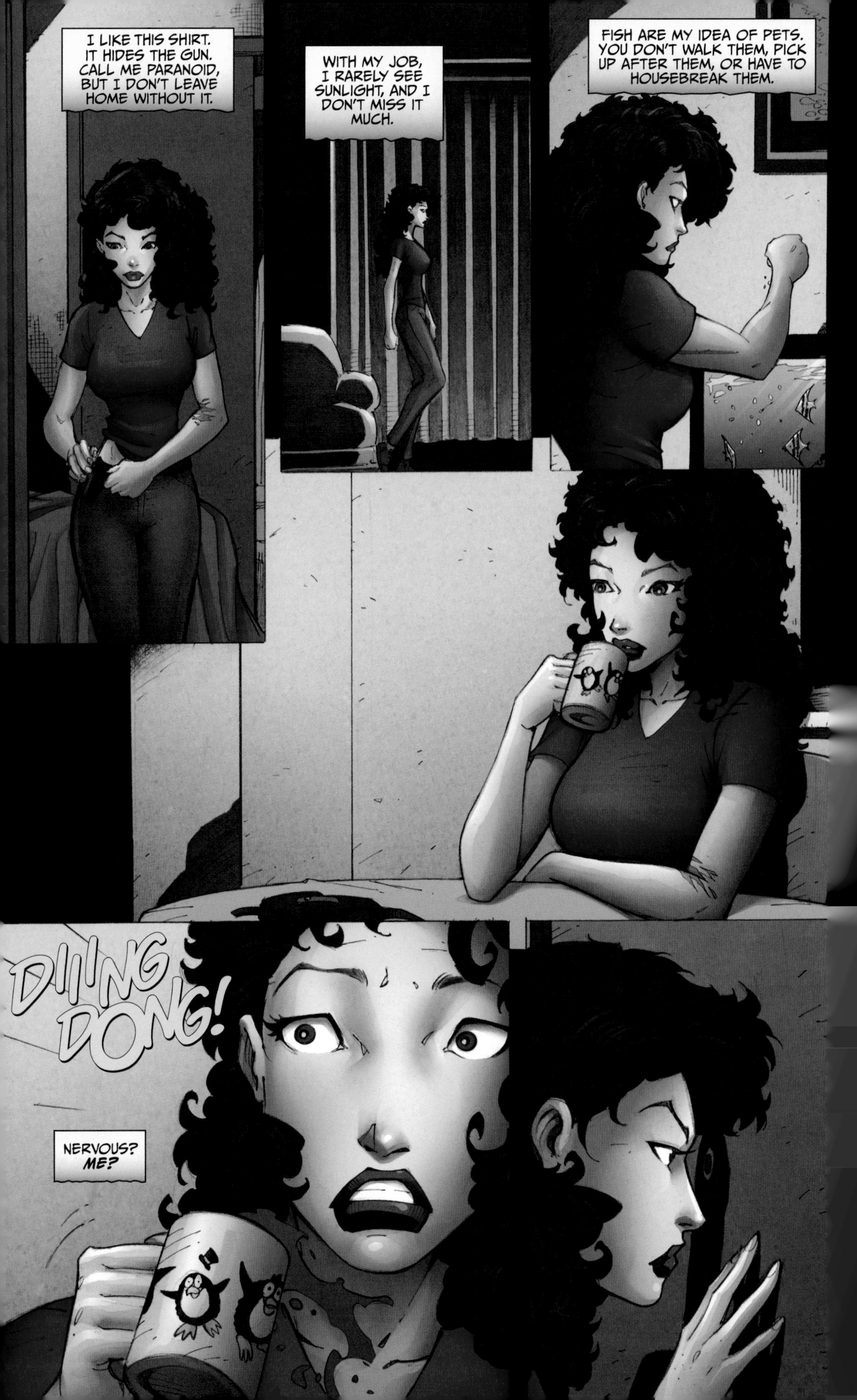
I LIKE THIS SHIRT. IT HIDES THE GUN. CALL ME PARANOID, BUT I DON'T LEAVE HOME WITHOUT IT.
WITH MY JOB, I RARELY SEE SUNLIGHT, AND I DON'T MISS IT MUCH.
FISH ARE MY IDEA OF PETS. YOU DON'T WALK THEM, PICK UP AFTER THEM, OR HAVE TO HOUSEBREAK THEM.
DIIING DONG!
NERVOUS? *ME?*

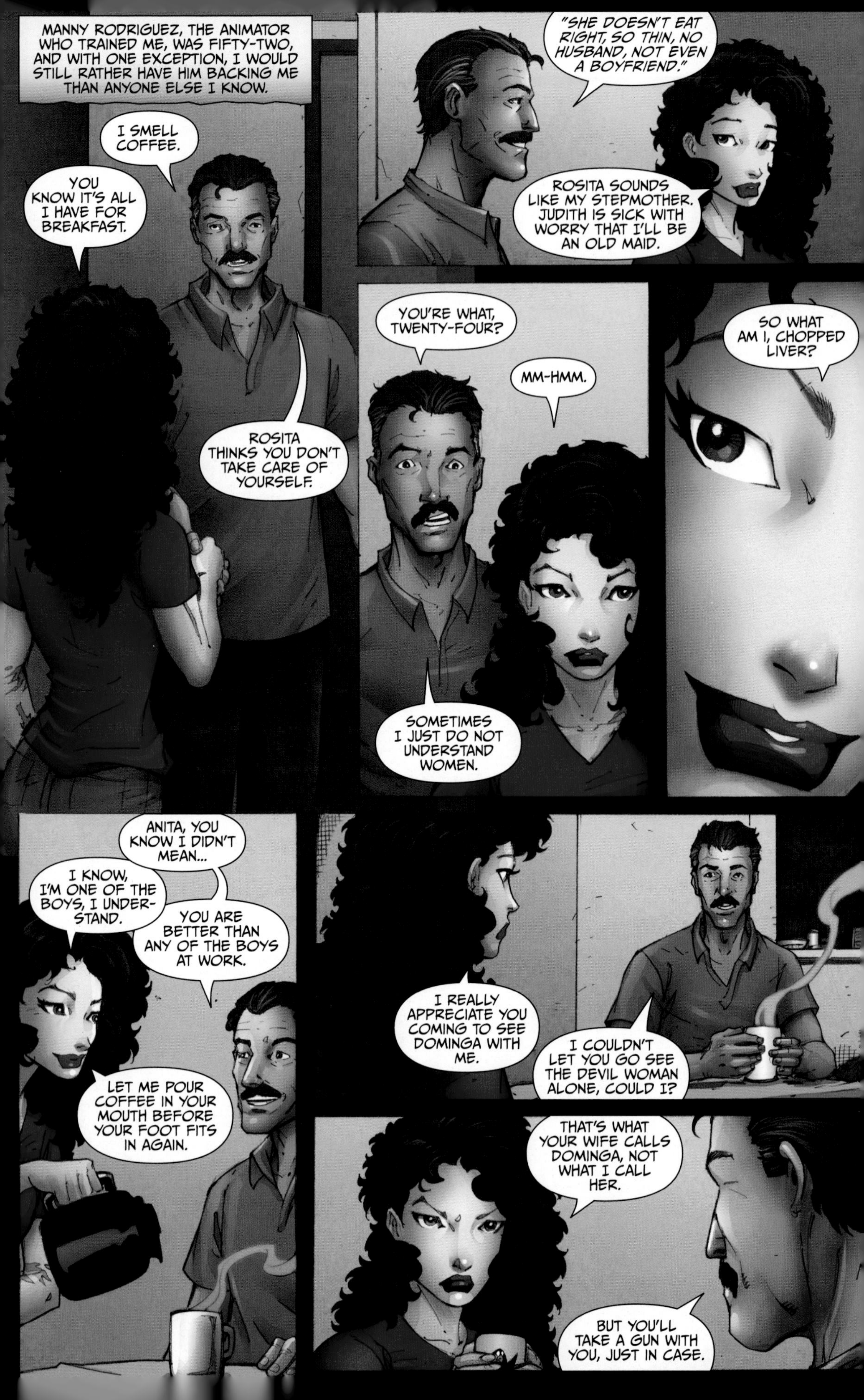
MANNY RODRIGUEZ, THE ANIMATOR WHO TRAINED ME, WAS FIFTY-TWO, AND WITH ONE EXCEPTION, I WOULD STILL RATHER HAVE HIM BACKING ME THAN ANYONE ELSE I KNOW.
I SMELL COFFEE.
YOU KNOW IT'S ALL I HAVE FOR BREAKFAST.
ROSITA THINKS YOU DON'T TAKE CARE OF YOURSELF.
"SHE DOESN'T EAT RIGHT, SO THIN, NO HUSBAND, NOT EVEN A BOYFRIEND."
ROSITA SOUNDS LIKE MY STEPMOTHER. JUDITH IS SICK WITH WORRY THAT I'LL BE AN OLD MAID.
YOU'RE WHAT, TWENTY-FOUR?
MM-HMM.
SOMETIMES I JUST DO NOT UNDERSTAND WOMEN.
SO WHAT AM I, CHOPPED LIVER?
ANITA, YOU KNOW I DIDN'T MEAN...
I KNOW, I'M ONE OF THE BOYS, I UNDER-STAND.
YOU ARE BETTER THAN ANY OF THE BOYS AT WORK.
LET ME POUR COFFEE IN YOUR MOUTH BEFORE YOUR FOOT FITS IN AGAIN.
I REALLY APPRECIATE YOU COMING TO SEE DOMINGA WITH ME.
I COULDN'T LET YOU GO SEE THE DEVIL WOMAN ALONE, COULD I?
THAT'S WHAT YOUR WIFE CALLS DOMINGA, NOT WHAT I CALL HER.
BUT YOU'LL TAKE A GUN WITH YOU, JUST IN CASE.

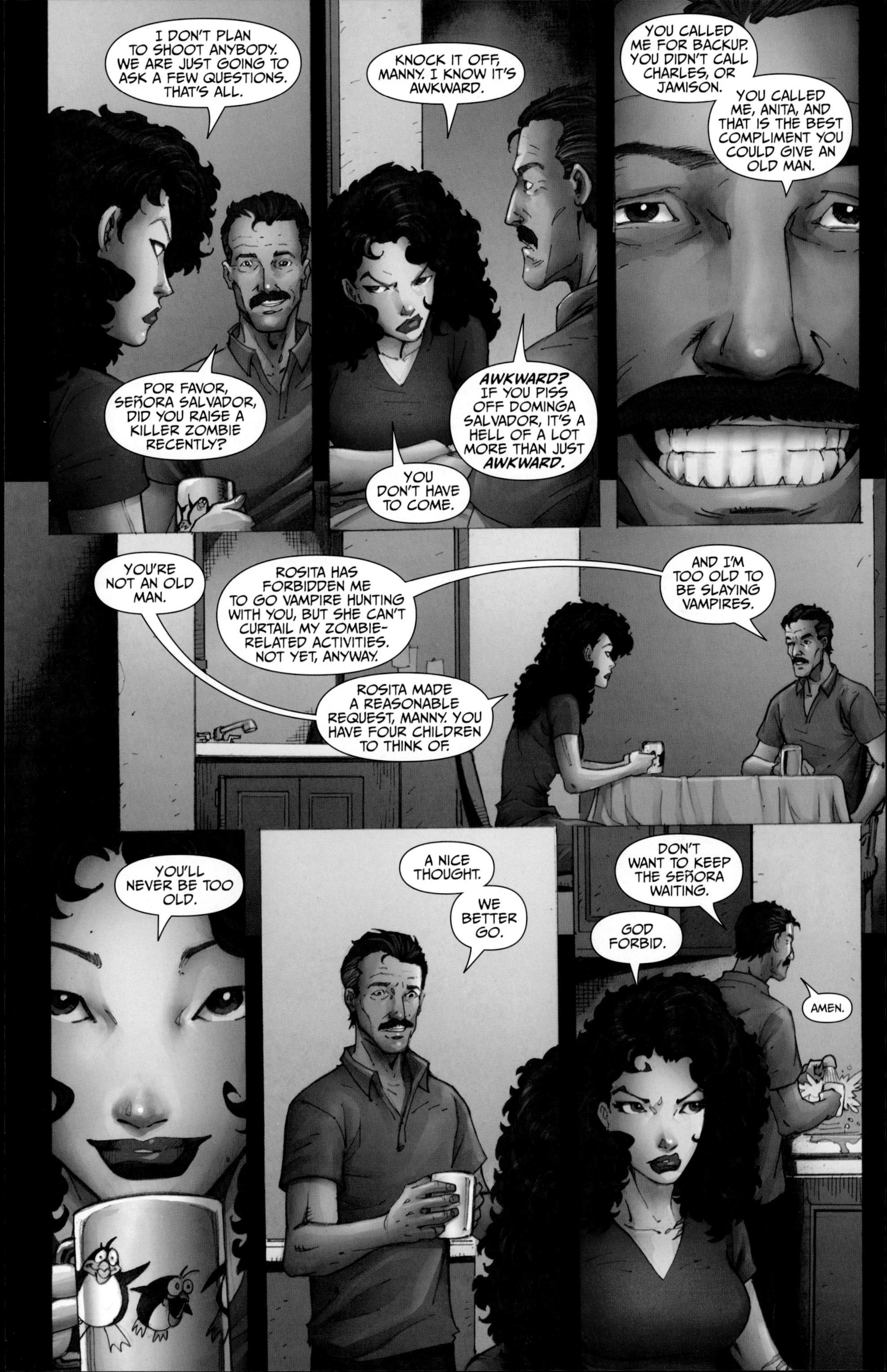
I DON'T PLAN TO SHOOT ANYBODY. WE ARE JUST GOING TO ASK A FEW QUESTIONS. THAT'S ALL.
POR FAVOR, SEÑORA SALVADOR, DID YOU RAISE A KILLER ZOMBIE RECENTLY?
KNOCK IT OFF, MANNY. I KNOW IT'S AWKWARD.
AWKWARD? IF YOU PISS OFF DOMINGA SALVADOR, IT'S A HELL OF A LOT MORE THAN JUST AWKWARD.
YOU DON'T HAVE TO COME.
YOU CALLED ME FOR BACKUP. YOU DIDN'T CALL CHARLES, OR JAMISON.
YOU CALLED ME, ANITA, AND THAT IS THE BEST COMPLIMENT YOU COULD GIVE AN OLD MAN.
YOU'RE NOT AN OLD MAN.
AND I'M TOO OLD TO BE SLAYING VAMPIRES.
ROSITA HAS FORBIDDEN ME TO GO VAMPIRE HUNTING WITH YOU, BUT SHE CAN'T CURTAIL MY ZOMBIE-RELATED ACTIVITIES. NOT YET, ANYWAY.
ROSITA MADE A REASONABLE REQUEST, MANNY. YOU HAVE FOUR CHILDREN TO THINK OF.
YOU'LL NEVER BE TOO OLD.
A NICE THOUGHT.
WE BETTER GO.
DON'T WANT TO KEEP THE SEÑORA WAITING.
GOD FORBID.
AMEN.

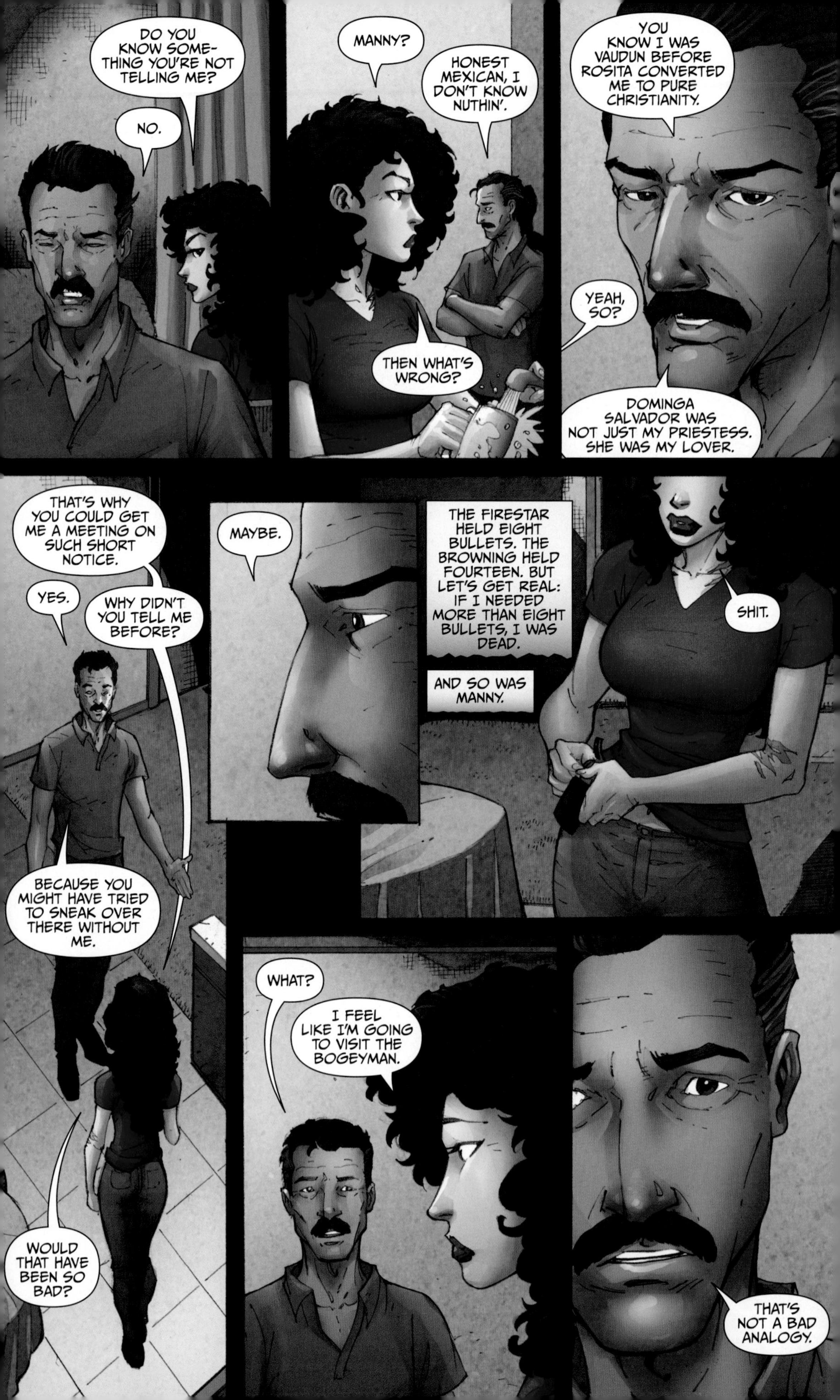
DO YOU KNOW SOME-THING YOU'RE NOT TELLING ME?
NO.
MANNY?
HONEST MEXICAN, I DON'T KNOW NUTHIN'.
THEN WHAT'S WRONG?
YOU KNOW I WAS VAUDUN BEFORE ROSITA CONVERTED ME TO PURE CHRISTIANITY.
YEAH, SO?
DOMINGA SALVADOR WAS NOT JUST MY PRIESTESS. SHE WAS MY LOVER.
THAT'S WHY YOU COULD GET ME A MEETING ON SUCH SHORT NOTICE.
YES.
WHY DIDN'T YOU TELL ME BEFORE?
BECAUSE YOU MIGHT HAVE TRIED TO SNEAK OVER THERE WITHOUT ME.
WOULD THAT HAVE BEEN SO BAD?
MAYBE.
THE FIRESTAR HELD EIGHT BULLETS. THE BROWNING HELD FOURTEEN. BUT LET'S GET REAL: IF I NEEDED MORE THAN EIGHT BULLETS, I WAS DEAD.
AND SO WAS MANNY.
SHIT.
WHAT?
I FEEL LIKE I'M GOING TO VISIT THE BOGEYMAN.
THAT'S NOT A BAD ANALOGY.

ONE BLOCK OVER FROM SEÑORA SALVADOR'S NEIGHBORHOOD YOU COULD GET YOURSELF SHOT FOR WEARING THE WRONG COLOR OF JACKET.

BUT EVEN TEENAGERS WITH AUTOMATIC PISTOLS FEAR THINGS YOU CAN'T STOP WITH BULLETS NO MATTER HOW GOOD A SHOT YOU ARE.

BULLETS, EVEN SILVER-PLATED, WILL NOT KILL A ZOMBIE. YOU CAN HACK THE DAMN THING TO PIECES AND THE PARTS WILL STILL CRAWL AFTER YOU.

I'VE SEEN IT. IT AIN'T PRETTY.

THERE ARE STORIES OF ONE GANG WHO THOUGHT IT HAD PROTECTION AGAINST GRIS-GRIS.

SOME PEOPLE SAY THE GANG'S EX-LEADER IS STILL DOWN IN DOMINGA'S BASEMENT, OBEYING AN OCCASIONAL ORDER.

BUENOS DIAS, ANTONIO. IT HAS BEEN A LONG TIME.

MY GRAND-MOTHER SAYS I MUST LET YOU IN.

SHE IS A WISE WOMAN.

SHE IS THE SEÑORA.

WHO IS THIS?

SEÑORITA ANITA BLAKE.

NICE TO MEET YOU.

I MUST CHECK YOU FOR WEAPONS, MANUEL.

I UNDERSTAND.

WHAT IS TAKING SO LONG, ANTONIO?

I AM SEARCHING HIM FOR WEAPONS.

SHE IS READY TO SEE YOU BOTH.

HE HADN'T BOTHERED TO CHECK ME FOR WEAPONS. SOMETIMES BEING UNDERESTIMATED WAS A GOOD THING.

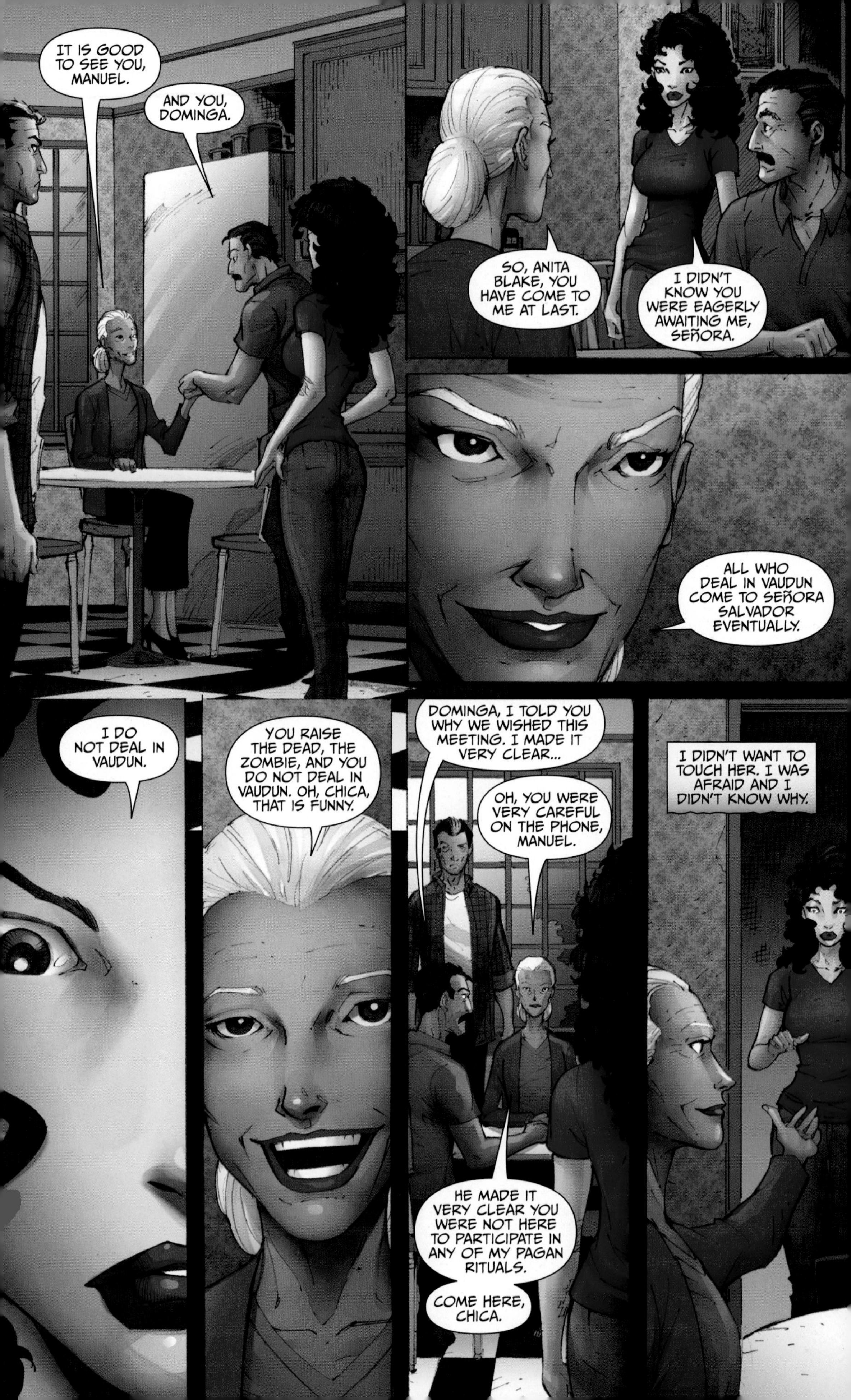
IT IS GOOD TO SEE YOU, MANUEL.
AND YOU, DOMINGA.
SO, ANITA BLAKE, YOU HAVE COME TO ME AT LAST.
I DIDN'T KNOW YOU WERE EAGERLY AWAITING ME, SEÑORA.
ALL WHO DEAL IN VAUDUN COME TO SEÑORA SALVADOR EVENTUALLY.
I DO NOT DEAL IN VAUDUN.
YOU RAISE THE DEAD, THE ZOMBIE, AND YOU DO NOT DEAL IN VAUDUN. OH, CHICA, THAT IS FUNNY.
DOMINGA, I TOLD YOU WHY WE WISHED THIS MEETING. I MADE IT VERY CLEAR...
OH, YOU WERE VERY CAREFUL ON THE PHONE, MANUEL.
HE MADE IT VERY CLEAR YOU WERE NOT HERE TO PARTICIPATE IN ANY OF MY PAGAN RITUALS.
COME HERE, CHICA.
I DIDN'T WANT TO TOUCH HER. I WAS AFRAID AND I DIDN'T KNOW WHY.

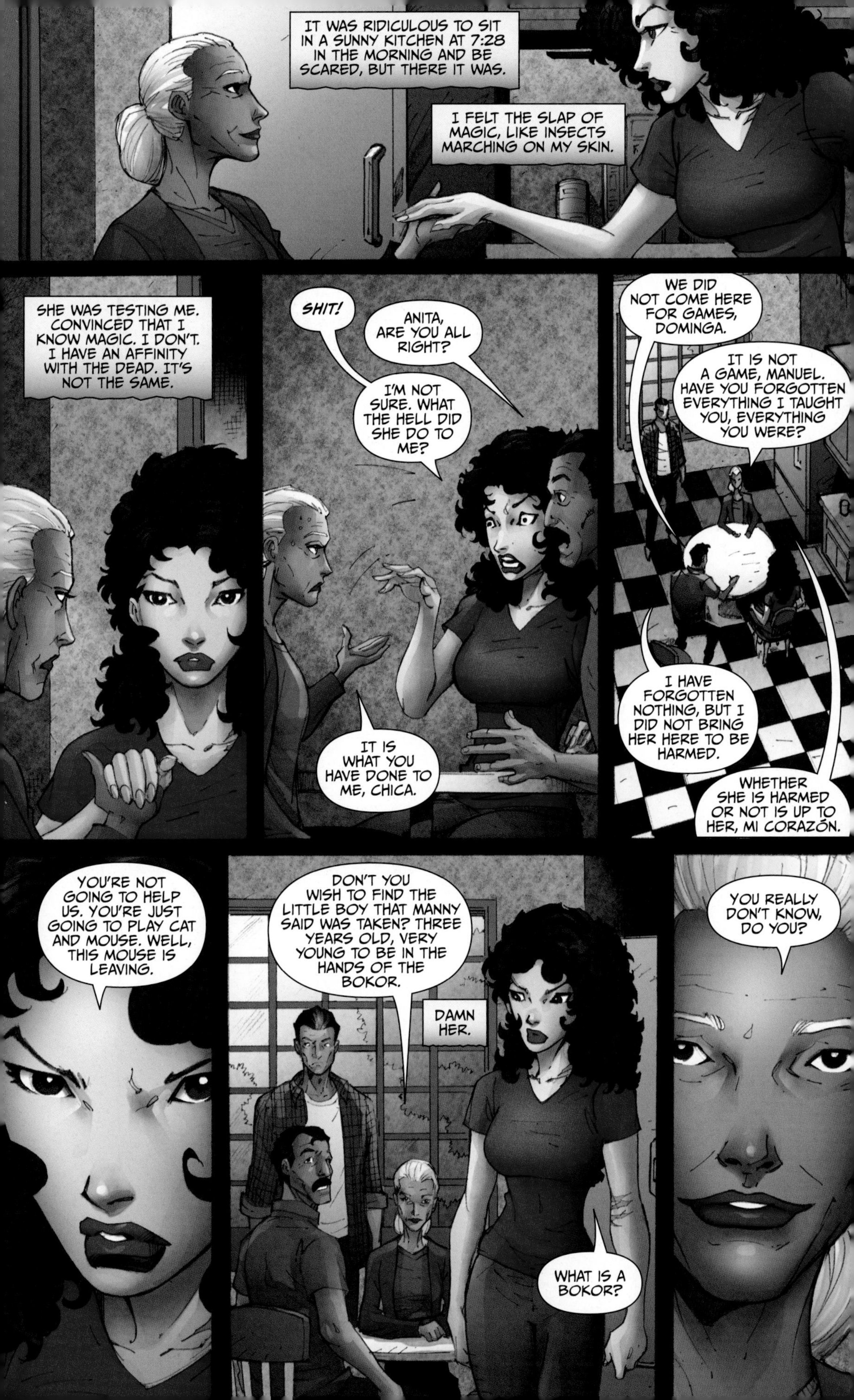
IT WAS RIDICULOUS TO SIT IN A SUNNY KITCHEN AT 7:28 IN THE MORNING AND BE SCARED, BUT THERE IT WAS.
I FELT THE SLAP OF MAGIC, LIKE INSECTS MARCHING ON MY SKIN.
SHE WAS TESTING ME. CONVINCED THAT I KNOW MAGIC. I DON'T. I HAVE AN AFFINITY WITH THE DEAD. IT'S NOT THE SAME.
SHIT!
ANITA, ARE YOU ALL RIGHT?
I'M NOT SURE. WHAT THE HELL DID SHE DO TO ME?
IT IS WHAT YOU HAVE DONE TO ME, CHICA.
WE DID NOT COME HERE FOR GAMES, DOMINGA.
IT IS NOT A GAME, MANUEL. HAVE YOU FORGOTTEN EVERYTHING I TAUGHT YOU, EVERYTHING YOU WERE?
I HAVE FORGOTTEN NOTHING, BUT I DID NOT BRING HER HERE TO BE HARMED.
WHETHER SHE IS HARMED OR NOT IS UP TO HER, MI CORAZÓN.
YOU'RE NOT GOING TO HELP US. YOU'RE JUST GOING TO PLAY CAT AND MOUSE. WELL, THIS MOUSE IS LEAVING.
DON'T YOU WISH TO FIND THE LITTLE BOY THAT MANNY SAID WAS TAKEN? THREE YEARS OLD, VERY YOUNG TO BE IN THE HANDS OF THE BOKOR.
DAMN HER.
WHAT IS A BOKOR?
YOU REALLY DON'T KNOW, DO YOU?

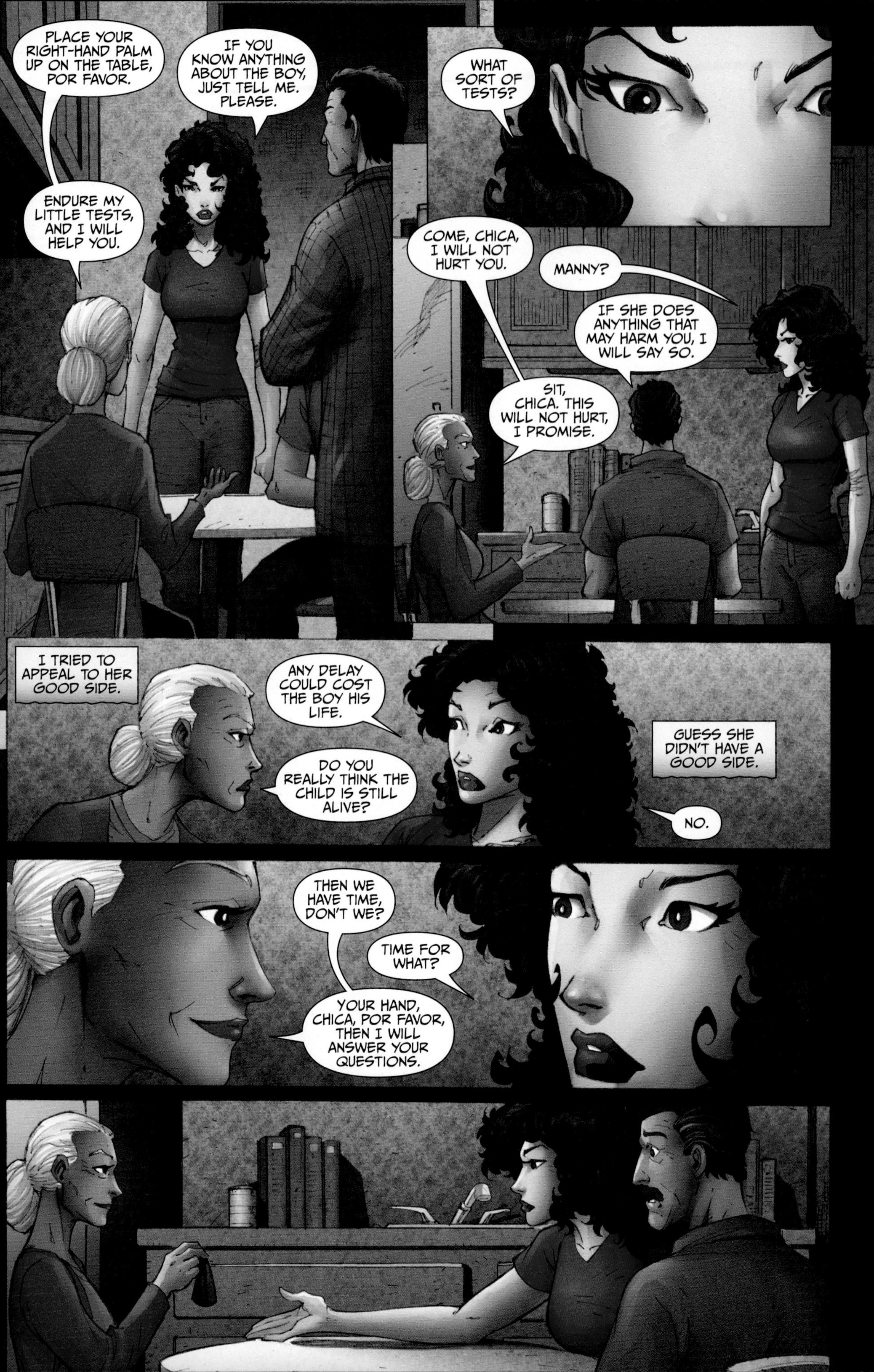
PLACE YOUR RIGHT-HAND PALM UP ON THE TABLE, POR FAVOR.
IF YOU KNOW ANYTHING ABOUT THE BOY, JUST TELL ME. PLEASE.
ENDURE MY LITTLE TESTS, AND I WILL HELP YOU.
WHAT SORT OF TESTS?
COME, CHICA, I WILL NOT HURT YOU.
MANNY?
IF SHE DOES ANYTHING THAT MAY HARM YOU, I WILL SAY SO.
SIT, CHICA. THIS WILL NOT HURT, I PROMISE.
I TRIED TO APPEAL TO HER GOOD SIDE.
ANY DELAY COULD COST THE BOY HIS LIFE.
DO YOU REALLY THINK THE CHILD IS STILL ALIVE?
GUESS SHE DIDN'T HAVE A GOOD SIDE.
NO.
THEN WE HAVE TIME, DON'T WE?
TIME FOR WHAT?
YOUR HAND, CHICA, POR FAVOR, THEN I WILL ANSWER YOUR QUESTIONS.

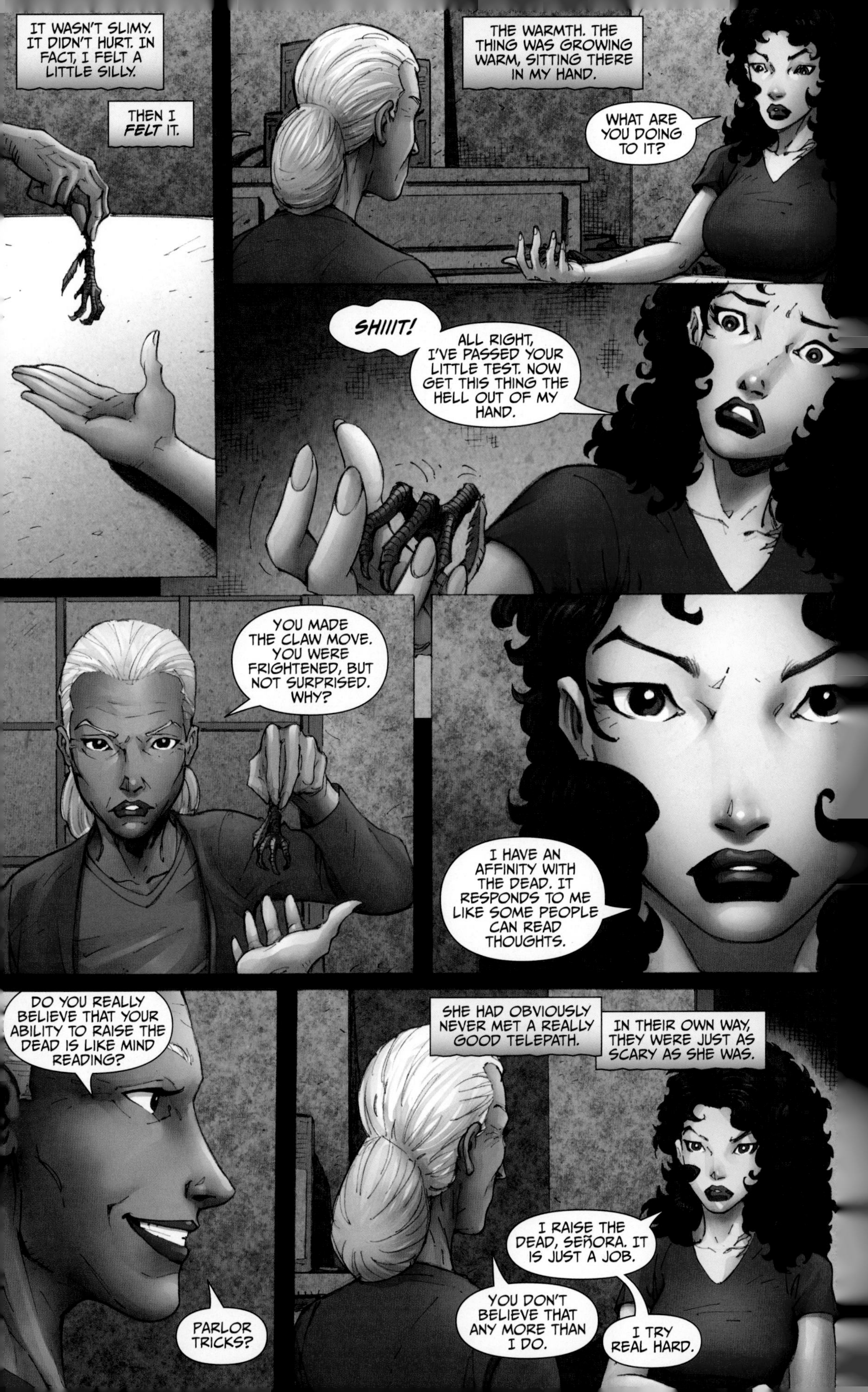
IT WASN'T SLIMY. IT DIDN'T HURT. IN FACT, I FELT A LITTLE SILLY.
THEN I *FELT* IT.
THE WARMTH. THE THING WAS GROWING WARM, SITTING THERE IN MY HAND.
WHAT ARE YOU DOING TO IT?
SHIIIT!
ALL RIGHT, I'VE PASSED YOUR LITTLE TEST. NOW GET THIS THING THE HELL OUT OF MY HAND.
YOU MADE THE CLAW MOVE. YOU WERE FRIGHTENED, BUT NOT SURPRISED. WHY?
I HAVE AN AFFINITY WITH THE DEAD. IT RESPONDS TO ME LIKE SOME PEOPLE CAN READ THOUGHTS.
DO YOU REALLY BELIEVE THAT YOUR ABILITY TO RAISE THE DEAD IS LIKE MIND READING?
PARLOR TRICKS?
SHE HAD OBVIOUSLY NEVER MET A REALLY GOOD TELEPATH.
IN THEIR OWN WAY, THEY WERE JUST AS SCARY AS SHE WAS.
I RAISE THE DEAD, SEÑORA. IT IS JUST A JOB.
YOU DON'T BELIEVE THAT ANY MORE THAN I DO.
I TRY REAL HARD.

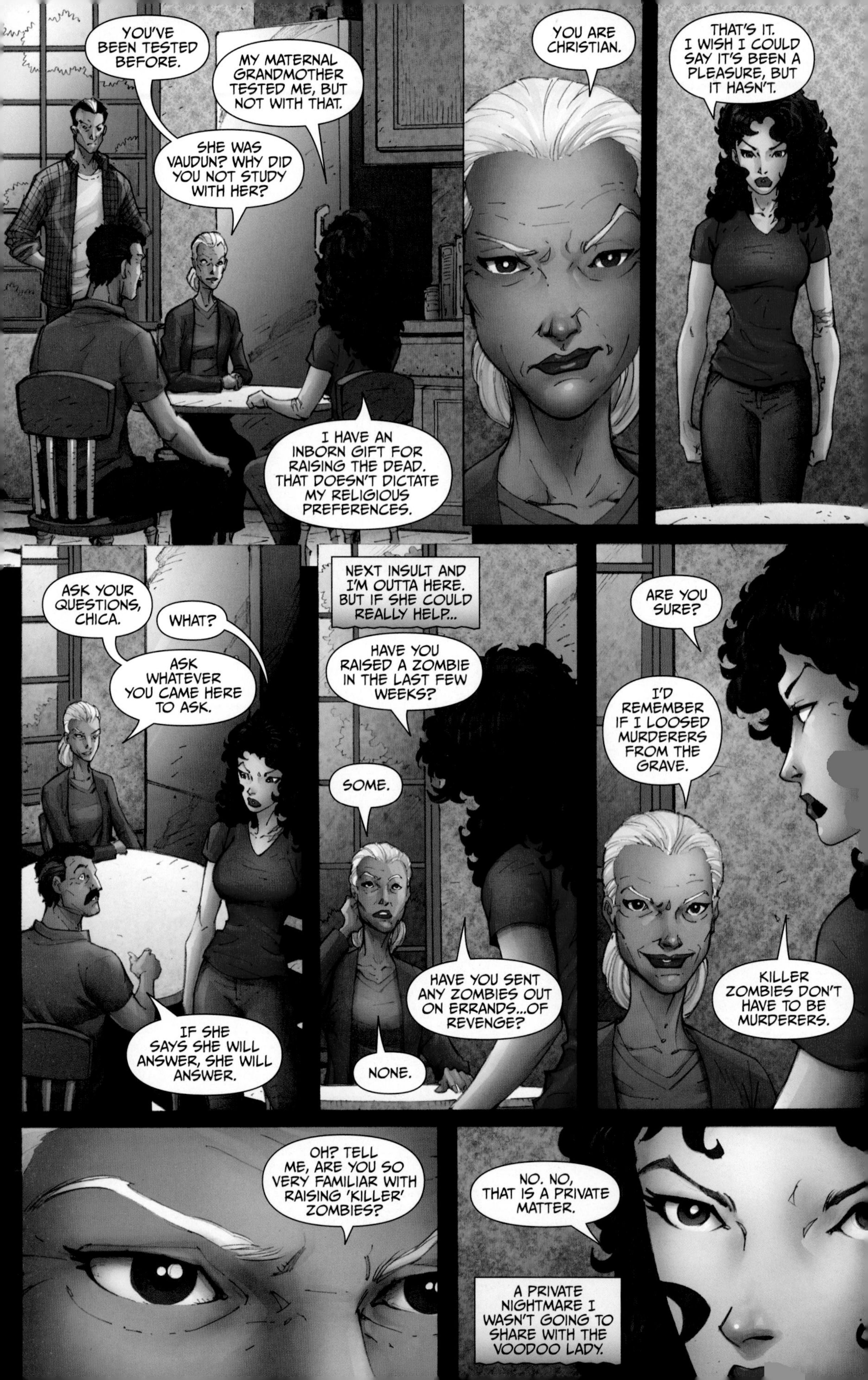
YOU'VE BEEN TESTED BEFORE.
MY MATERNAL GRANDMOTHER TESTED ME, BUT NOT WITH THAT.
SHE WAS VAUDUN? WHY DID YOU NOT STUDY WITH HER?
I HAVE AN INBORN GIFT FOR RAISING THE DEAD. THAT DOESN'T DICTATE MY RELIGIOUS PREFERENCES.
YOU ARE CHRISTIAN.
THAT'S IT. I WISH I COULD SAY IT'S BEEN A PLEASURE, BUT IT HASN'T.
ASK YOUR QUESTIONS, CHICA.
WHAT?
ASK WHATEVER YOU CAME HERE TO ASK.
IF SHE SAYS SHE WILL ANSWER, SHE WILL ANSWER.
NEXT INSULT AND I'M OUTTA HERE. BUT IF SHE COULD REALLY HELP...
HAVE YOU RAISED A ZOMBIE IN THE LAST FEW WEEKS?
SOME.
HAVE YOU SENT ANY ZOMBIES OUT ON ERRANDS...OF REVENGE?
NONE.
ARE YOU SURE?
I'D REMEMBER IF I LOOSED MURDERERS FROM THE GRAVE.
KILLER ZOMBIES DON'T HAVE TO BE MURDERERS.
OH? TELL ME, ARE YOU SO VERY FAMILIAR WITH RAISING 'KILLER' ZOMBIES?
NO. NO, THAT IS A PRIVATE MATTER.
A PRIVATE NIGHTMARE I WASN'T GOING TO SHARE WITH THE VOODOO LADY.

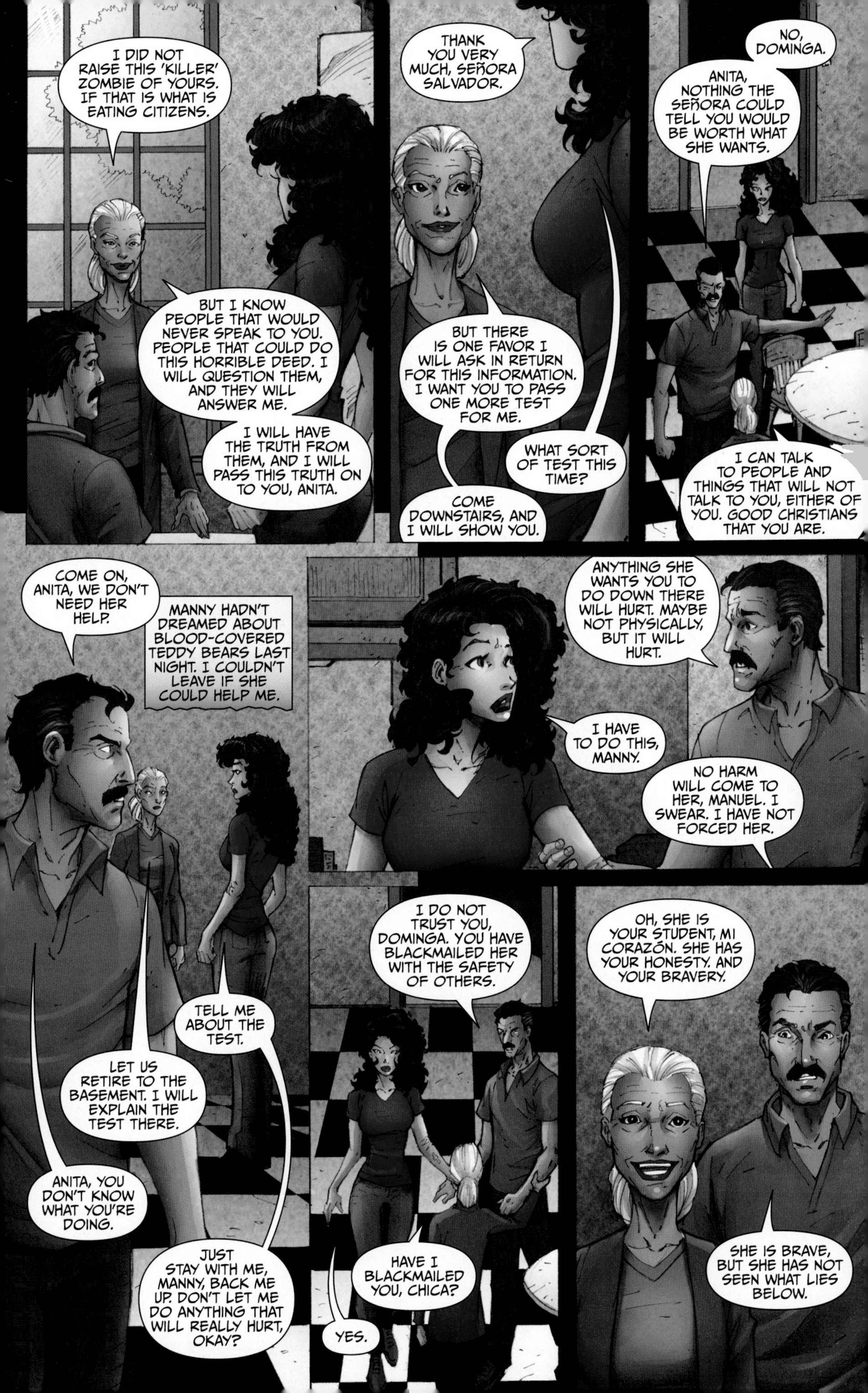
I DID NOT RAISE THIS 'KILLER' ZOMBIE OF YOURS. IF THAT IS WHAT IS EATING CITIZENS.
BUT I KNOW PEOPLE THAT WOULD NEVER SPEAK TO YOU. PEOPLE THAT COULD DO THIS HORRIBLE DEED. I WILL QUESTION THEM, AND THEY WILL ANSWER ME.
I WILL HAVE THE TRUTH FROM THEM, AND I WILL PASS THIS TRUTH ON TO YOU, ANITA.
THANK YOU VERY MUCH, SEÑORA SALVADOR.
BUT THERE IS ONE FAVOR I WILL ASK IN RETURN FOR THIS INFORMATION. I WANT YOU TO PASS ONE MORE TEST FOR ME.
WHAT SORT OF TEST THIS TIME?
COME DOWNSTAIRS, AND I WILL SHOW YOU.
NO, DOMINGA.
ANITA, NOTHING THE SEÑORA COULD TELL YOU WOULD BE WORTH WHAT SHE WANTS.
I CAN TALK TO PEOPLE AND THINGS THAT WILL NOT TALK TO YOU, EITHER OF YOU. GOOD CHRISTIANS THAT YOU ARE.
COME ON, ANITA, WE DON'T NEED HER HELP.
MANNY HADN'T DREAMED ABOUT BLOOD-COVERED TEDDY BEARS LAST NIGHT. I COULDN'T LEAVE IF SHE COULD HELP ME.
TELL ME ABOUT THE TEST.
LET US RETIRE TO THE BASEMENT. I WILL EXPLAIN THE TEST THERE.
ANITA, YOU DON'T KNOW WHAT YOU'RE DOING.
JUST STAY WITH ME, MANNY, BACK ME UP. DON'T LET ME DO ANYTHING THAT WILL REALLY HURT, OKAY?
ANYTHING SHE WANTS YOU TO DO DOWN THERE WILL HURT. MAYBE NOT PHYSICALLY, BUT IT WILL HURT.
I HAVE TO DO THIS, MANNY.
NO HARM WILL COME TO HER, MANUEL. I SWEAR. I HAVE NOT FORCED HER.
I DO NOT TRUST YOU, DOMINGA. YOU HAVE BLACKMAILED HER WITH THE SAFETY OF OTHERS.
HAVE I BLACKMAILED YOU, CHICA?
YES.
OH, SHE IS YOUR STUDENT, MI CORAZÓN. SHE HAS YOUR HONESTY. AND YOUR BRAVERY.
SHE IS BRAVE, BUT SHE HAS NOT SEEN WHAT LIES BELOW.

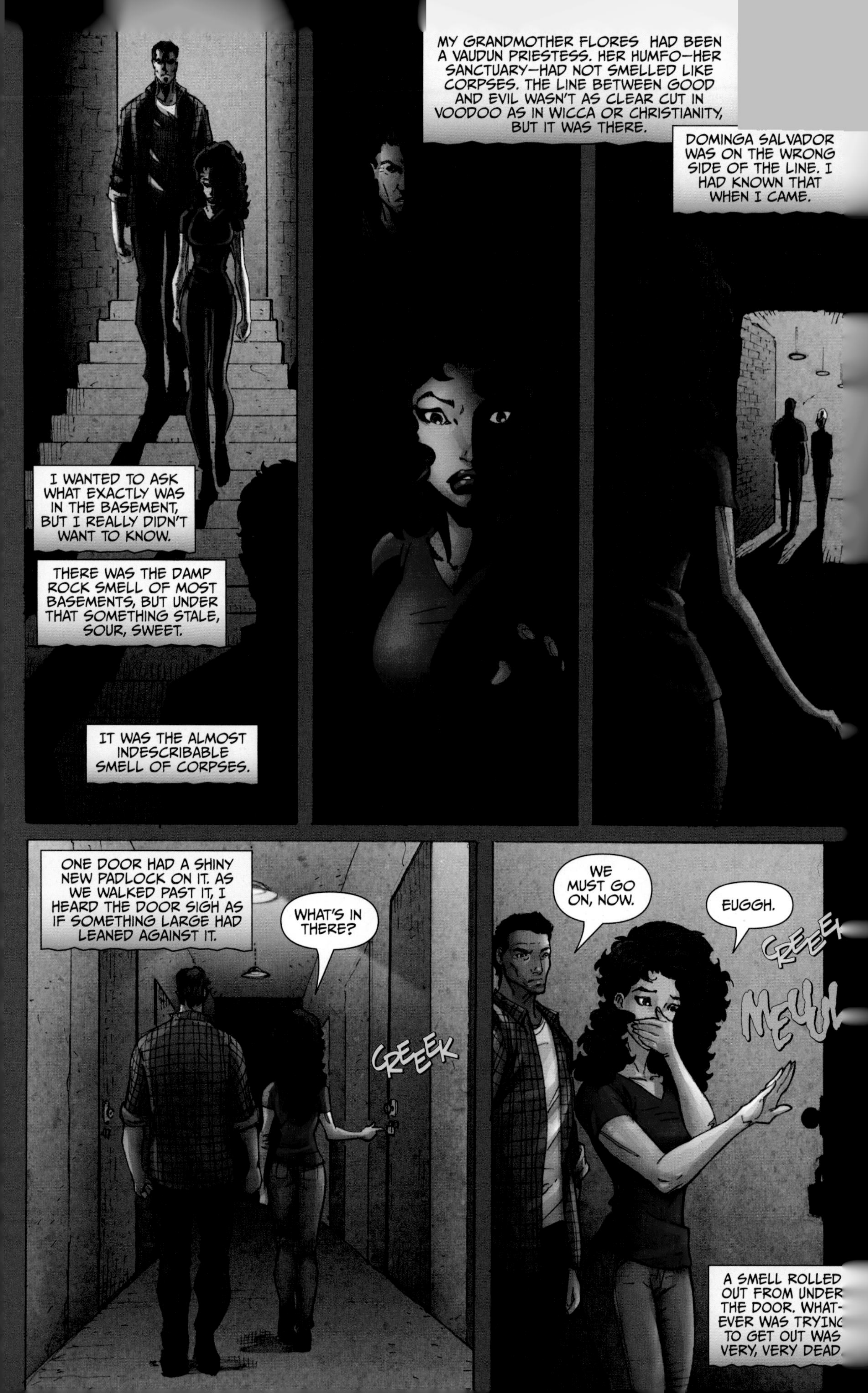
MY GRANDMOTHER FLORES HAD BEEN A VAUDUN PRIESTESS. HER HUMFO—HER SANCTUARY—HAD NOT SMELLED LIKE CORPSES. THE LINE BETWEEN GOOD AND EVIL WASN'T AS CLEAR CUT IN VOODOO AS IN WICCA OR CHRISTIANITY, BUT IT WAS THERE.
DOMINGA SALVADOR WAS ON THE WRONG SIDE OF THE LINE. I HAD KNOWN THAT WHEN I CAME.
I WANTED TO ASK WHAT EXACTLY WAS IN THE BASEMENT, BUT I REALLY DIDN'T WANT TO KNOW.
THERE WAS THE DAMP ROCK SMELL OF MOST BASEMENTS, BUT UNDER THAT SOMETHING STALE, SOUR, SWEET.
IT WAS THE ALMOST INDESCRIBABLE SMELL OF CORPSES.
ONE DOOR HAD A SHINY NEW PADLOCK ON IT. AS WE WALKED PAST IT, I HEARD THE DOOR SIGH AS IF SOMETHING LARGE HAD LEANED AGAINST IT.
WHAT'S IN THERE?
CREEEK
WE MUST GO ON, NOW.
EUGGH.
CREEEK
MEUUU
A SMELL ROLLED OUT FROM UNDER THE DOOR. WHAT-EVER WAS TRYING TO GET OUT WAS VERY, VERY DEAD.

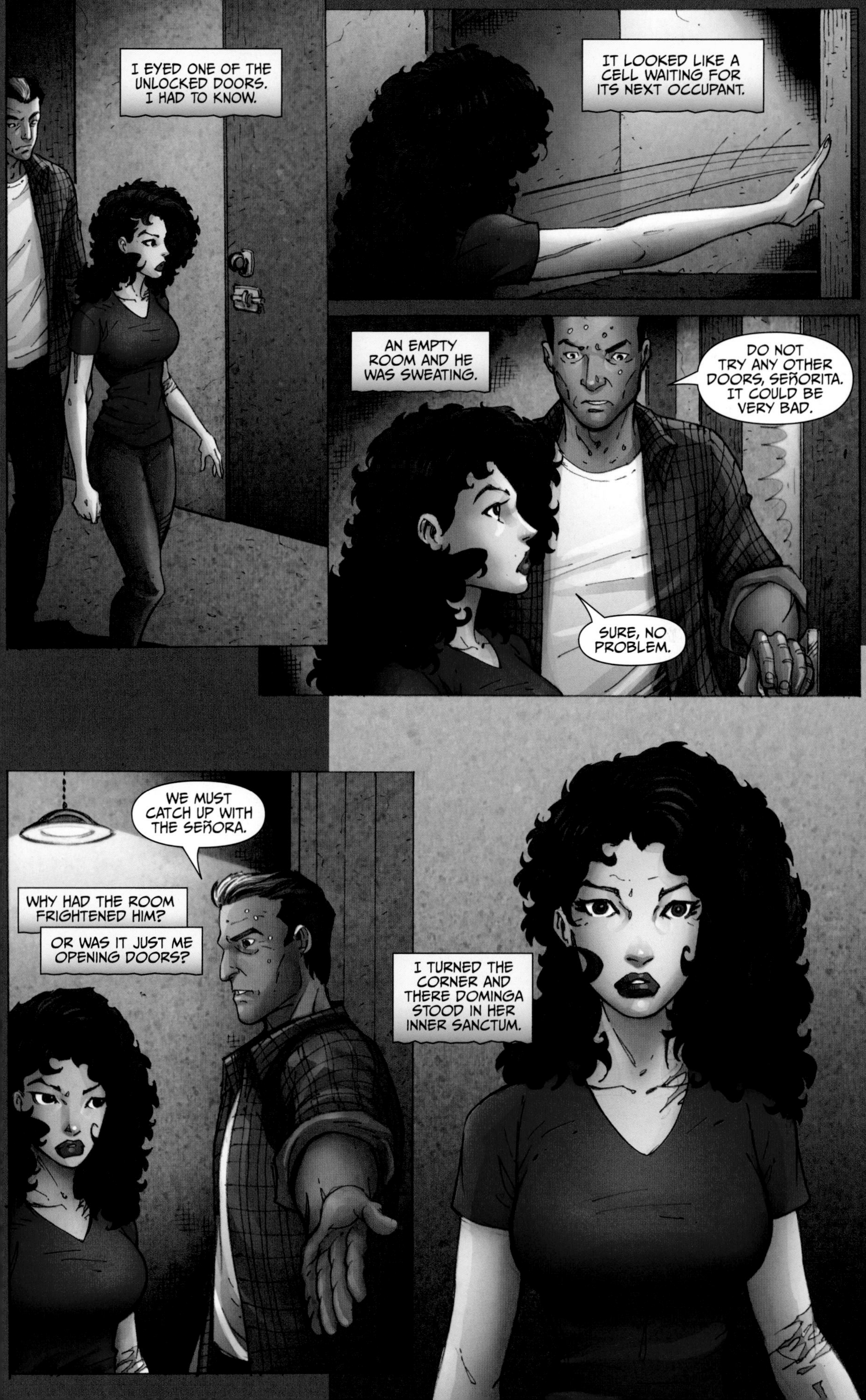
I EYED ONE OF THE UNLOCKED DOORS. I HAD TO KNOW.
IT LOOKED LIKE A CELL WAITING FOR ITS NEXT OCCUPANT.
AN EMPTY ROOM AND HE WAS SWEATING.
DO NOT TRY ANY OTHER DOORS, SEÑORITA. IT COULD BE VERY BAD.
SURE, NO PROBLEM.
WE MUST CATCH UP WITH THE SEÑORA.
WHY HAD THE ROOM FRIGHTENED HIM?
OR WAS IT JUST ME OPENING DOORS?
I TURNED THE CORNER AND THERE DOMINGA STOOD IN HER INNER SANCTUM.

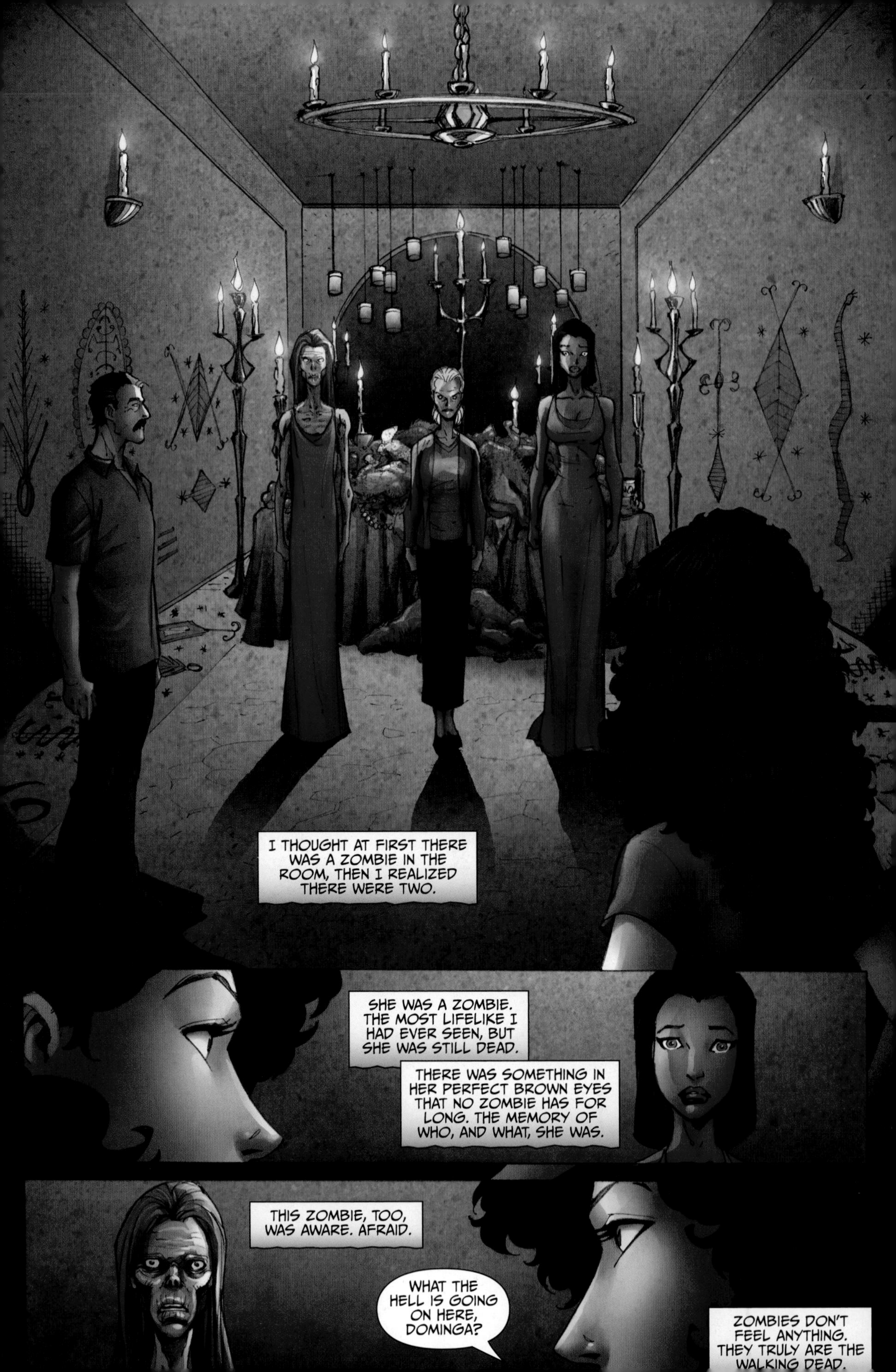
I THOUGHT AT FIRST THERE WAS A ZOMBIE IN THE ROOM, THEN I REALIZED THERE WERE TWO.
SHE WAS A ZOMBIE. THE MOST LIFELIKE I HAD EVER SEEN, BUT SHE WAS STILL DEAD.
THERE WAS SOMETHING IN HER PERFECT BROWN EYES THAT NO ZOMBIE HAS FOR LONG. THE MEMORY OF WHO, AND WHAT, SHE WAS.
THIS ZOMBIE, TOO, WAS AWARE. AFRAID.
WHAT THE HELL IS GOING ON HERE, DOMINGA?
ZOMBIES DON'T FEEL ANYTHING. THEY TRULY ARE THE WALKING DEAD.

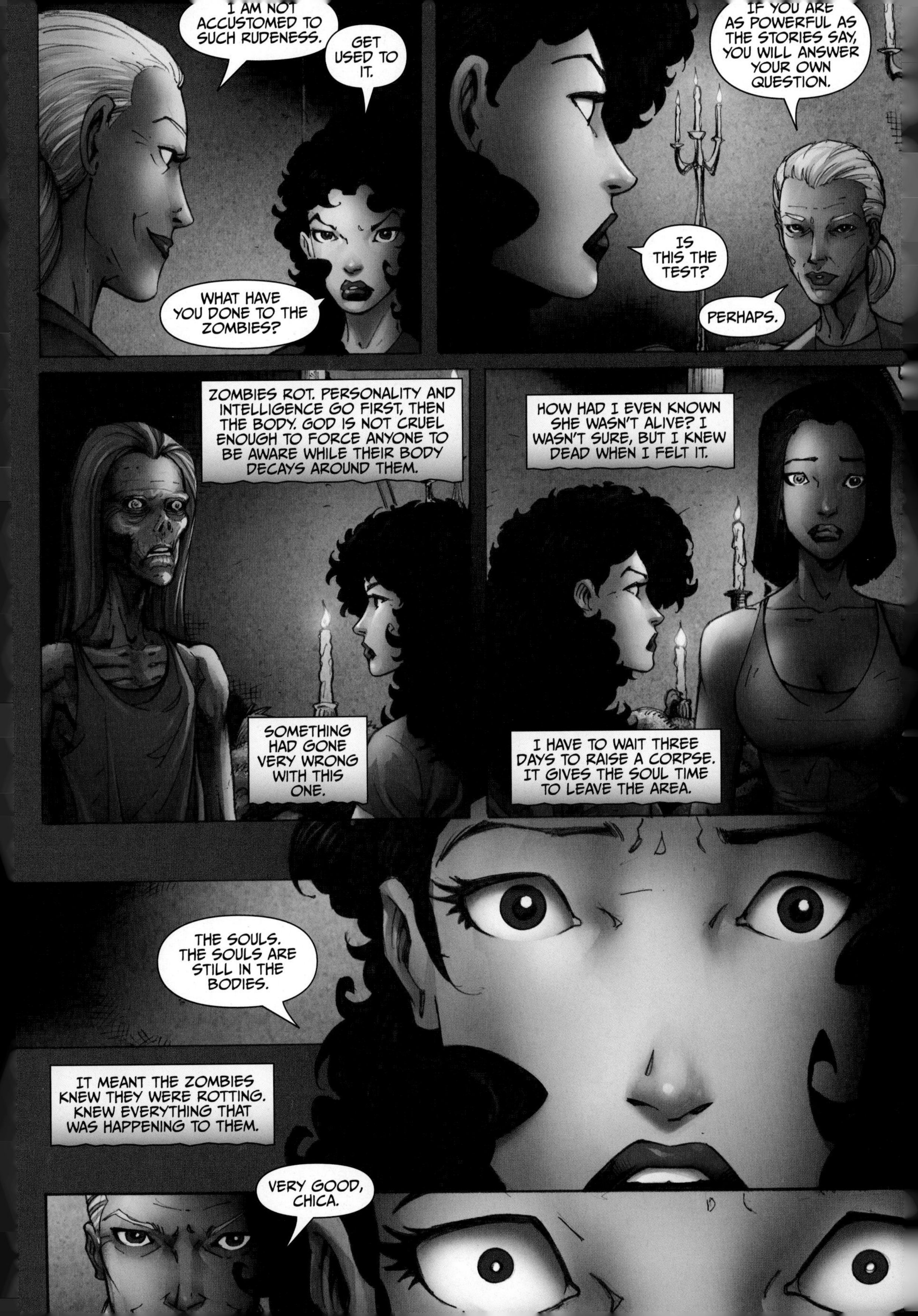
I AM NOT ACCUSTOMED TO SUCH RUDENESS.
GET USED TO IT.
WHAT HAVE YOU DONE TO THE ZOMBIES?
IF YOU ARE AS POWERFUL AS THE STORIES SAY, YOU WILL ANSWER YOUR OWN QUESTION.
IS THIS THE TEST?
PERHAPS.
ZOMBIES ROT. PERSONALITY AND INTELLIGENCE GO FIRST, THEN THE BODY. GOD IS NOT CRUEL ENOUGH TO FORCE ANYONE TO BE AWARE WHILE THEIR BODY DECAYS AROUND THEM.
SOMETHING HAD GONE VERY WRONG WITH THIS ONE.
HOW HAD I EVEN KNOWN SHE WASN'T ALIVE? I WASN'T SURE, BUT I KNEW DEAD WHEN I FELT IT.
I HAVE TO WAIT THREE DAYS TO RAISE A CORPSE. IT GIVES THE SOUL TIME TO LEAVE THE AREA.
THE SOULS. THE SOULS ARE STILL IN THE BODIES.
IT MEANT THE ZOMBIES KNEW THEY WERE ROTTING. KNEW EVERYTHING THAT WAS HAPPENING TO THEM.
VERY GOOD, CHICA.

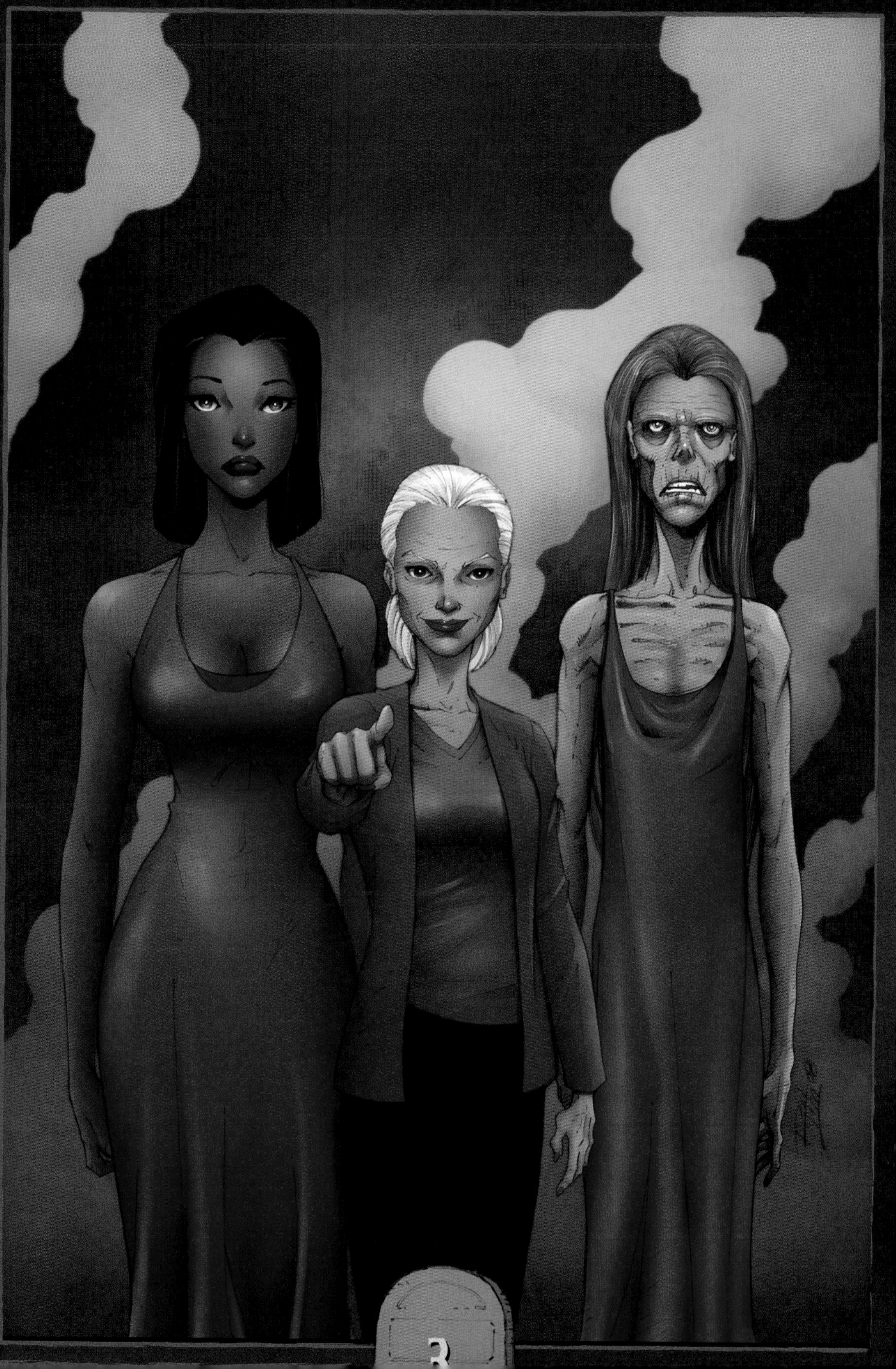

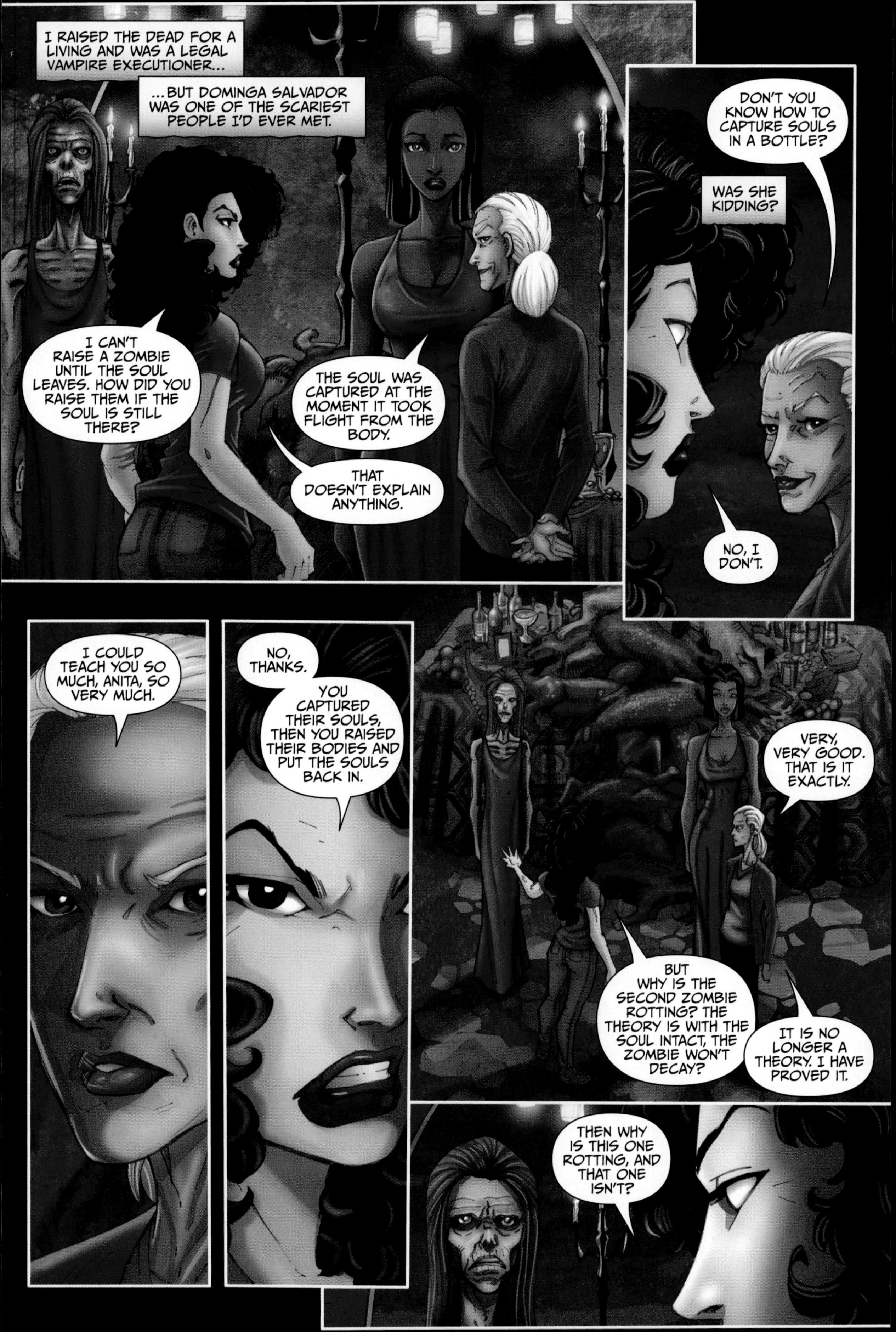
I RAISED THE DEAD FOR A LIVING AND WAS A LEGAL VAMPIRE EXECUTIONER...
...BUT DOMINGA SALVADOR WAS ONE OF THE SCARIEST PEOPLE I'D EVER MET.
I CAN'T RAISE A ZOMBIE UNTIL THE SOUL LEAVES. HOW DID YOU RAISE THEM IF THE SOUL IS STILL THERE?
THE SOUL WAS CAPTURED AT THE MOMENT IT TOOK FLIGHT FROM THE BODY.
THAT DOESN'T EXPLAIN ANYTHING.
DON'T YOU KNOW HOW TO CAPTURE SOULS IN A BOTTLE?
WAS SHE KIDDING?
NO, I DON'T.
I COULD TEACH YOU SO MUCH, ANITA, SO VERY MUCH.
NO, THANKS.
YOU CAPTURED THEIR SOULS, THEN YOU RAISED THEIR BODIES AND PUT THE SOULS BACK IN.
VERY, VERY GOOD. THAT IS IT EXACTLY.
BUT WHY IS THE SECOND ZOMBIE ROTTING? THE THEORY IS WITH THE SOUL INTACT, THE ZOMBIE WON'T DECAY?
IT IS NO LONGER A THEORY. I HAVE PROVED IT.
THEN WHY IS THIS ONE ROTTING, AND THAT ONE ISN'T?

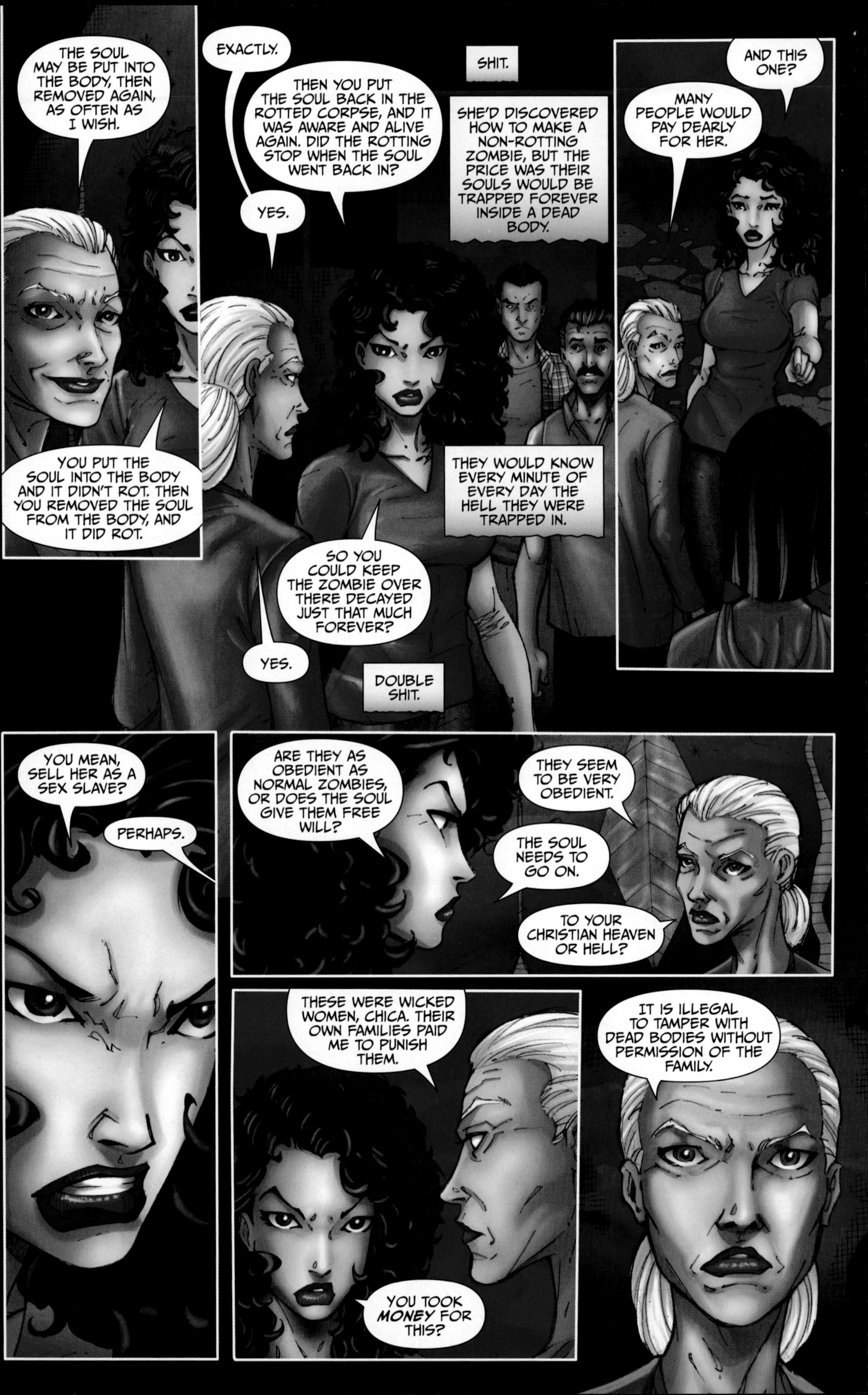

THE SOUL MAY BE PUT INTO THE BODY, THEN REMOVED AGAIN, AS OFTEN AS I WISH.
YOU PUT THE SOUL INTO THE BODY AND IT DIDN'T ROT. THEN YOU REMOVED THE SOUL FROM THE BODY, AND IT DID ROT.
EXACTLY.
THEN YOU PUT THE SOUL BACK IN THE ROTTED CORPSE, AND IT WAS AWARE AND ALIVE AGAIN. DID THE ROTTING STOP WHEN THE SOUL WENT BACK IN?
YES.
SO YOU COULD KEEP THE ZOMBIE OVER THERE DECAYED JUST THAT MUCH FOREVER?
YES.
SHIT.
SHE'D DISCOVERED HOW TO MAKE A NON-ROTTING ZOMBIE, BUT THE PRICE WAS THEIR SOULS WOULD BE TRAPPED FOREVER INSIDE A DEAD BODY.
THEY WOULD KNOW EVERY MINUTE OF EVERY DAY THE HELL THEY WERE TRAPPED IN.
DOUBLE SHIT.
AND THIS ONE?
MANY PEOPLE WOULD PAY DEARLY FOR HER.
YOU MEAN, SELL HER AS A SEX SLAVE?
PERHAPS.
ARE THEY AS OBEDIENT AS NORMAL ZOMBIES, OR DOES THE SOUL GIVE THEM FREE WILL?
THEY SEEM TO BE VERY OBEDIENT.
THE SOUL NEEDS TO GO ON.
TO YOUR CHRISTIAN HEAVEN OR HELL?
THESE WERE WICKED WOMEN, CHICA. THEIR OWN FAMILIES PAID ME TO PUNISH THEM.
YOU TOOK *MONEY* FOR THIS?
IT IS ILLEGAL TO TAMPER WITH DEAD BODIES WITHOUT PERMISSION OF THE FAMILY.

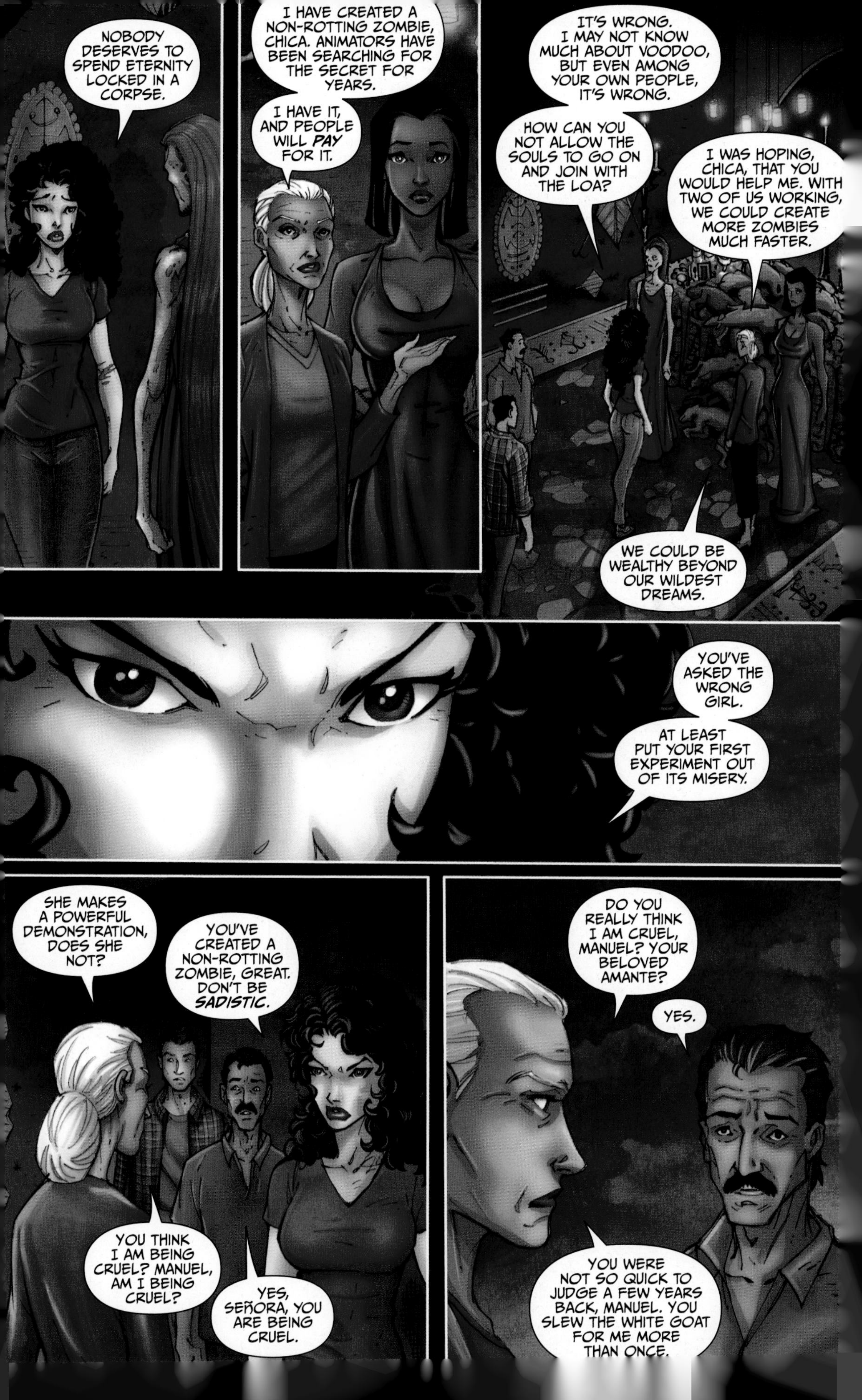
NOBODY DESERVES TO SPEND ETERNITY LOCKED IN A CORPSE.
I HAVE CREATED A NON-ROTTING ZOMBIE, CHICA. ANIMATORS HAVE BEEN SEARCHING FOR THE SECRET FOR YEARS.
I HAVE IT, AND PEOPLE WILL *PAY* FOR IT.
IT'S WRONG. I MAY NOT KNOW MUCH ABOUT VOODOO, BUT EVEN AMONG YOUR OWN PEOPLE, IT'S WRONG.
HOW CAN YOU NOT ALLOW THE SOULS TO GO ON AND JOIN WITH THE LOA?
I WAS HOPING, CHICA, THAT YOU WOULD HELP ME. WITH TWO OF US WORKING, WE COULD CREATE MORE ZOMBIES MUCH FASTER.
WE COULD BE WEALTHY BEYOND OUR WILDEST DREAMS.
YOU'VE ASKED THE WRONG GIRL.
AT LEAST PUT YOUR FIRST EXPERIMENT OUT OF ITS MISERY.
SHE MAKES A POWERFUL DEMONSTRATION, DOES SHE NOT?
YOU'VE CREATED A NON-ROTTING ZOMBIE, GREAT. DON'T BE *SADISTIC*.
YOU THINK I AM BEING CRUEL? MANUEL, AM I BEING CRUEL?
YES, SEÑORA, YOU ARE BEING CRUEL.
DO YOU REALLY THINK I AM CRUEL, MANUEL? YOUR BELOVED AMANTE?
YES.
YOU WERE NOT SO QUICK TO JUDGE A FEW YEARS BACK, MANUEL. YOU SLEW THE WHITE GOAT FOR ME MORE THAN ONCE.

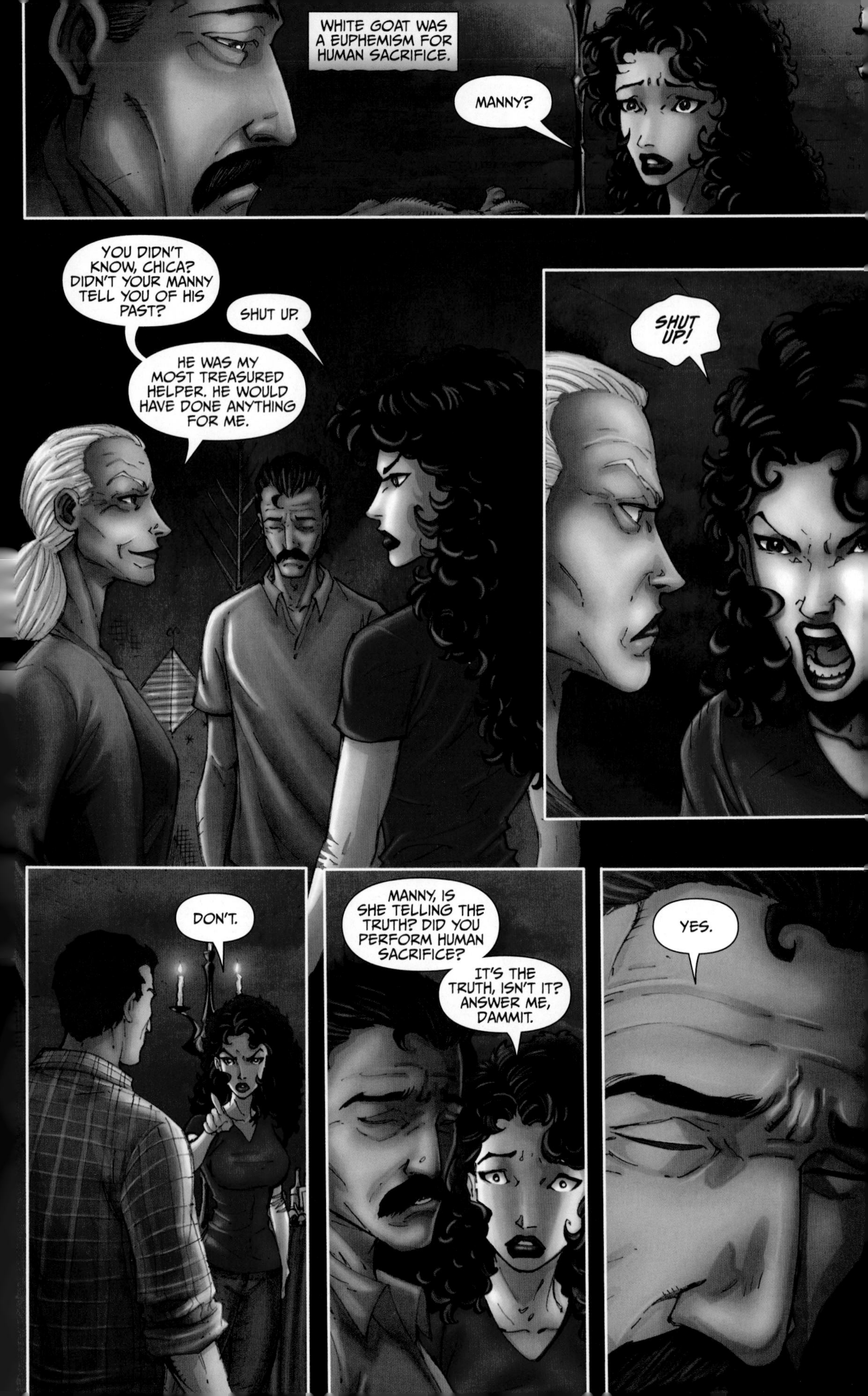
WHITE GOAT WAS A EUPHEMISM FOR HUMAN SACRIFICE.
MANNY?
YOU DIDN'T KNOW, CHICA? DIDN'T YOUR MANNY TELL YOU OF HIS PAST?
HE WAS MY MOST TREASURED HELPER. HE WOULD HAVE DONE ANYTHING FOR ME.
SHUT UP.
SHUT UP!
DON'T.
MANNY, IS SHE TELLING THE TRUTH? DID YOU PERFORM HUMAN SACRIFICE?
IT'S THE TRUTH, ISN'T IT? ANSWER ME, DAMMIT.
YES.

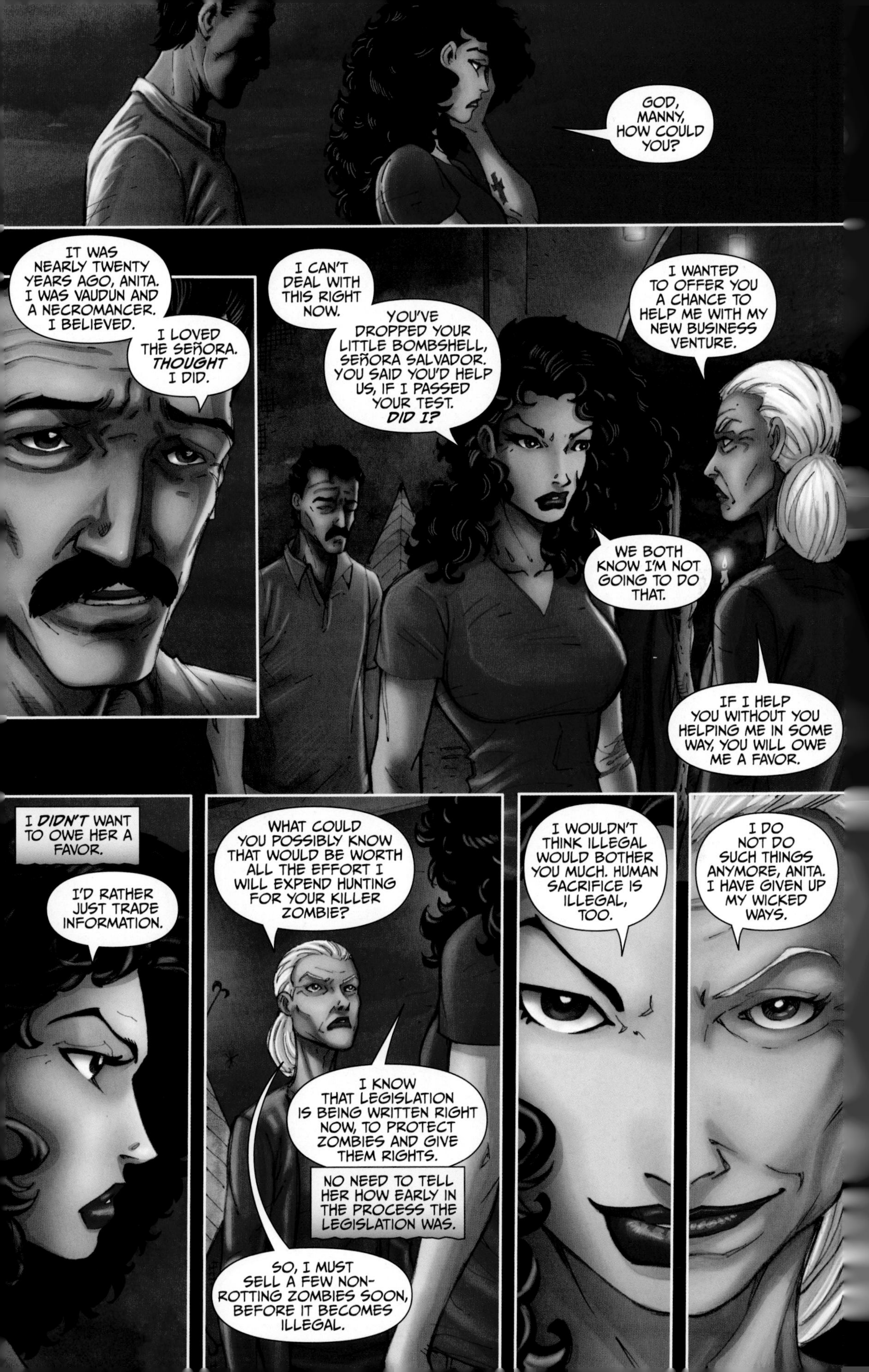
GOD, MANNY, HOW COULD YOU?
IT WAS NEARLY TWENTY YEARS AGO, ANITA. I WAS VAUDUN AND A NECROMANCER. I BELIEVED.
I LOVED THE SEÑORA. *THOUGHT* I DID.
I CAN'T DEAL WITH THIS RIGHT NOW.
YOU'VE DROPPED YOUR LITTLE BOMBSHELL, SEÑORA SALVADOR. YOU SAID YOU'D HELP US, IF I PASSED YOUR TEST. ***DID I?***
I WANTED TO OFFER YOU A CHANCE TO HELP ME WITH MY NEW BUSINESS VENTURE.
WE BOTH KNOW I'M NOT GOING TO DO THAT.
IF I HELP YOU WITHOUT YOU HELPING ME IN SOME WAY, YOU WILL OWE ME A FAVOR.
I *DIDN'T* WANT TO OWE HER A FAVOR.
I'D RATHER JUST TRADE INFORMATION.
WHAT COULD YOU POSSIBLY KNOW THAT WOULD BE WORTH ALL THE EFFORT I WILL EXPEND HUNTING FOR YOUR KILLER ZOMBIE?
I KNOW THAT LEGISLATION IS BEING WRITTEN RIGHT NOW, TO PROTECT ZOMBIES AND GIVE THEM RIGHTS.
NO NEED TO TELL HER HOW EARLY IN THE PROCESS THE LEGISLATION WAS.
SO, I MUST SELL A FEW NON-ROTTING ZOMBIES SOON, BEFORE IT BECOMES ILLEGAL.
I WOULDN'T THINK ILLEGAL WOULD BOTHER YOU MUCH. HUMAN SACRIFICE IS ILLEGAL, TOO.
I DO NOT DO SUCH THINGS ANYMORE, ANITA. I HAVE GIVEN UP MY WICKED WAYS.

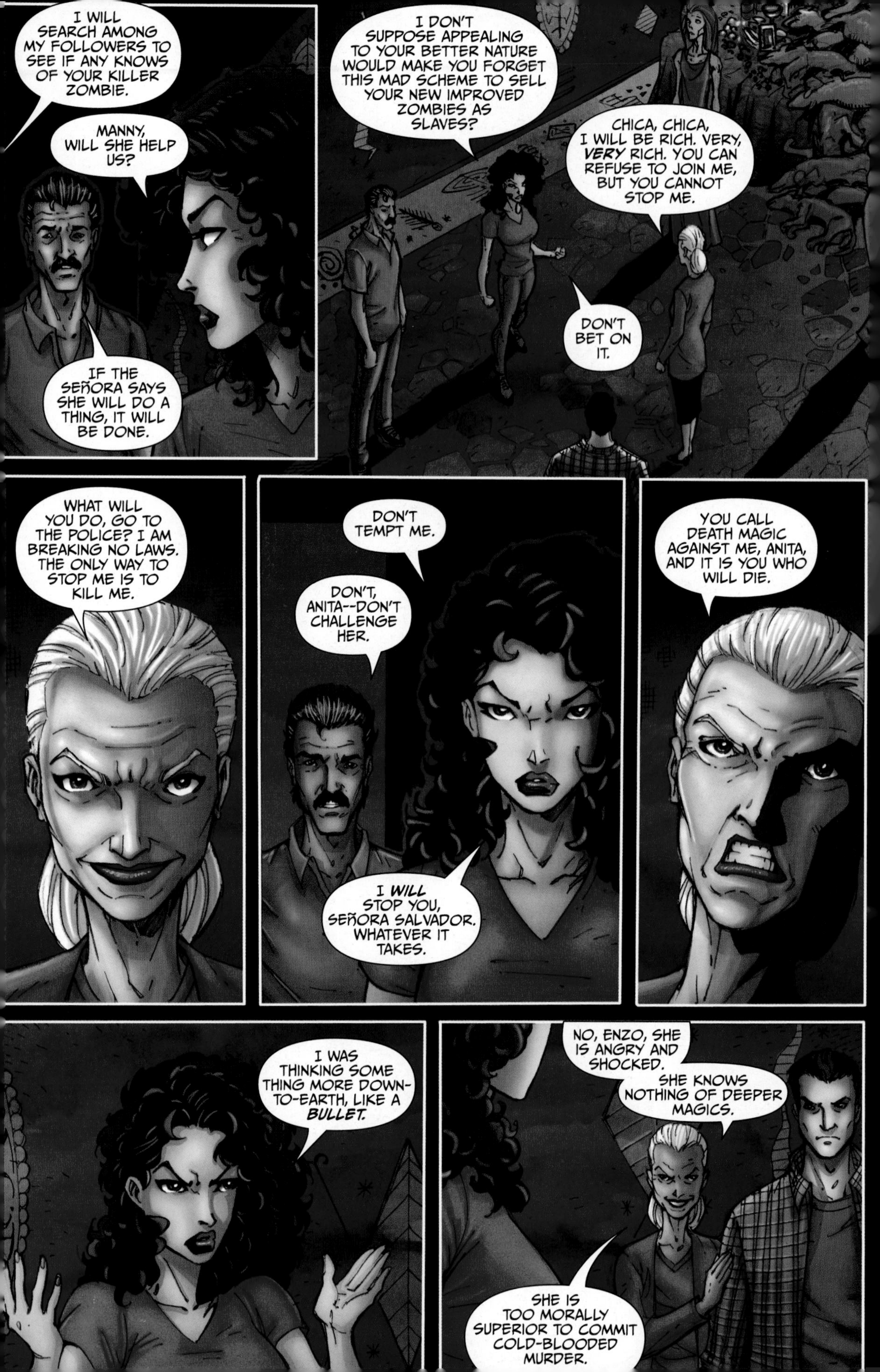
I WILL SEARCH AMONG MY FOLLOWERS TO SEE IF ANY KNOWS OF YOUR KILLER ZOMBIE.
MANNY, WILL SHE HELP US?
IF THE SEÑORA SAYS SHE WILL DO A THING, IT WILL BE DONE.
I DON'T SUPPOSE APPEALING TO YOUR BETTER NATURE WOULD MAKE YOU FORGET THIS MAD SCHEME TO SELL YOUR NEW IMPROVED ZOMBIES AS SLAVES?
CHICA, CHICA, I WILL BE RICH. VERY, *VERY* RICH. YOU CAN REFUSE TO JOIN ME, BUT YOU CANNOT STOP ME.
DON'T BET ON IT.
WHAT WILL YOU DO, GO TO THE POLICE? I AM BREAKING NO LAWS. THE ONLY WAY TO STOP ME IS TO KILL ME.
DON'T TEMPT ME.
DON'T, ANITA--DON'T CHALLENGE HER.
I *WILL* STOP YOU, SEÑORA SALVADOR. WHATEVER IT TAKES.
YOU CALL DEATH MAGIC AGAINST ME, ANITA, AND IT IS YOU WHO WILL DIE.
I WAS THINKING SOME THING MORE DOWN-TO-EARTH, LIKE A *BULLET.*
NO, ENZO, SHE IS ANGRY AND SHOCKED.
SHE KNOWS NOTHING OF DEEPER MAGICS.
SHE IS TOO MORALLY SUPERIOR TO COMMIT COLD-BLOODED MURDER.

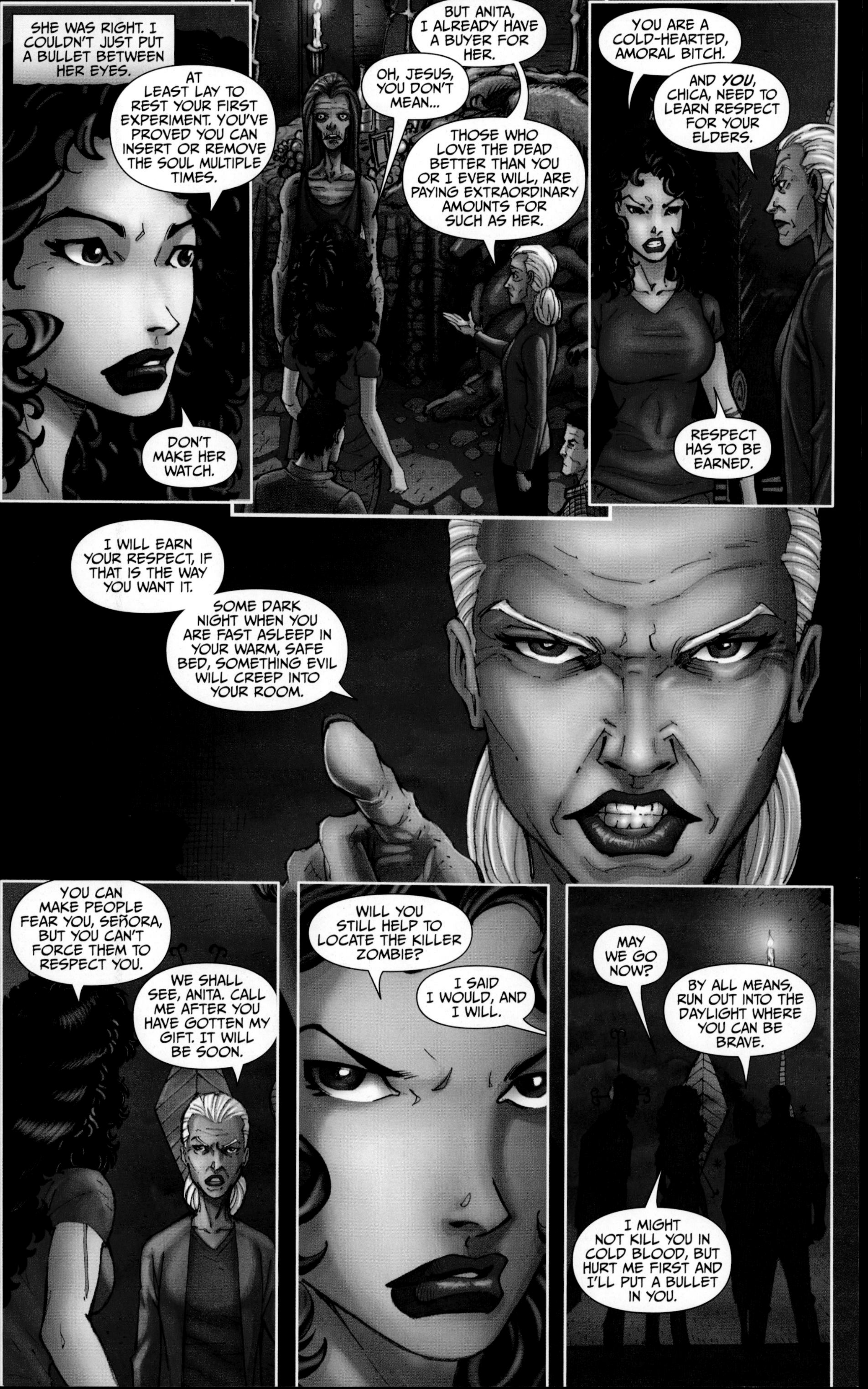

SHE WAS RIGHT. I COULDN'T JUST PUT A BULLET BETWEEN HER EYES.
AT LEAST LAY TO REST YOUR FIRST EXPERIMENT. YOU'VE PROVED YOU CAN INSERT OR REMOVE THE SOUL MULTIPLE TIMES.
DON'T MAKE HER WATCH.
BUT ANITA, I ALREADY HAVE A BUYER FOR HER.
OH, JESUS, YOU DON'T MEAN...
THOSE WHO LOVE THE DEAD BETTER THAN YOU OR I EVER WILL, ARE PAYING EXTRAORDINARY AMOUNTS FOR SUCH AS HER.
YOU ARE A COLD-HEARTED, AMORAL BITCH.
AND *YOU*, CHICA, NEED TO LEARN RESPECT FOR YOUR ELDERS.
RESPECT HAS TO BE EARNED.
I WILL EARN YOUR RESPECT, IF THAT IS THE WAY YOU WANT IT.
SOME DARK NIGHT WHEN YOU ARE FAST ASLEEP IN YOUR WARM, SAFE BED, SOMETHING EVIL WILL CREEP INTO YOUR ROOM.
YOU CAN MAKE PEOPLE FEAR YOU, SEÑORA, BUT YOU CAN'T FORCE THEM TO RESPECT YOU.
WE SHALL SEE, ANITA. CALL ME AFTER YOU HAVE GOTTEN MY GIFT. IT WILL BE SOON.
WILL YOU STILL HELP TO LOCATE THE KILLER ZOMBIE?
I SAID I WOULD, AND I WILL.
MAY WE GO NOW?
BY ALL MEANS, RUN OUT INTO THE DAYLIGHT WHERE YOU CAN BE BRAVE.
I MIGHT NOT KILL YOU IN COLD BLOOD, BUT HURT ME FIRST AND I'LL PUT A BULLET IN YOU.

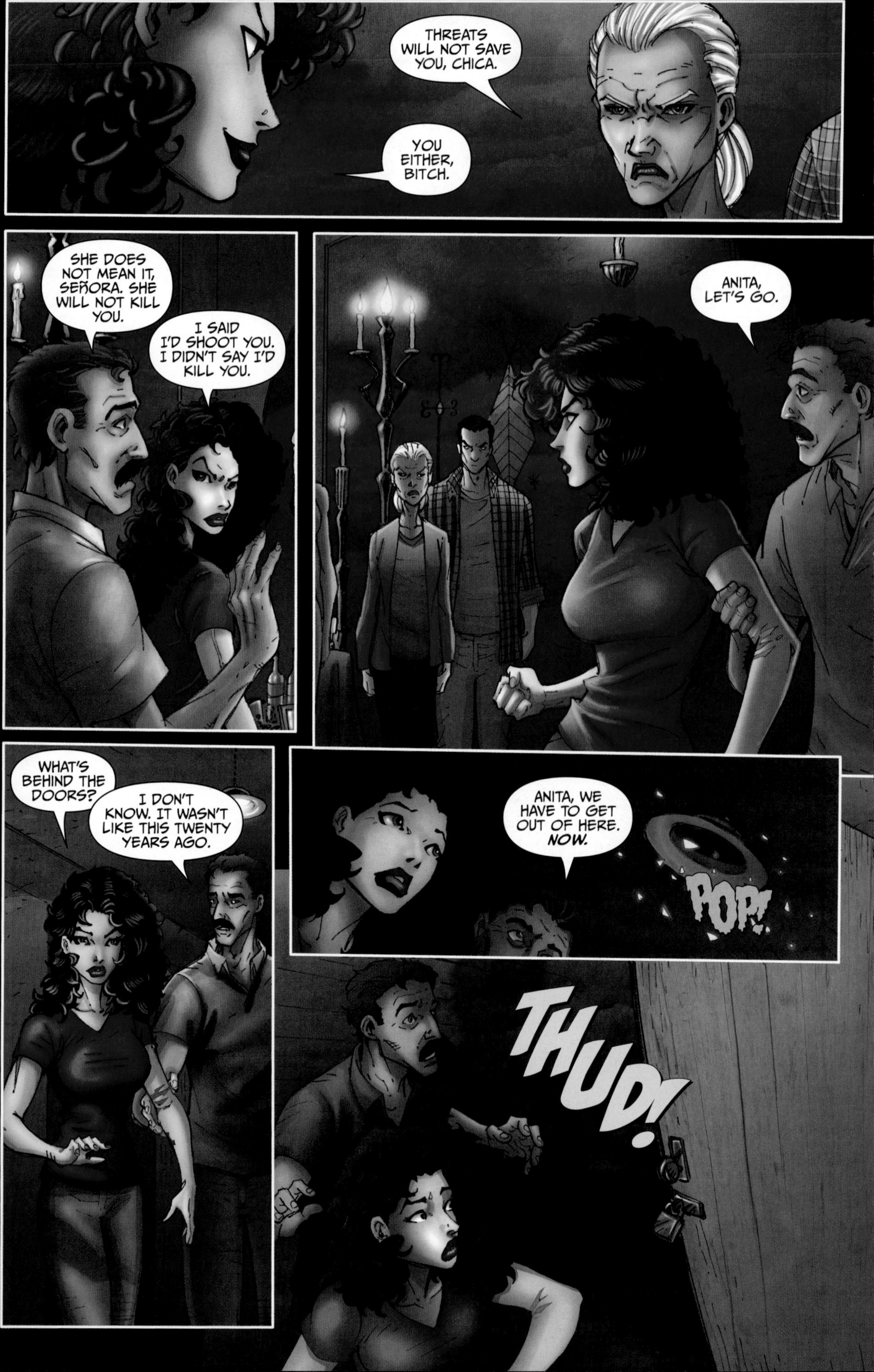
THREATS WILL NOT SAVE YOU, CHICA.
YOU EITHER, BITCH.
SHE DOES NOT MEAN IT, SEÑORA. SHE WILL NOT KILL YOU.
I SAID I'D SHOOT YOU. I DIDN'T SAY I'D KILL YOU.
ANITA, LET'S GO.
WHAT'S BEHIND THE DOORS?
I DON'T KNOW. IT WASN'T LIKE THIS TWENTY YEARS AGO.
ANITA, WE HAVE TO GET OUT OF HERE. *NOW.*
POP!
THUD!

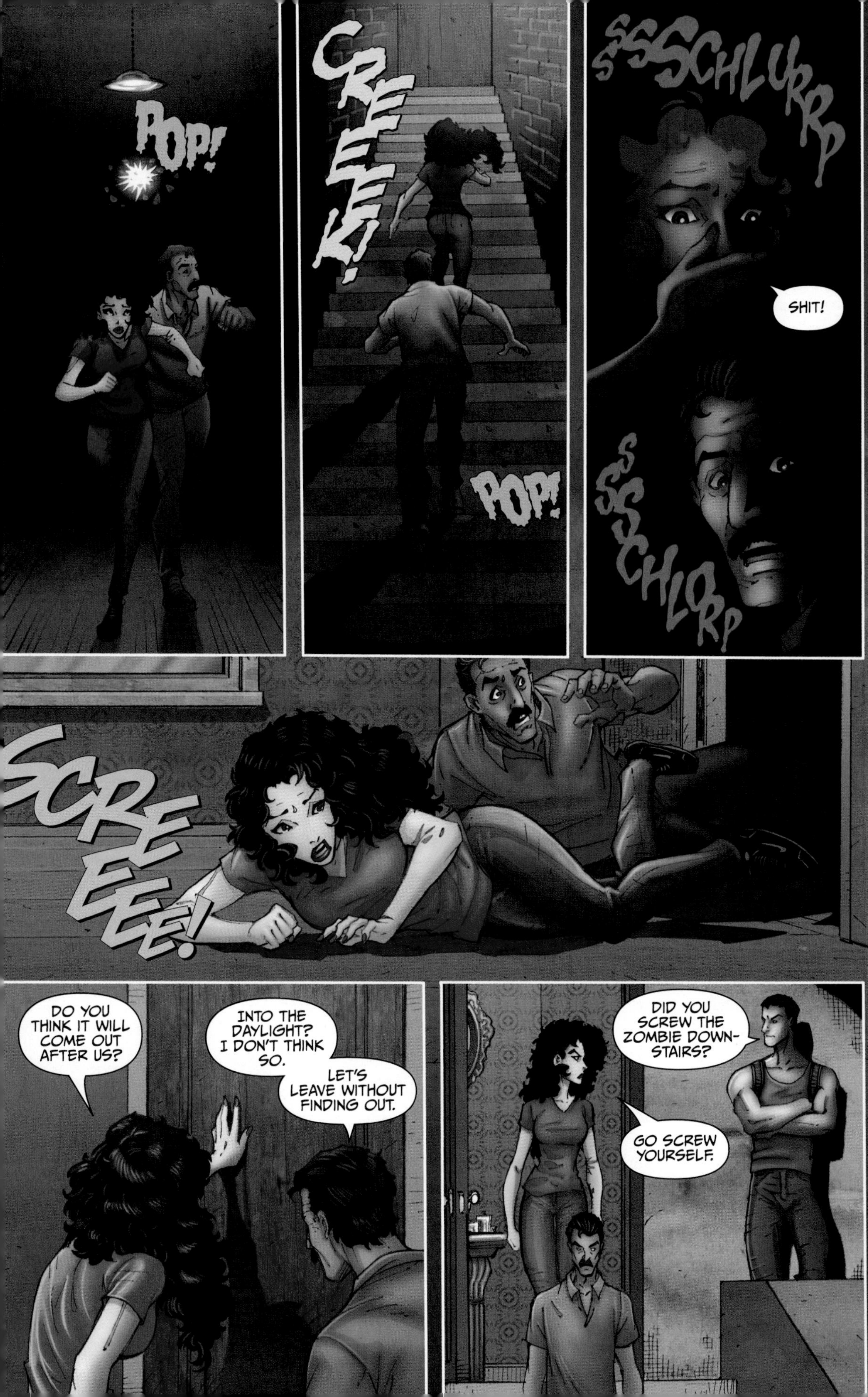
POP!
CREEEK!
POP!
SSSCHLURRP
SHIT!
SSSCHLORP
SCREEEEE!
DO YOU THINK IT WILL COME OUT AFTER US?
INTO THE DAYLIGHT? I DON'T THINK SO.
LET'S LEAVE WITHOUT FINDING OUT.
DID YOU SCREW THE ZOMBIE DOWN-STAIRS?
GO SCREW YOURSELF.

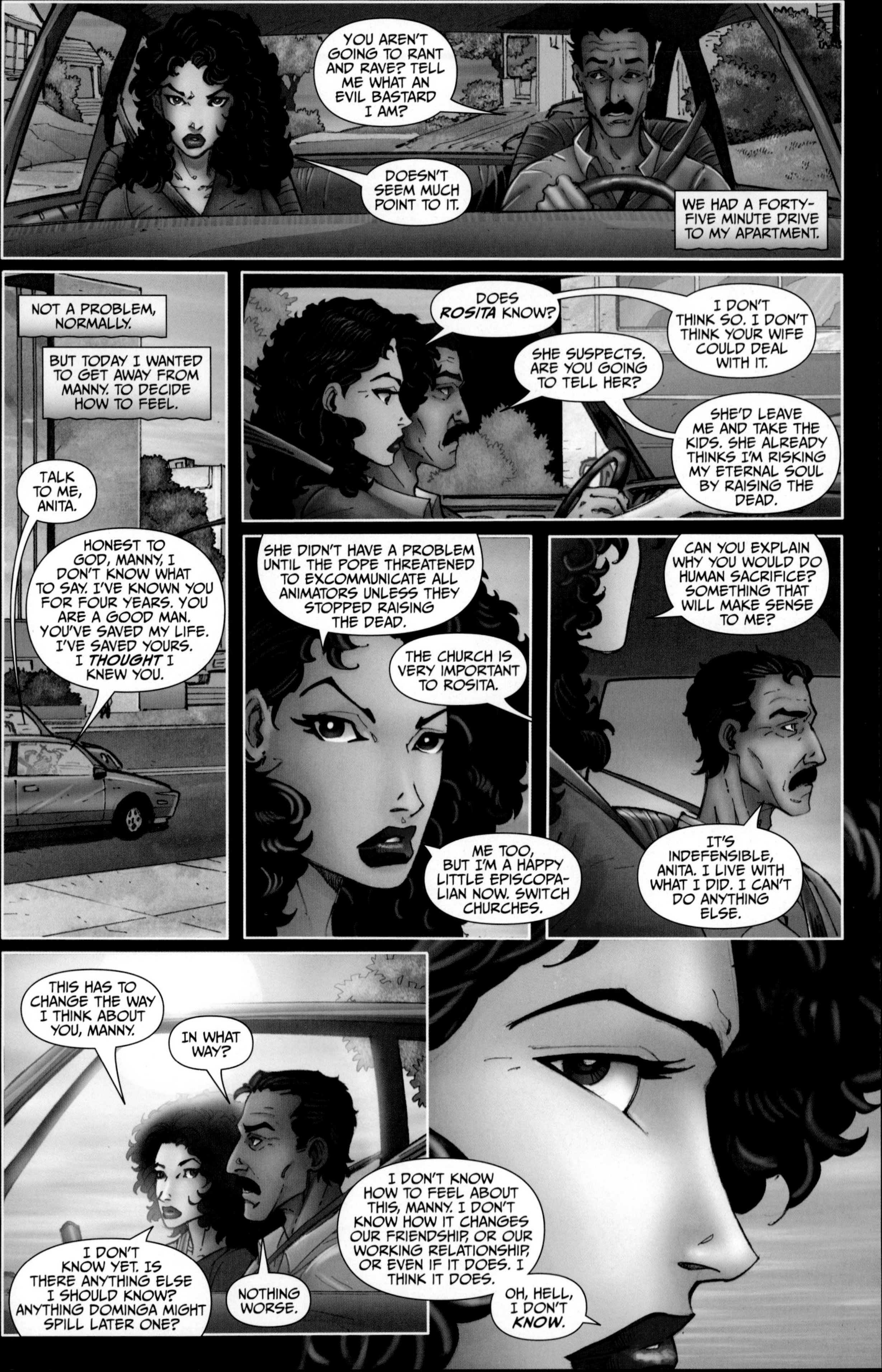

YOU AREN'T GOING TO RANT AND RAVE? TELL ME WHAT AN EVIL BASTARD I AM?
DOESN'T SEEM MUCH POINT TO IT.
WE HAD A FORTY-FIVE MINUTE DRIVE TO MY APARTMENT.
NOT A PROBLEM, NORMALLY.
BUT TODAY I WANTED TO GET AWAY FROM MANNY. TO DECIDE HOW TO FEEL.
TALK TO ME, ANITA.
HONEST TO GOD, MANNY, I DON'T KNOW WHAT TO SAY. I'VE KNOWN YOU FOR FOUR YEARS. YOU ARE A GOOD MAN. YOU'VE SAVED MY LIFE. I'VE SAVED YOURS. I *THOUGHT* I KNEW YOU.
DOES *ROSITA* KNOW?
I DON'T THINK SO. I DON'T THINK YOUR WIFE COULD DEAL WITH IT.
SHE SUSPECTS. ARE YOU GOING TO TELL HER?
SHE'D LEAVE ME AND TAKE THE KIDS. SHE ALREADY THINKS I'M RISKING MY ETERNAL SOUL BY RAISING THE DEAD.
SHE DIDN'T HAVE A PROBLEM UNTIL THE POPE THREATENED TO EXCOMMUNICATE ALL ANIMATORS UNLESS THEY STOPPED RAISING THE DEAD.
THE CHURCH IS VERY IMPORTANT TO ROSITA.
ME TOO, BUT I'M A HAPPY LITTLE EPISCOPA-LIAN NOW. SWITCH CHURCHES.
CAN YOU EXPLAIN WHY YOU WOULD DO HUMAN SACRIFICE? SOMETHING THAT WILL MAKE SENSE TO ME?
IT'S INDEFENSIBLE, ANITA. I LIVE WITH WHAT I DID. I CAN'T DO ANYTHING ELSE.
THIS HAS TO CHANGE THE WAY I THINK ABOUT YOU, MANNY.
IN WHAT WAY?
I DON'T KNOW YET. IS THERE ANYTHING ELSE I SHOULD KNOW? ANYTHING DOMINGA MIGHT SPILL LATER ONE?
NOTHING WORSE.
I DON'T KNOW HOW TO FEEL ABOUT THIS, MANNY. I DON'T KNOW HOW IT CHANGES OUR FRIENDSHIP, OR OUR WORKING RELATIONSHIP, OR EVEN IF IT DOES. I THINK IT DOES.
OH, HELL, I DON'T *KNOW*.

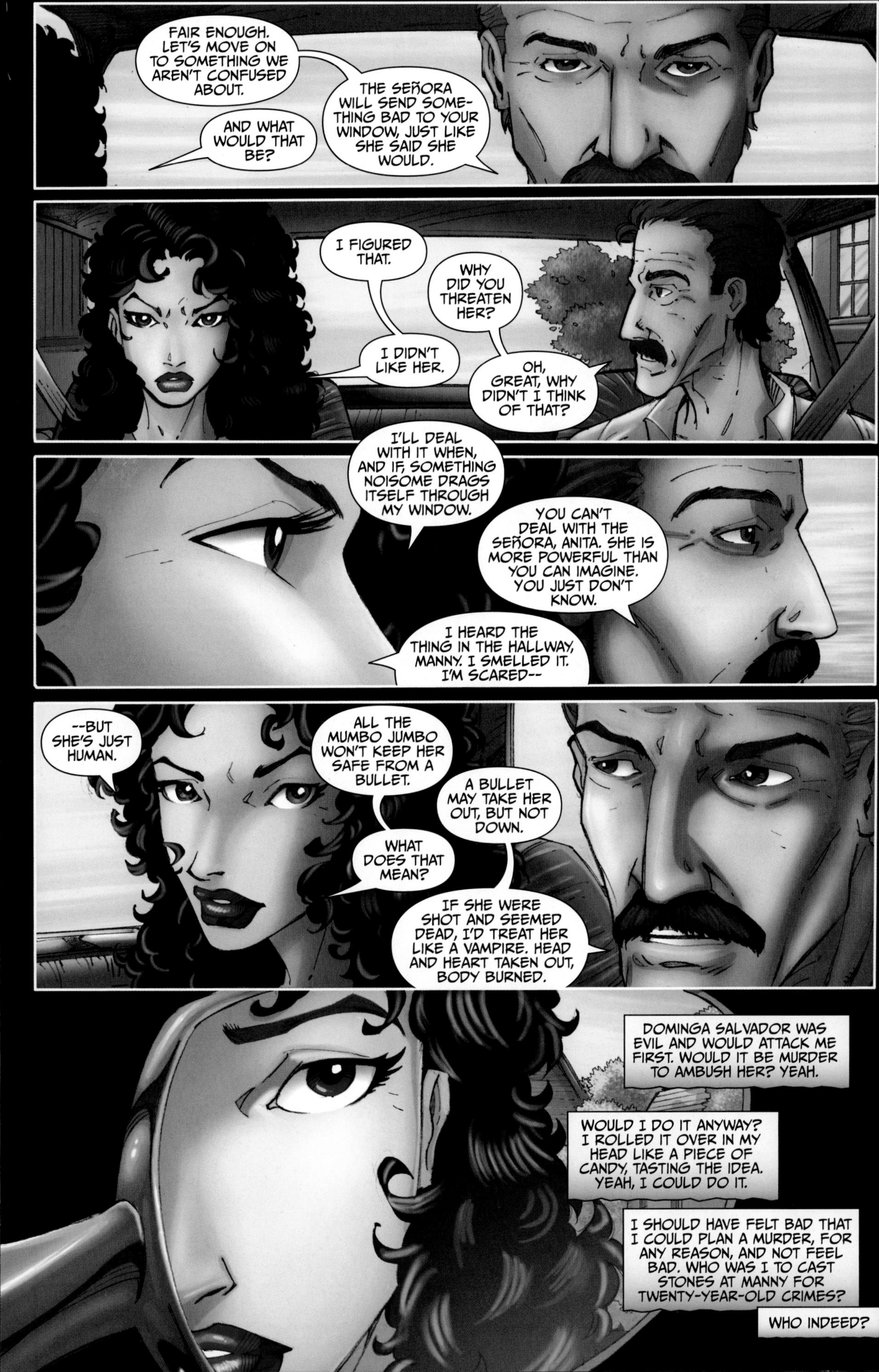
FAIR ENOUGH. LET'S MOVE ON TO SOMETHING WE AREN'T CONFUSED ABOUT.
AND WHAT WOULD THAT BE?
THE SEÑORA WILL SEND SOME-THING BAD TO YOUR WINDOW, JUST LIKE SHE SAID SHE WOULD.
I FIGURED THAT.
I DIDN'T LIKE HER.
WHY DID YOU THREATEN HER?
OH, GREAT, WHY DIDN'T I THINK OF THAT?
I'LL DEAL WITH IT WHEN, AND IF, SOMETHING NOISOME DRAGS ITSELF THROUGH MY WINDOW.
YOU CAN'T DEAL WITH THE SEÑORA, ANITA. SHE IS MORE POWERFUL THAN YOU CAN IMAGINE. YOU JUST DON'T KNOW.
I HEARD THE THING IN THE HALLWAY, MANNY. I SMELLED IT. I'M SCARED--
--BUT SHE'S JUST HUMAN.
ALL THE MUMBO JUMBO WON'T KEEP HER SAFE FROM A BULLET.
A BULLET MAY TAKE HER OUT, BUT NOT DOWN.
WHAT DOES THAT MEAN?
IF SHE WERE SHOT AND SEEMED DEAD, I'D TREAT HER LIKE A VAMPIRE. HEAD AND HEART TAKEN OUT, BODY BURNED.
DOMINGA SALVADOR WAS EVIL AND WOULD ATTACK ME FIRST. WOULD IT BE MURDER TO AMBUSH HER? YEAH.
WOULD I DO IT ANYWAY? I ROLLED IT OVER IN MY HEAD LIKE A PIECE OF CANDY, TASTING THE IDEA. YEAH, I COULD DO IT.
I SHOULD HAVE FELT BAD THAT I COULD PLAN A MURDER, FOR ANY REASON, AND NOT FEEL BAD. WHO WAS I TO CAST STONES AT MANNY FOR TWENTY-YEAR-OLD CRIMES?
WHO INDEED?

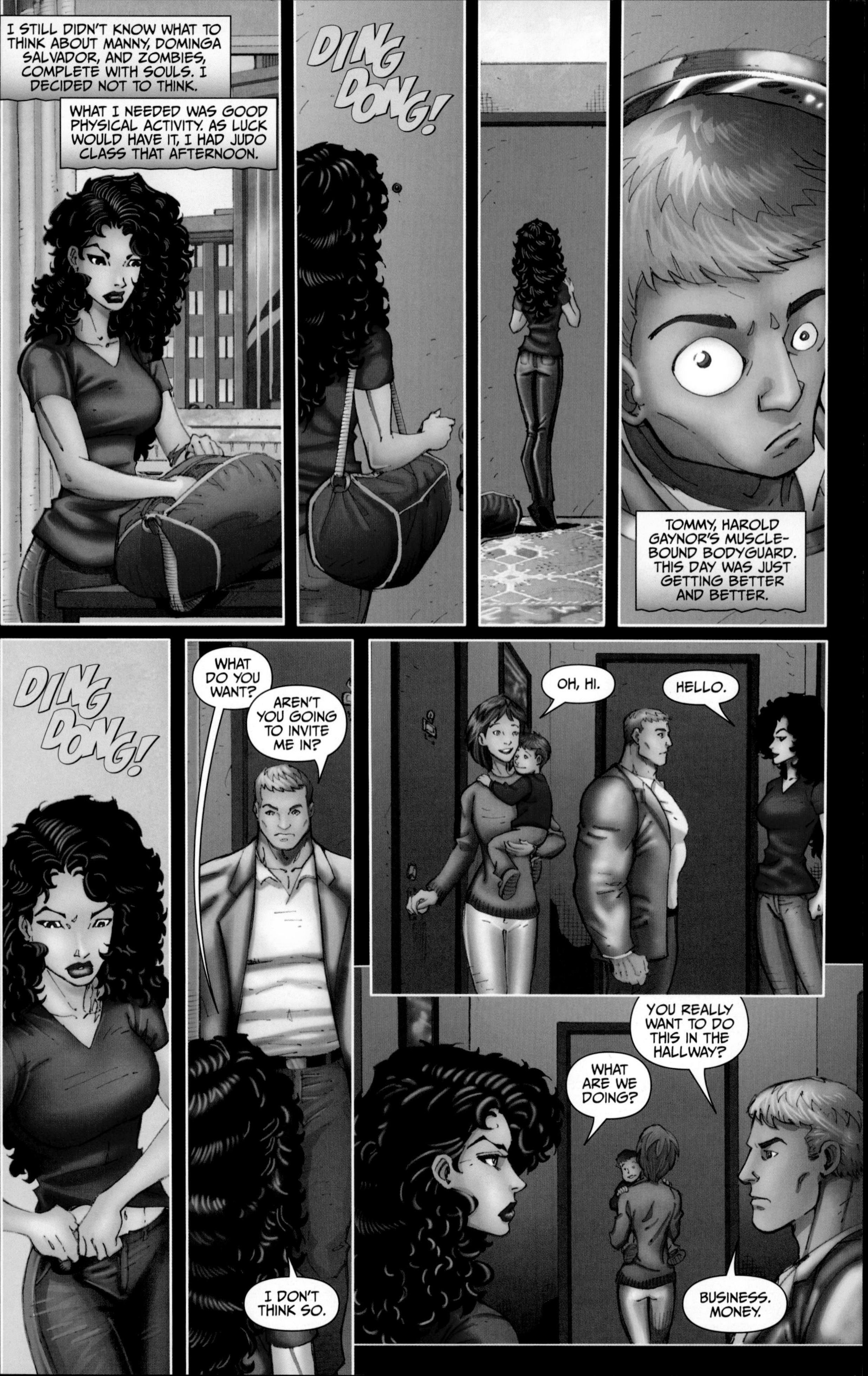
I STILL DIDN'T KNOW WHAT TO THINK ABOUT MANNY, DOMINGA SALVADOR, AND ZOMBIES, COMPLETE WITH SOULS. I DECIDED NOT TO THINK.
WHAT I NEEDED WAS GOOD PHYSICAL ACTIVITY. AS LUCK WOULD HAVE IT, I HAD JUDO CLASS THAT AFTERNOON.
DING DONG!
TOMMY, HAROLD GAYNOR'S MUSCLE-BOUND BODYGUARD. THIS DAY WAS JUST GETTING BETTER AND BETTER.
DING DONG!
WHAT DO YOU WANT?
AREN'T YOU GOING TO INVITE ME IN?
I DON'T THINK SO.
OH, HI.
HELLO.
YOU REALLY WANT TO DO THIS IN THE HALLWAY?
WHAT ARE WE DOING?
BUSINESS. MONEY.

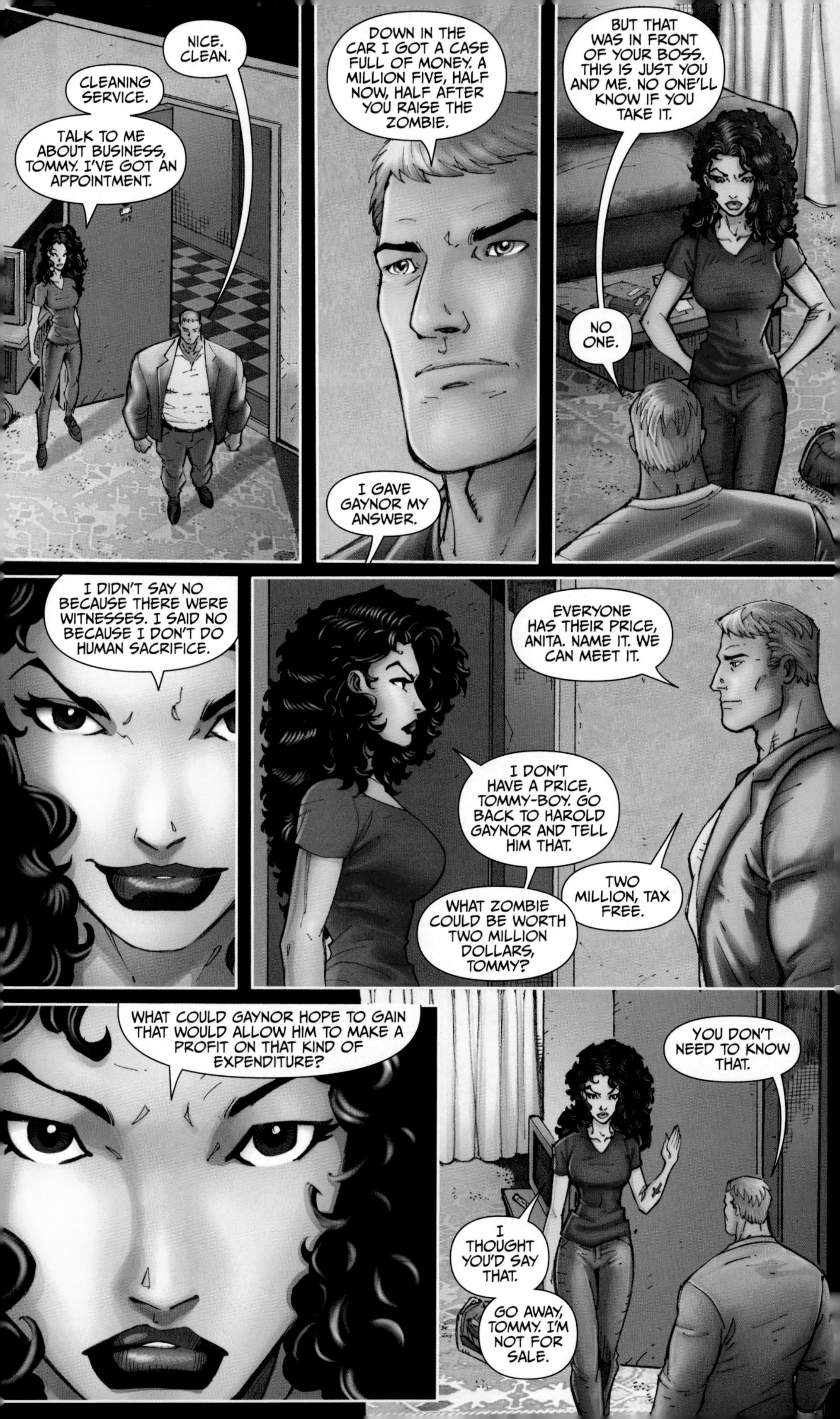
NICE. CLEAN.
CLEANING SERVICE.
TALK TO ME ABOUT BUSINESS, TOMMY. I'VE GOT AN APPOINTMENT.
DOWN IN THE CAR I GOT A CASE FULL OF MONEY. A MILLION FIVE, HALF NOW, HALF AFTER YOU RAISE THE ZOMBIE.
I GAVE GAYNOR MY ANSWER.
BUT THAT WAS IN FRONT OF YOUR BOSS. THIS IS JUST YOU AND ME. NO ONE'LL KNOW IF YOU TAKE IT.
NO ONE.
I DIDN'T SAY NO BECAUSE THERE WERE WITNESSES. I SAID NO BECAUSE I DON'T DO HUMAN SACRIFICE.
EVERYONE HAS THEIR PRICE, ANITA. NAME IT. WE CAN MEET IT.
I DON'T HAVE A PRICE, TOMMY-BOY. GO BACK TO HAROLD GAYNOR AND TELL HIM THAT.
TWO MILLION, TAX FREE.
WHAT ZOMBIE COULD BE WORTH TWO MILLION DOLLARS, TOMMY?
WHAT COULD GAYNOR HOPE TO GAIN THAT WOULD ALLOW HIM TO MAKE A PROFIT ON THAT KIND OF EXPENDITURE?
YOU DON'T NEED TO KNOW THAT.
I THOUGHT YOU'D SAY THAT.
GO AWAY, TOMMY. I'M NOT FOR SALE.

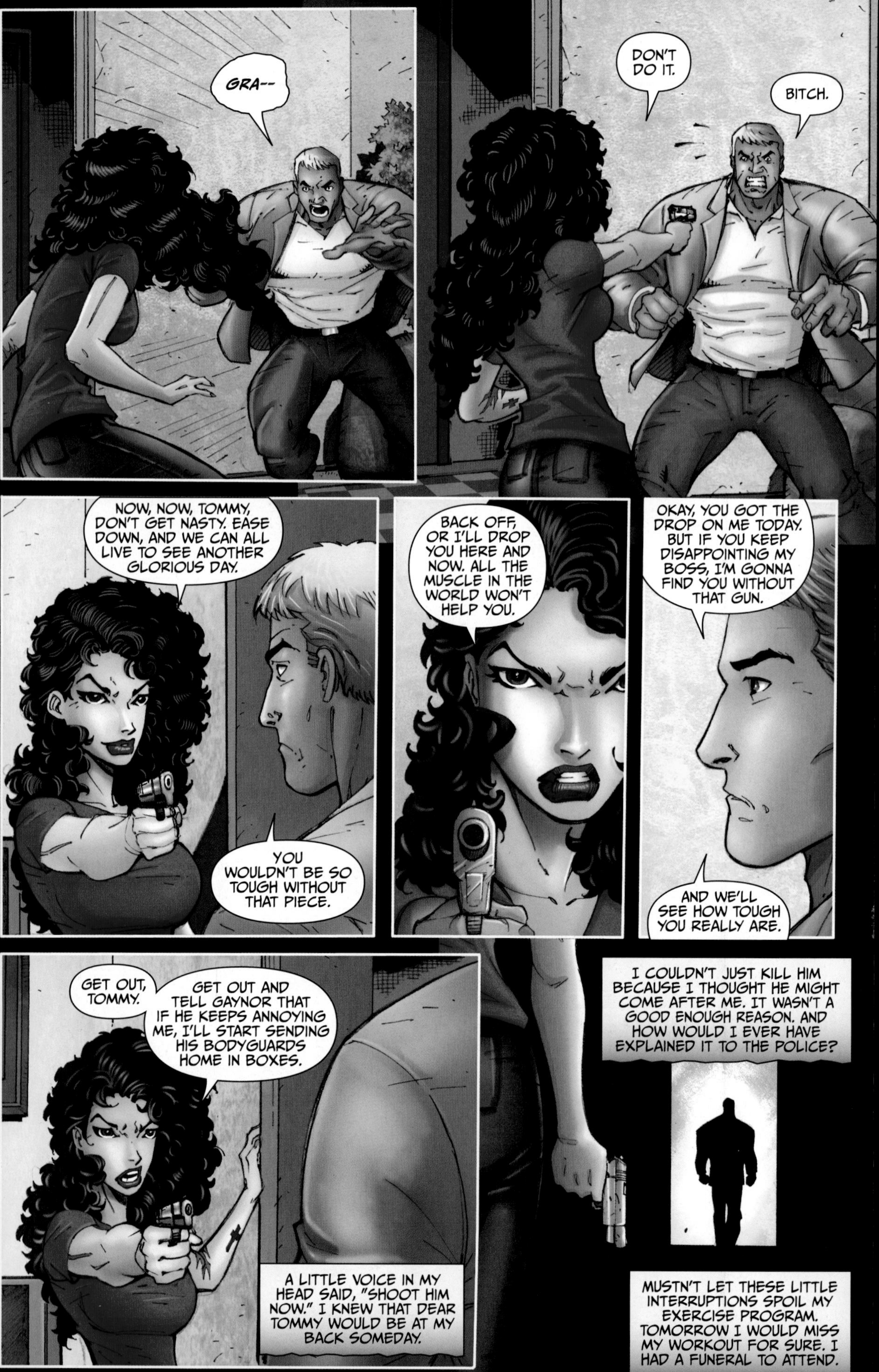
GRA--
DON'T DO IT.
BITCH.
NOW, NOW, TOMMY, DON'T GET NASTY. EASE DOWN, AND WE CAN ALL LIVE TO SEE ANOTHER GLORIOUS DAY.
YOU WOULDN'T BE SO TOUGH WITHOUT THAT PIECE.
BACK OFF, OR I'LL DROP YOU HERE AND NOW. ALL THE MUSCLE IN THE WORLD WON'T HELP YOU.
OKAY, YOU GOT THE DROP ON ME TODAY. BUT IF YOU KEEP DISAPPOINTING MY BOSS, I'M GONNA FIND YOU WITHOUT THAT GUN.
AND WE'LL SEE HOW TOUGH YOU REALLY ARE.
GET OUT, TOMMY.
GET OUT AND TELL GAYNOR THAT IF HE KEEPS ANNOYING ME, I'LL START SENDING HIS BODYGUARDS HOME IN BOXES.
A LITTLE VOICE IN MY HEAD SAID, "SHOOT HIM NOW." I KNEW THAT DEAR TOMMY WOULD BE AT MY BACK SOMEDAY.
I COULDN'T JUST KILL HIM BECAUSE I THOUGHT HE MIGHT COME AFTER ME. IT WASN'T A GOOD ENOUGH REASON. AND HOW WOULD I EVER HAVE EXPLAINED IT TO THE POLICE?
MUSTN'T LET THESE LITTLE INTERRUPTIONS SPOIL MY EXERCISE PROGRAM. TOMORROW I WOULD MISS MY WORKOUT FOR SURE. I HAD A FUNERAL TO ATTEND.

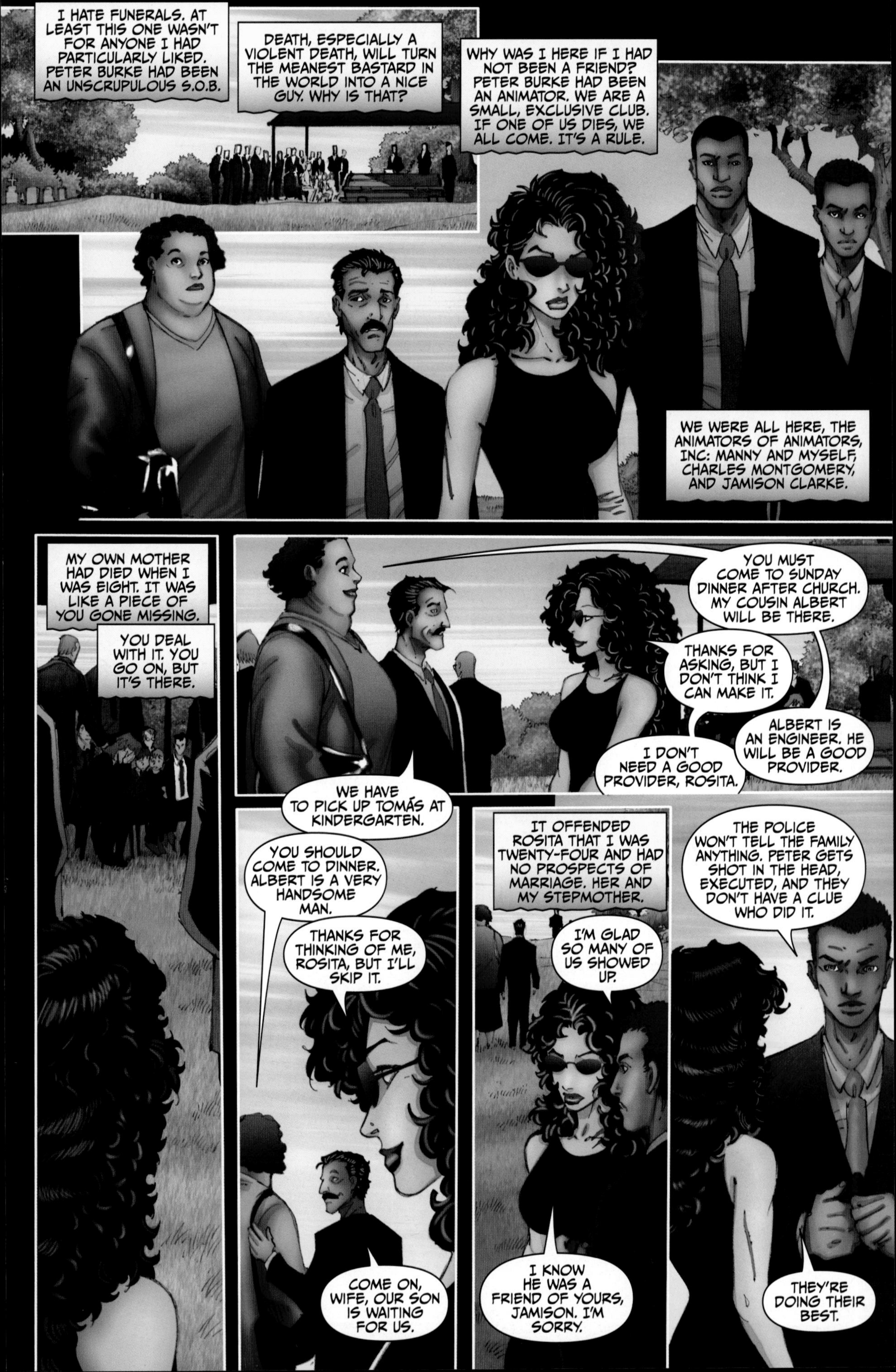
I HATE FUNERALS. AT LEAST THIS ONE WASN'T FOR ANYONE I HAD PARTICULARLY LIKED. PETER BURKE HAD BEEN AN UNSCRUPULOUS S.O.B.
DEATH, ESPECIALLY A VIOLENT DEATH, WILL TURN THE MEANEST BASTARD IN THE WORLD INTO A NICE GUY. WHY IS THAT?
WHY WAS I HERE IF I HAD NOT BEEN A FRIEND? PETER BURKE HAD BEEN AN ANIMATOR. WE ARE A SMALL, EXCLUSIVE CLUB. IF ONE OF US DIES, WE ALL COME. IT'S A RULE.
WE WERE ALL HERE, THE ANIMATORS OF ANIMATORS, INC: MANNY AND MYSELF, CHARLES MONTGOMERY, AND JAMISON CLARKE.
MY OWN MOTHER HAD DIED WHEN I WAS EIGHT. IT WAS LIKE A PIECE OF YOU GONE MISSING.
YOU DEAL WITH IT. YOU GO ON, BUT IT'S THERE.
YOU MUST COME TO SUNDAY DINNER AFTER CHURCH. MY COUSIN ALBERT WILL BE THERE.
THANKS FOR ASKING, BUT I DON'T THINK I CAN MAKE IT.
ALBERT IS AN ENGINEER. HE WILL BE A GOOD PROVIDER.
I DON'T NEED A GOOD PROVIDER, ROSITA.
WE HAVE TO PICK UP TOMÁS AT KINDERGARTEN.
YOU SHOULD COME TO DINNER. ALBERT IS A VERY HANDSOME MAN.
THANKS FOR THINKING OF ME, ROSITA, BUT I'LL SKIP IT.
COME ON, WIFE, OUR SON IS WAITING FOR US.
IT OFFENDED ROSITA THAT I WAS TWENTY-FOUR AND HAD NO PROSPECTS OF MARRIAGE. HER AND MY STEPMOTHER.
I'M GLAD SO MANY OF US SHOWED UP.
I KNOW HE WAS A FRIEND OF YOURS, JAMISON. I'M SORRY.
THE POLICE WON'T TELL THE FAMILY ANYTHING. PETER GETS SHOT IN THE HEAD, EXECUTED, AND THEY DON'T HAVE A CLUE WHO DID IT.
THEY'RE DOING THEIR BEST.

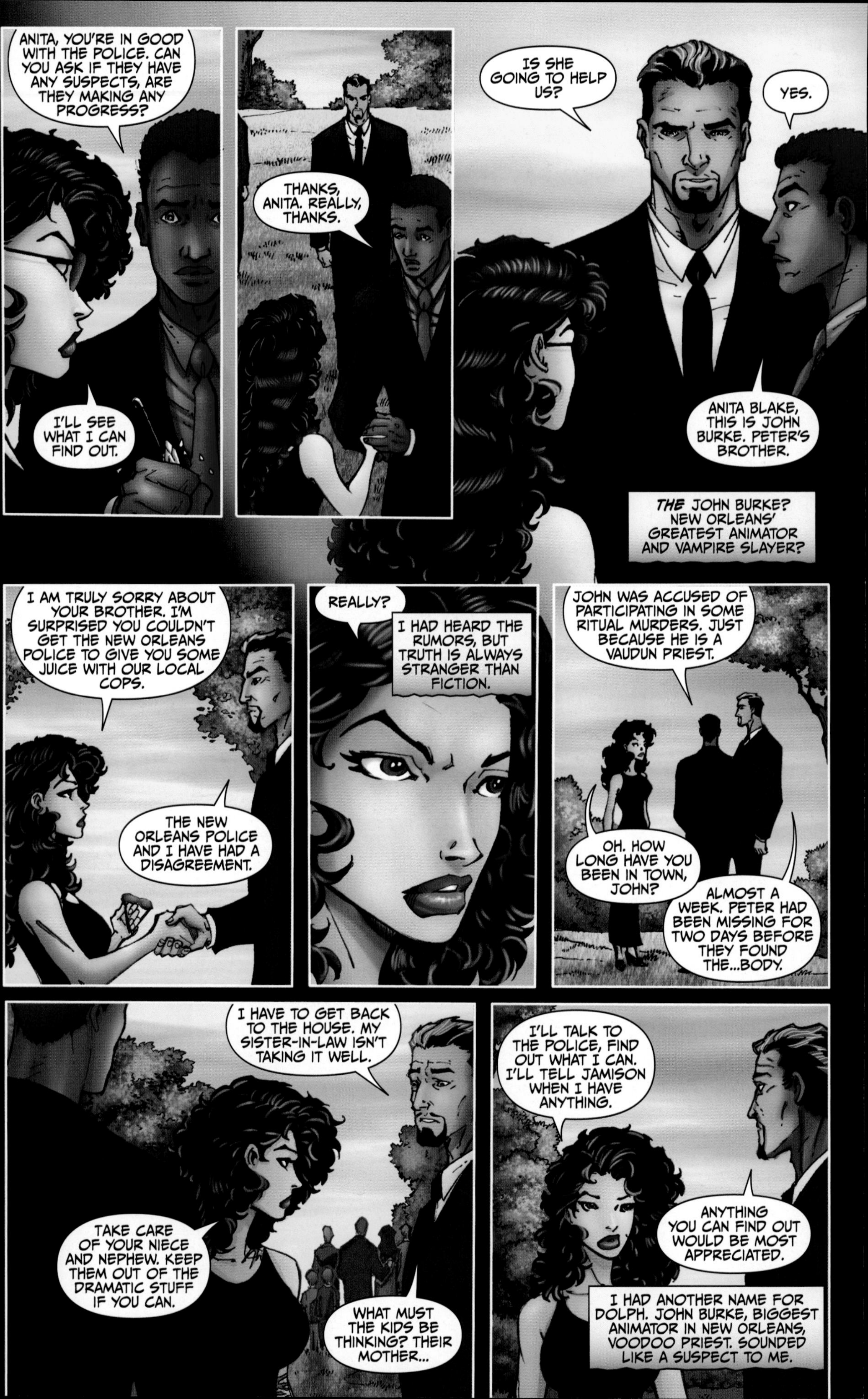
ANITA, YOU'RE IN GOOD WITH THE POLICE. CAN YOU ASK IF THEY HAVE ANY SUSPECTS, ARE THEY MAKING ANY PROGRESS?
I'LL SEE WHAT I CAN FIND OUT.
THANKS, ANITA. REALLY, THANKS.
IS SHE GOING TO HELP US?
YES.
ANITA BLAKE, THIS IS JOHN BURKE. PETER'S BROTHER.
THE JOHN BURKE? NEW ORLEANS' GREATEST ANIMATOR AND VAMPIRE SLAYER?
I AM TRULY SORRY ABOUT YOUR BROTHER. I'M SURPRISED YOU COULDN'T GET THE NEW ORLEANS POLICE TO GIVE YOU SOME JUICE WITH OUR LOCAL COPS.
THE NEW ORLEANS POLICE AND I HAVE HAD A DISAGREEMENT.
REALLY?
I HAD HEARD THE RUMORS, BUT TRUTH IS ALWAYS STRANGER THAN FICTION.
JOHN WAS ACCUSED OF PARTICIPATING IN SOME RITUAL MURDERS. JUST BECAUSE HE IS A VAUDUN PRIEST.
OH. HOW LONG HAVE YOU BEEN IN TOWN, JOHN?
ALMOST A WEEK. PETER HAD BEEN MISSING FOR TWO DAYS BEFORE THEY FOUND THE...BODY.
I HAVE TO GET BACK TO THE HOUSE. MY SISTER-IN-LAW ISN'T TAKING IT WELL.
TAKE CARE OF YOUR NIECE AND NEPHEW. KEEP THEM OUT OF THE DRAMATIC STUFF IF YOU CAN.
WHAT MUST THE KIDS BE THINKING? THEIR MOTHER...
I'LL TALK TO THE POLICE, FIND OUT WHAT I CAN. I'LL TELL JAMISON WHEN I HAVE ANYTHING.
ANYTHING YOU CAN FIND OUT WOULD BE MOST APPRECIATED.
I HAD ANOTHER NAME FOR DOLPH. JOHN BURKE, BIGGEST ANIMATOR IN NEW ORLEANS, VOODOO PRIEST. SOUNDED LIKE A SUSPECT TO ME.

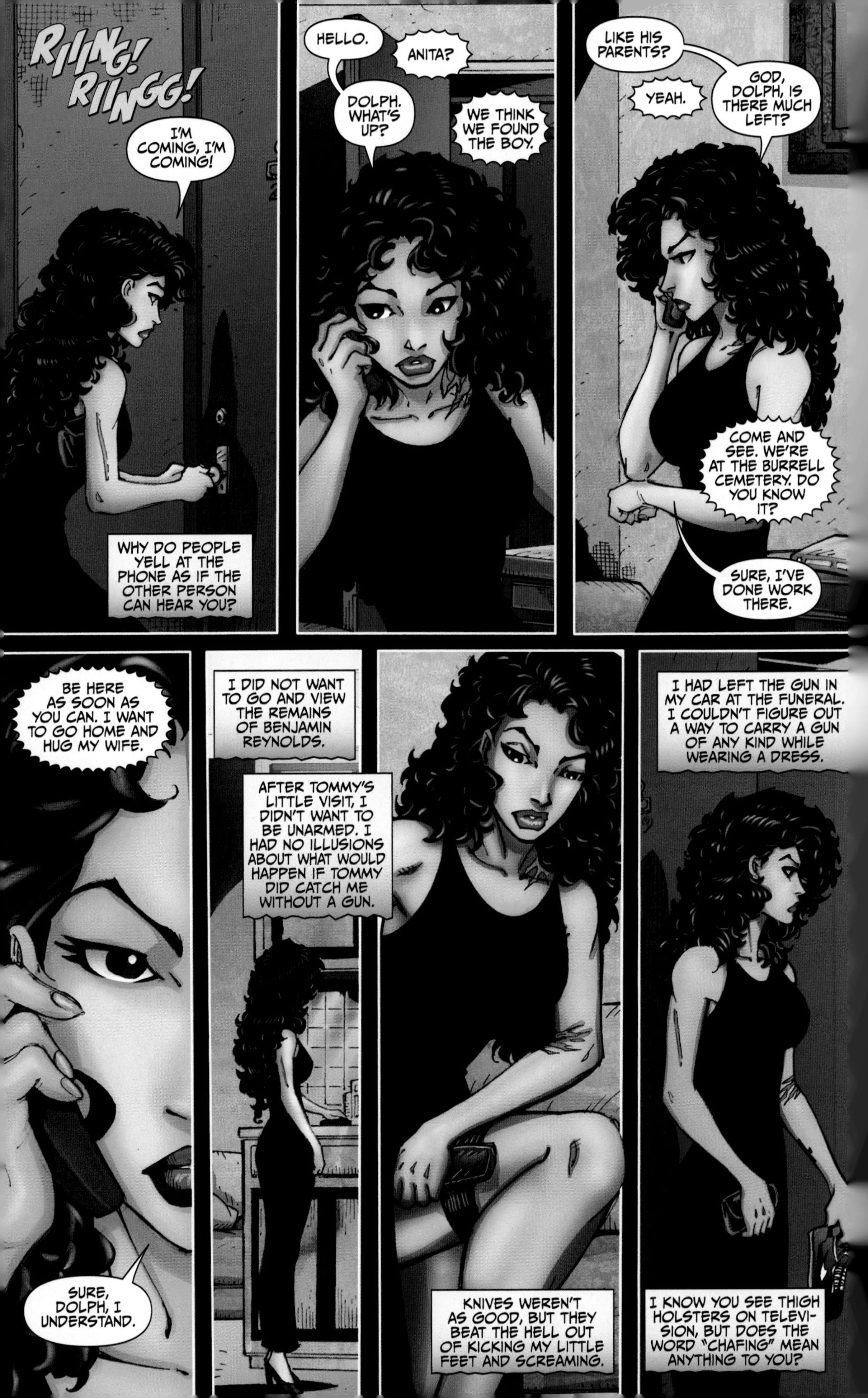
RIING! RIINGG!
I'M COMING, I'M COMING!
WHY DO PEOPLE YELL AT THE PHONE AS IF THE OTHER PERSON CAN HEAR YOU?
HELLO.
ANITA?
DOLPH. WHAT'S UP?
WE THINK WE FOUND THE BOY.
LIKE HIS PARENTS?
YEAH.
GOD, DOLPH, IS THERE MUCH LEFT?
COME AND SEE. WE'RE AT THE BURRELL CEMETERY. DO YOU KNOW IT?
SURE, I'VE DONE WORK THERE.
BE HERE AS SOON AS YOU CAN. I WANT TO GO HOME AND HUG MY WIFE.
SURE, DOLPH, I UNDERSTAND.
I DID NOT WANT TO GO AND VIEW THE REMAINS OF BENJAMIN REYNOLDS.
AFTER TOMMY'S LITTLE VISIT, I DIDN'T WANT TO BE UNARMED. I HAD NO ILLUSIONS ABOUT WHAT WOULD HAPPEN IF TOMMY DID CATCH ME WITHOUT A GUN.
KNIVES WEREN'T AS GOOD, BUT THEY BEAT THE HELL OUT OF KICKING MY LITTLE FEET AND SCREAMING.
I HAD LEFT THE GUN IN MY CAR AT THE FUNERAL. I COULDN'T FIGURE OUT A WAY TO CARRY A GUN OF ANY KIND WHILE WEARING A DRESS.
I KNOW YOU SEE THIGH HOLSTERS ON TELEVISION, BUT DOES THE WORD "CHAFING" MEAN ANYTHING TO YOU?

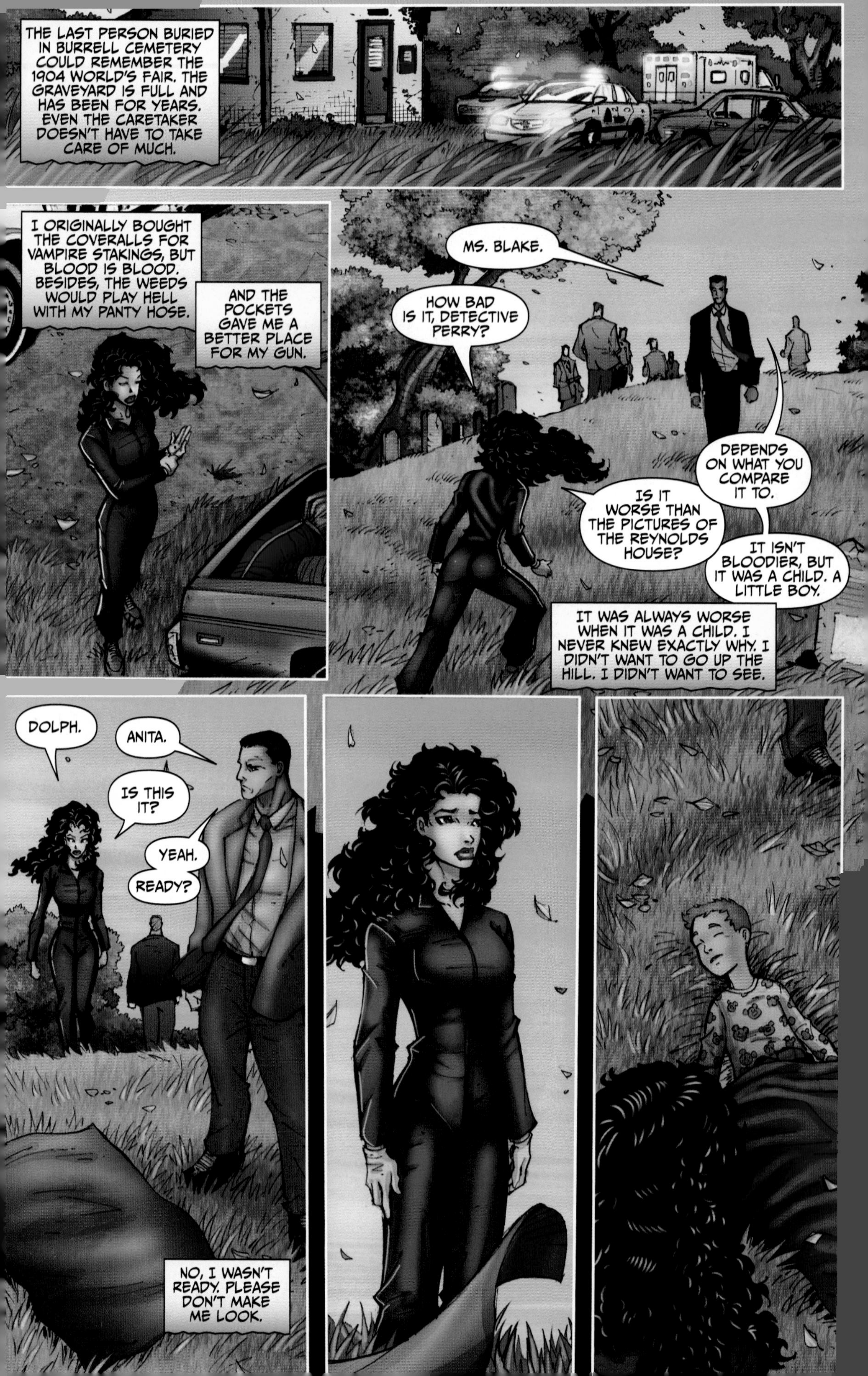
THE LAST PERSON BURIED IN BURRELL CEMETERY COULD REMEMBER THE 1904 WORLD'S FAIR. THE GRAVEYARD IS FULL AND HAS BEEN FOR YEARS. EVEN THE CARETAKER DOESN'T HAVE TO TAKE CARE OF MUCH.
I ORIGINALLY BOUGHT THE COVERALLS FOR VAMPIRE STAKINGS, BUT BLOOD IS BLOOD. BESIDES, THE WEEDS WOULD PLAY HELL WITH MY PANTY HOSE.
AND THE POCKETS GAVE ME A BETTER PLACE FOR MY GUN.
MS. BLAKE.
HOW BAD IS IT, DETECTIVE PERRY?
DEPENDS ON WHAT YOU COMPARE IT TO.
IS IT WORSE THAN THE PICTURES OF THE REYNOLDS HOUSE?
IT ISN'T BLOODIER, BUT IT WAS A CHILD. A LITTLE BOY.
IT WAS ALWAYS WORSE WHEN IT WAS A CHILD. I NEVER KNEW EXACTLY WHY. I DIDN'T WANT TO GO UP THE HILL. I DIDN'T WANT TO SEE.
DOLPH.
ANITA.
IS THIS IT?
YEAH.
READY?
NO, I WASN'T READY. PLEASE DON'T MAKE ME LOOK.

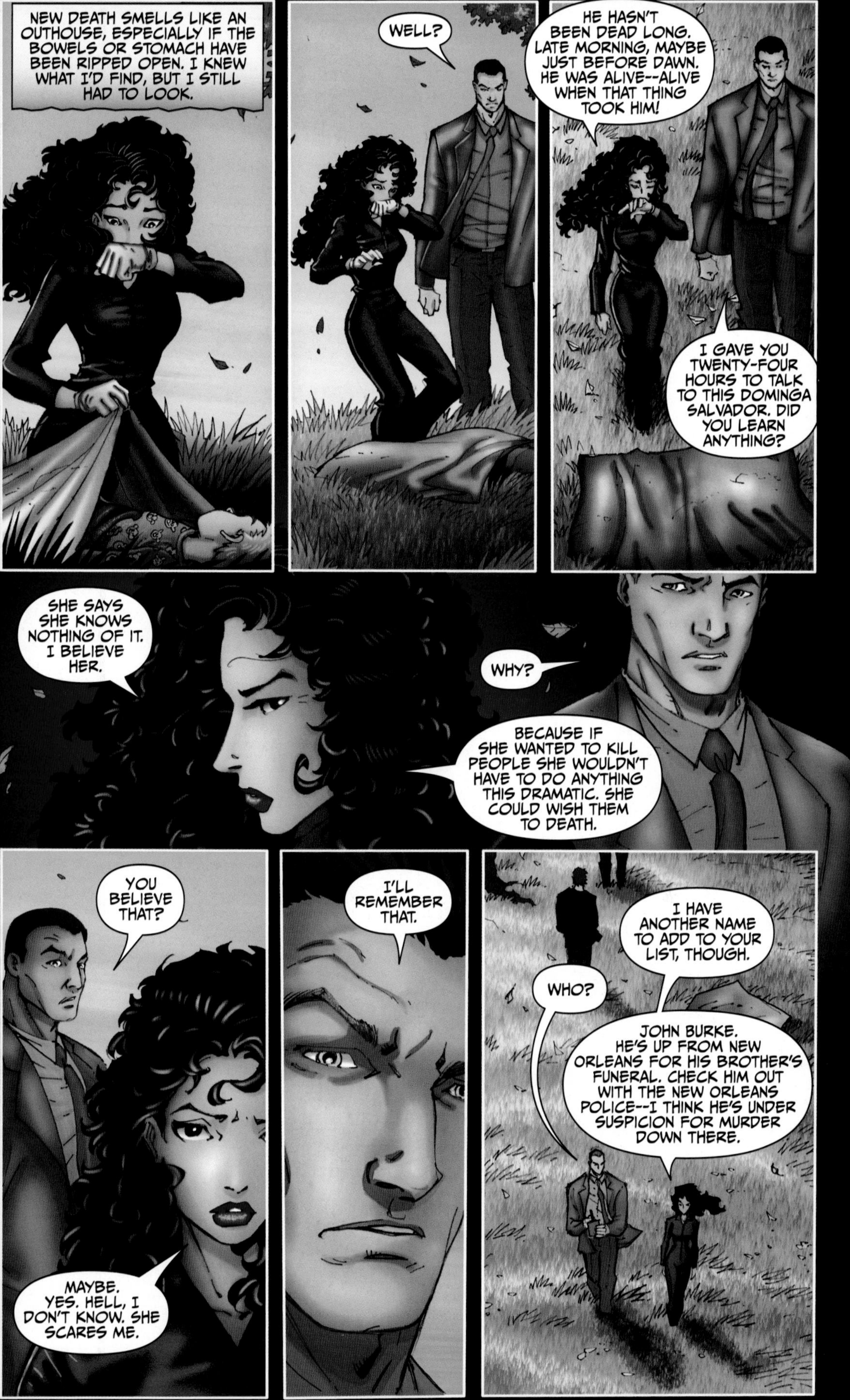
NEW DEATH SMELLS LIKE AN OUTHOUSE, ESPECIALLY IF THE BOWELS OR STOMACH HAVE BEEN RIPPED OPEN. I KNEW WHAT I'D FIND, BUT I STILL HAD TO LOOK.
WELL?
HE HASN'T BEEN DEAD LONG. LATE MORNING, MAYBE JUST BEFORE DAWN. HE WAS ALIVE--ALIVE WHEN THAT THING TOOK HIM!
I GAVE YOU TWENTY-FOUR HOURS TO TALK TO THIS DOMINGA SALVADOR. DID YOU LEARN ANYTHING?
SHE SAYS SHE KNOWS NOTHING OF IT. I BELIEVE HER.
WHY?
BECAUSE IF SHE WANTED TO KILL PEOPLE SHE WOULDN'T HAVE TO DO ANYTHING THIS DRAMATIC. SHE COULD WISH THEM TO DEATH.
YOU BELIEVE THAT?
MAYBE. YES. HELL, I DON'T KNOW. SHE SCARES ME.
I'LL REMEMBER THAT.
I HAVE ANOTHER NAME TO ADD TO YOUR LIST, THOUGH.
WHO?
JOHN BURKE. HE'S UP FROM NEW ORLEANS FOR HIS BROTHER'S FUNERAL. CHECK HIM OUT WITH THE NEW ORLEANS POLICE--I THINK HE'S UNDER SUSPICION FOR MURDER DOWN THERE.

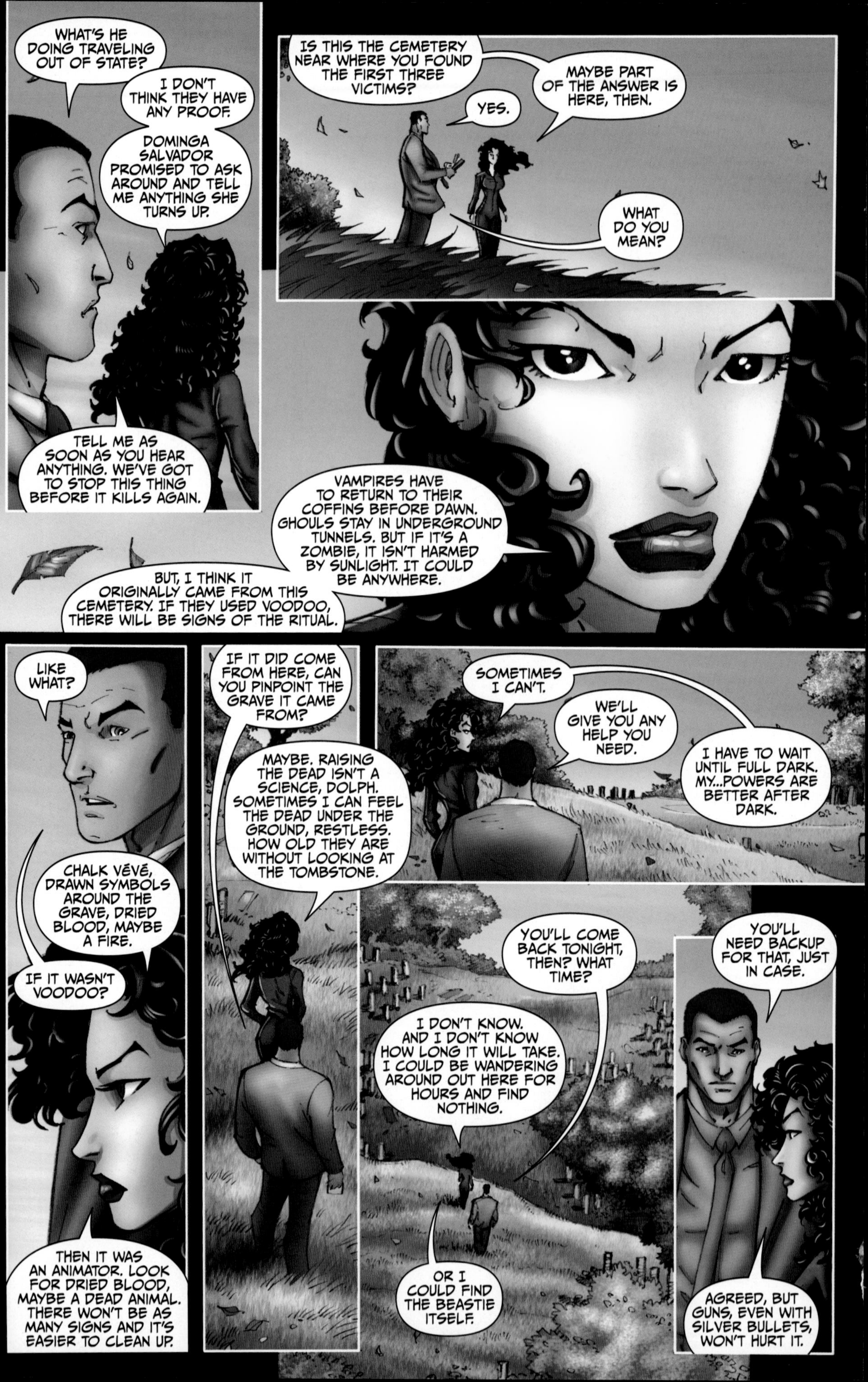
WHAT'S HE DOING TRAVELING OUT OF STATE?
I DON'T THINK THEY HAVE ANY PROOF.
DOMINGA SALVADOR PROMISED TO ASK AROUND AND TELL ME ANYTHING SHE TURNS UP.
TELL ME AS SOON AS YOU HEAR ANYTHING. WE'VE GOT TO STOP THIS THING BEFORE IT KILLS AGAIN.
IS THIS THE CEMETERY NEAR WHERE YOU FOUND THE FIRST THREE VICTIMS?
YES.
MAYBE PART OF THE ANSWER IS HERE, THEN.
WHAT DO YOU MEAN?
VAMPIRES HAVE TO RETURN TO THEIR COFFINS BEFORE DAWN. GHOULS STAY IN UNDERGROUND TUNNELS. BUT IF IT'S A ZOMBIE, IT ISN'T HARMED BY SUNLIGHT. IT COULD BE ANYWHERE.
BUT, I THINK IT ORIGINALLY CAME FROM THIS CEMETERY. IF THEY USED VOODOO, THERE WILL BE SIGNS OF THE RITUAL.
LIKE WHAT?
CHALK VÉVÉ, DRAWN SYMBOLS AROUND THE GRAVE, DRIED BLOOD, MAYBE A FIRE.
IF IT WASN'T VOODOO?
THEN IT WAS AN ANIMATOR. LOOK FOR DRIED BLOOD, MAYBE A DEAD ANIMAL. THERE WON'T BE AS MANY SIGNS AND IT'S EASIER TO CLEAN UP.
IF IT DID COME FROM HERE, CAN YOU PINPOINT THE GRAVE IT CAME FROM?
MAYBE. RAISING THE DEAD ISN'T A SCIENCE, DOLPH. SOMETIMES I CAN FEEL THE DEAD UNDER THE GROUND, RESTLESS. HOW OLD THEY ARE WITHOUT LOOKING AT THE TOMBSTONE.
SOMETIMES I CAN'T.
WE'LL GIVE YOU ANY HELP YOU NEED.
I HAVE TO WAIT UNTIL FULL DARK. MY...POWERS ARE BETTER AFTER DARK.
YOU'LL COME BACK TONIGHT, THEN? WHAT TIME?
I DON'T KNOW. AND I DON'T KNOW HOW LONG IT WILL TAKE. I COULD BE WANDERING AROUND OUT HERE FOR HOURS AND FIND NOTHING.
OR I COULD FIND THE BEASTIE ITSELF.
YOU'LL NEED BACKUP FOR THAT, JUST IN CASE.
AGREED, BUT GUNS, EVEN WITH SILVER BULLETS, WON'T HURT IT.

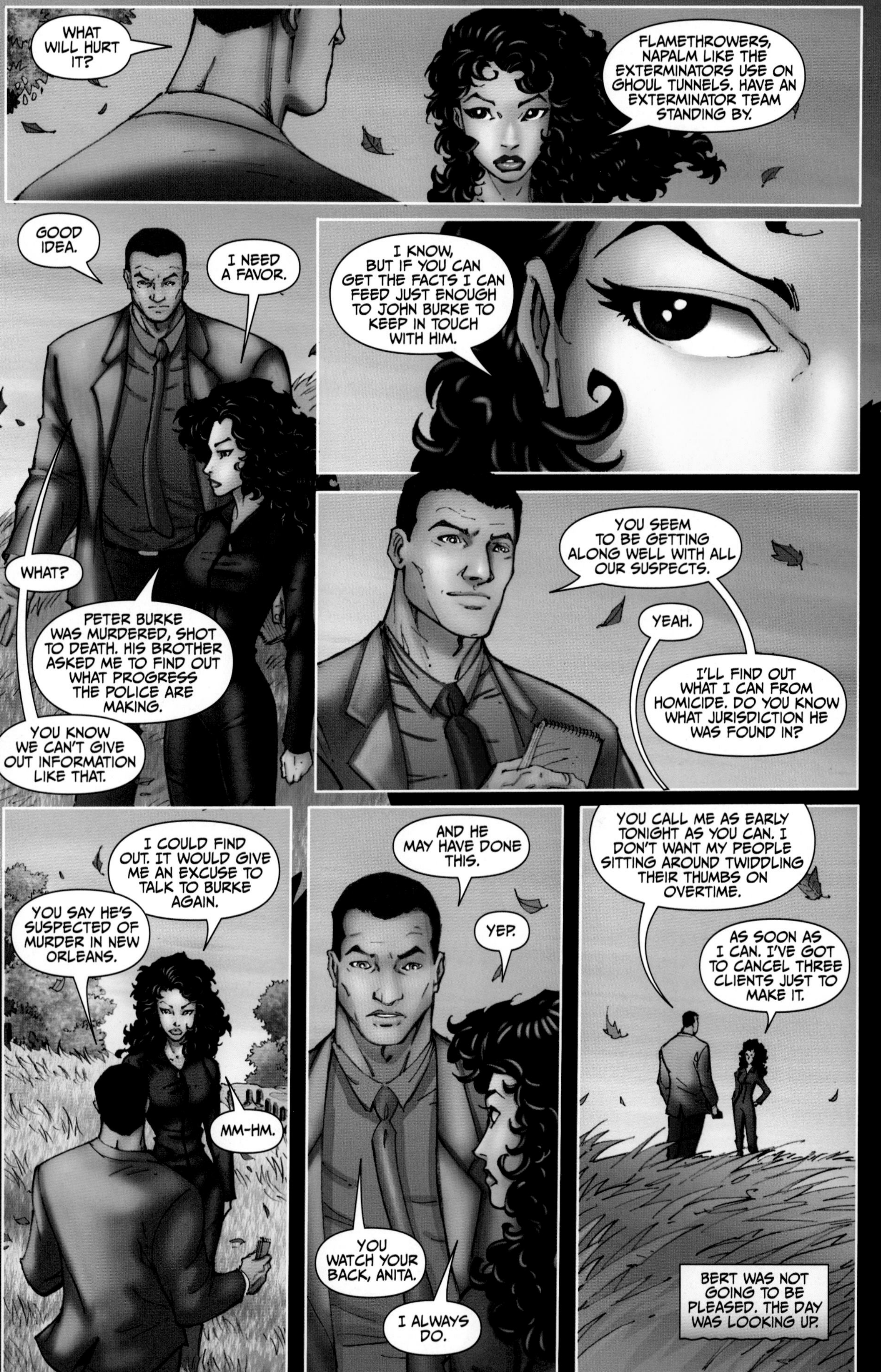

WHAT WILL HURT IT?
FLAMETHROWERS, NAPALM LIKE THE EXTERMINATORS USE ON GHOUL TUNNELS. HAVE AN EXTERMINATOR TEAM STANDING BY.
GOOD IDEA.
I NEED A FAVOR.
WHAT?
PETER BURKE WAS MURDERED, SHOT TO DEATH. HIS BROTHER ASKED ME TO FIND OUT WHAT PROGRESS THE POLICE ARE MAKING.
YOU KNOW WE CAN'T GIVE OUT INFORMATION LIKE THAT.
I KNOW, BUT IF YOU CAN GET THE FACTS I CAN FEED JUST ENOUGH TO JOHN BURKE TO KEEP IN TOUCH WITH HIM.
YOU SEEM TO BE GETTING ALONG WELL WITH ALL OUR SUSPECTS.
YEAH.
I'LL FIND OUT WHAT I CAN FROM HOMICIDE. DO YOU KNOW WHAT JURISDICTION HE WAS FOUND IN?
I COULD FIND OUT. IT WOULD GIVE ME AN EXCUSE TO TALK TO BURKE AGAIN.
YOU SAY HE'S SUSPECTED OF MURDER IN NEW ORLEANS.
MM-HM.
AND HE MAY HAVE DONE THIS.
YEP.
YOU WATCH YOUR BACK, ANITA.
I ALWAYS DO.
YOU CALL ME AS EARLY TONIGHT AS YOU CAN. I DON'T WANT MY PEOPLE SITTING AROUND TWIDDLING THEIR THUMBS ON OVERTIME.
AS SOON AS I CAN. I'VE GOT TO CANCEL THREE CLIENTS JUST TO MAKE IT.
BERT WAS NOT GOING TO BE PLEASED. THE DAY WAS LOOKING UP.

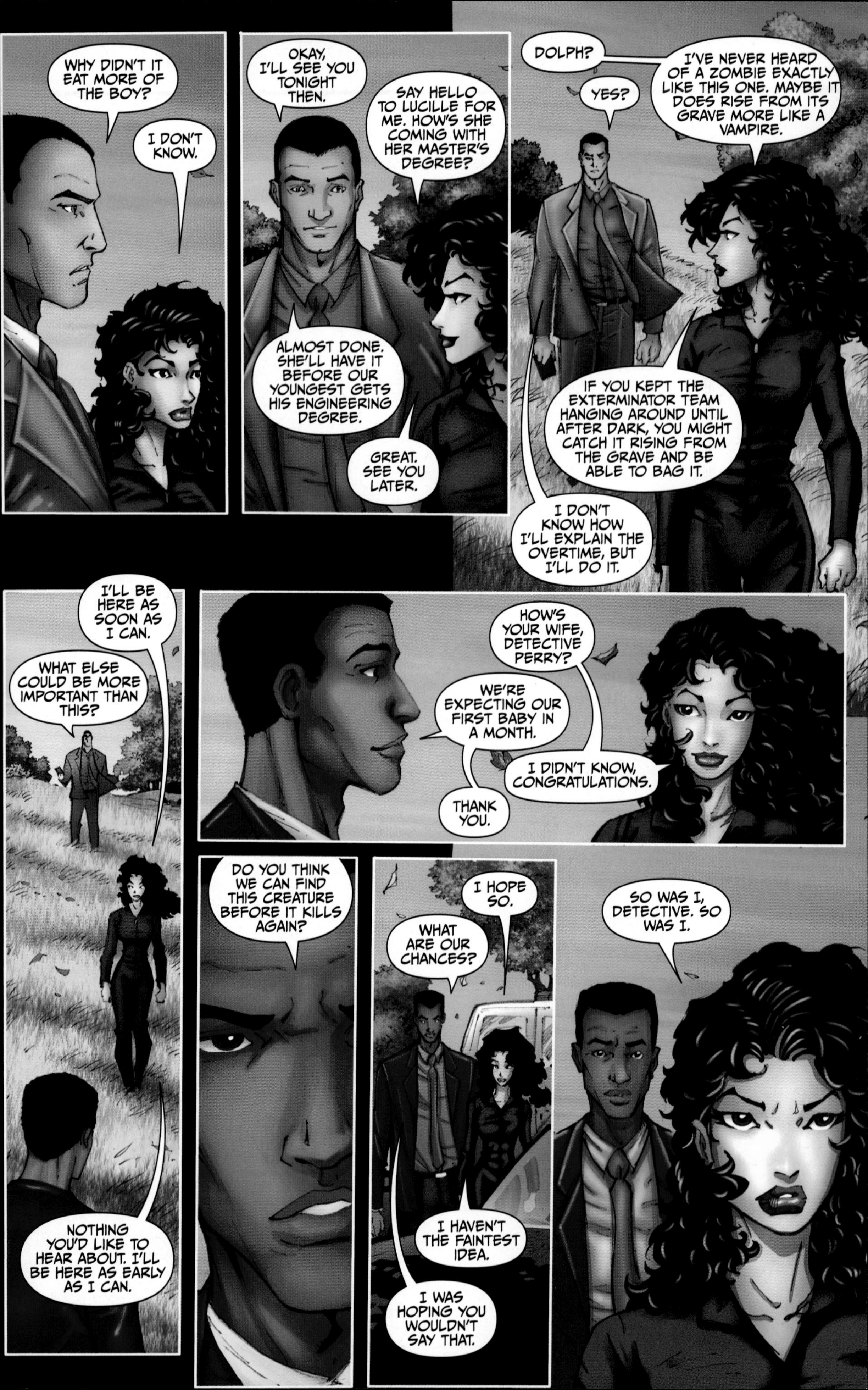

WHY DIDN'T IT EAT MORE OF THE BOY?
I DON'T KNOW.
OKAY, I'LL SEE YOU TONIGHT THEN.
SAY HELLO TO LUCILLE FOR ME. HOW'S SHE COMING WITH HER MASTER'S DEGREE?
ALMOST DONE. SHE'LL HAVE IT BEFORE OUR YOUNGEST GETS HIS ENGINEERING DEGREE.
GREAT. SEE YOU LATER.
DOLPH?
YES?
I'VE NEVER HEARD OF A ZOMBIE EXACTLY LIKE THIS ONE. MAYBE IT DOES RISE FROM ITS GRAVE MORE LIKE A VAMPIRE.
IF YOU KEPT THE EXTERMINATOR TEAM HANGING AROUND UNTIL AFTER DARK, YOU MIGHT CATCH IT RISING FROM THE GRAVE AND BE ABLE TO BAG IT.
I DON'T KNOW HOW I'LL EXPLAIN THE OVERTIME, BUT I'LL DO IT.
I'LL BE HERE AS SOON AS I CAN.
WHAT ELSE COULD BE MORE IMPORTANT THAN THIS?
NOTHING YOU'D LIKE TO HEAR ABOUT. I'LL BE HERE AS EARLY AS I CAN.
HOW'S YOUR WIFE, DETECTIVE PERRY?
WE'RE EXPECTING OUR FIRST BABY IN A MONTH.
I DIDN'T KNOW, CONGRATULATIONS.
THANK YOU.
DO YOU THINK WE CAN FIND THIS CREATURE BEFORE IT KILLS AGAIN?
I HOPE SO.
WHAT ARE OUR CHANCES?
I HAVEN'T THE FAINTEST IDEA.
I WAS HOPING YOU WOULDN'T SAY THAT.
SO WAS I, DETECTIVE. SO WAS I.

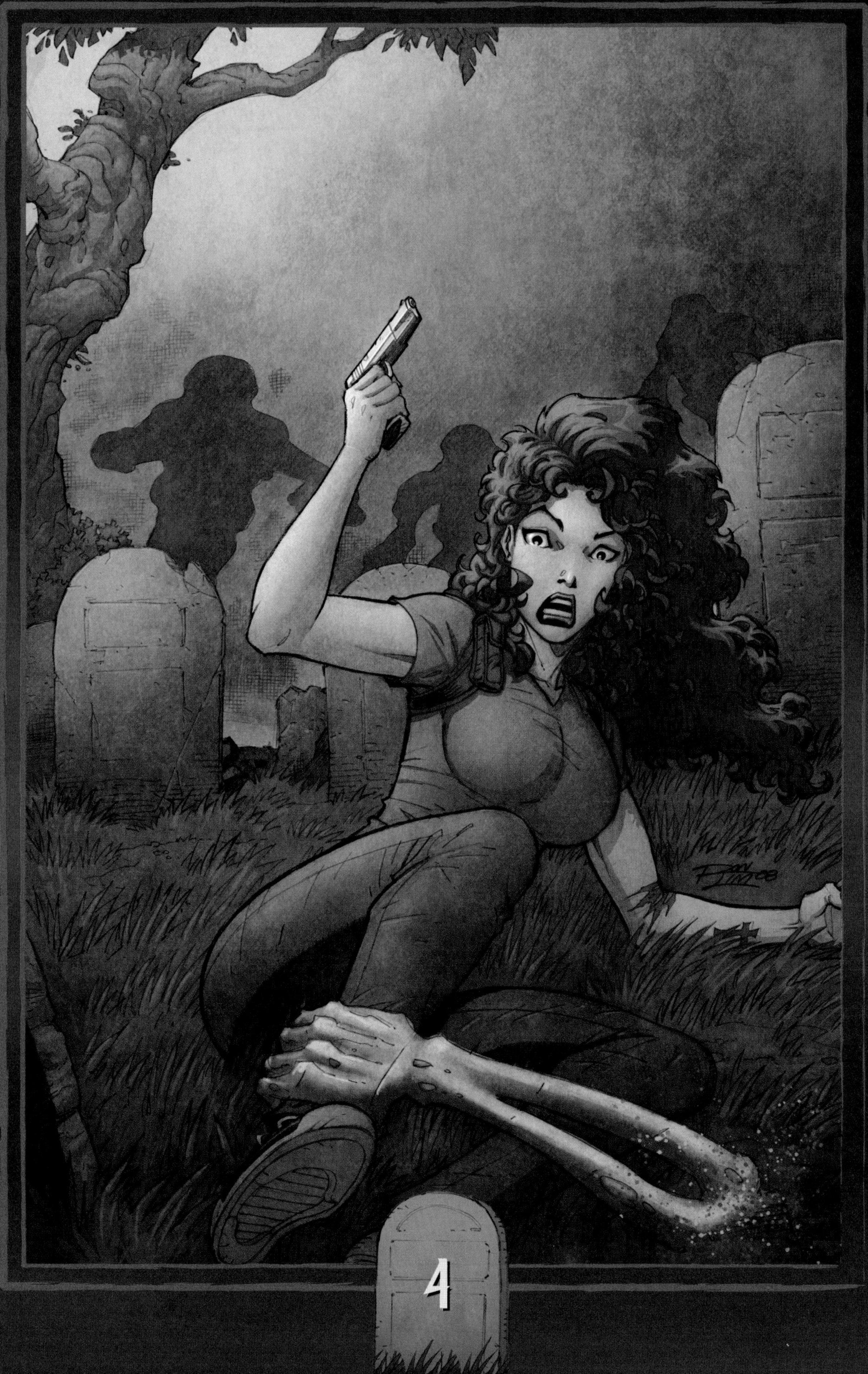
4

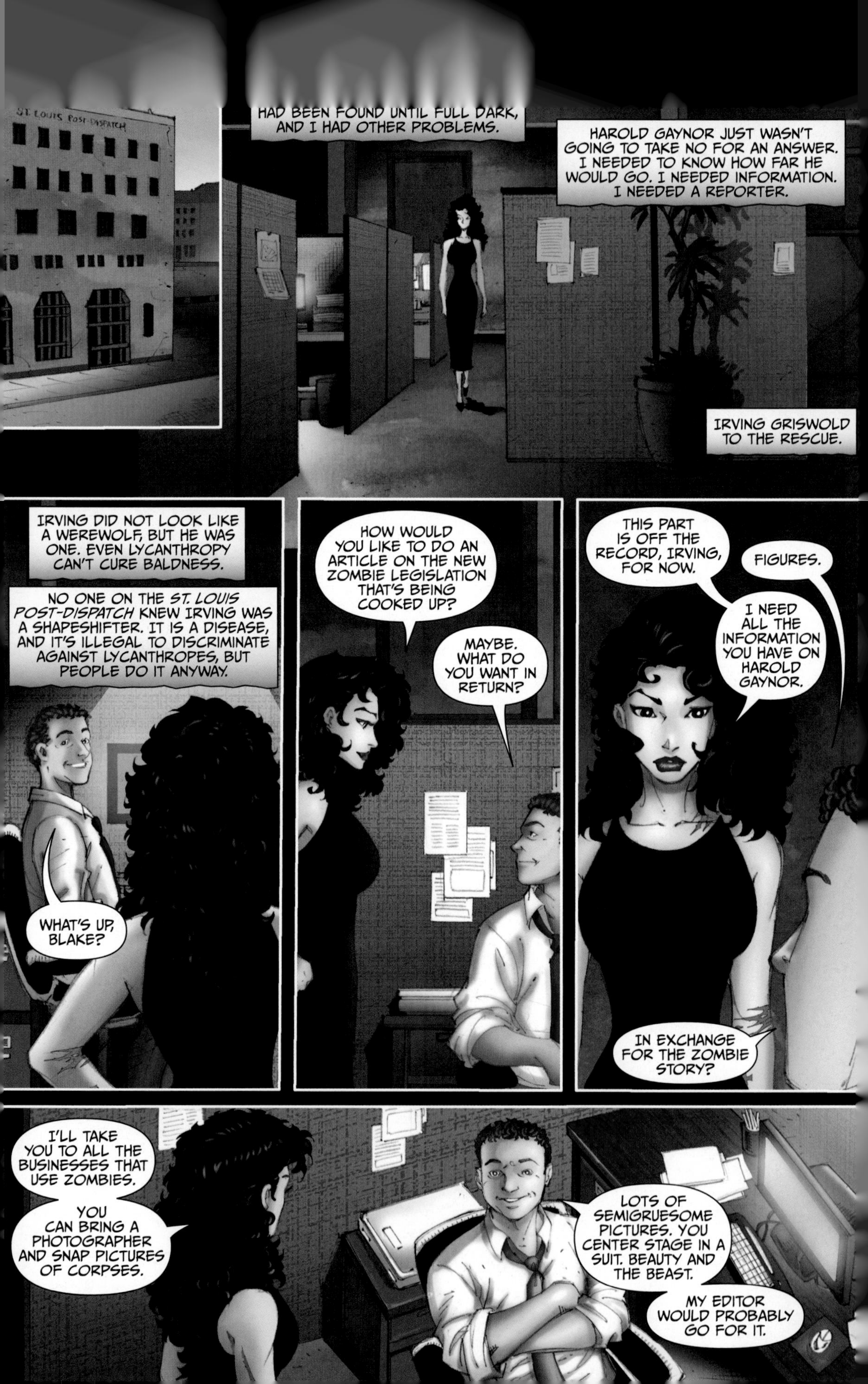

ST. LOUIS POST-DISPATCH
HAD BEEN FOUND UNTIL FULL DARK, AND I HAD OTHER PROBLEMS.
HAROLD GAYNOR JUST WASN'T GOING TO TAKE NO FOR AN ANSWER. I NEEDED TO KNOW HOW FAR HE WOULD GO. I NEEDED INFORMATION. I NEEDED A REPORTER.
IRVING GRISWOLD TO THE RESCUE.
IRVING DID NOT LOOK LIKE A WEREWOLF, BUT HE WAS ONE. EVEN LYCANTHROPY CAN'T CURE BALDNESS.
NO ONE ON THE *ST. LOUIS POST-DISPATCH* KNEW IRVING WAS A SHAPESHIFTER. IT IS A DISEASE, AND IT'S ILLEGAL TO DISCRIMINATE AGAINST LYCANTHROPES, BUT PEOPLE DO IT ANYWAY.
WHAT'S UP, BLAKE?
HOW WOULD YOU LIKE TO DO AN ARTICLE ON THE NEW ZOMBIE LEGISLATION THAT'S BEING COOKED UP?
MAYBE. WHAT DO YOU WANT IN RETURN?
THIS PART IS OFF THE RECORD, IRVING, FOR NOW.
FIGURES.
I NEED ALL THE INFORMATION YOU HAVE ON HAROLD GAYNOR.
IN EXCHANGE FOR THE ZOMBIE STORY?
I'LL TAKE YOU TO ALL THE BUSINESSES THAT USE ZOMBIES.
YOU CAN BRING A PHOTOGRAPHER AND SNAP PICTURES OF CORPSES.
LOTS OF SEMIGRUESOME PICTURES. YOU CENTER STAGE IN A SUIT. BEAUTY AND THE BEAST.
MY EDITOR WOULD PROBABLY GO FOR IT.

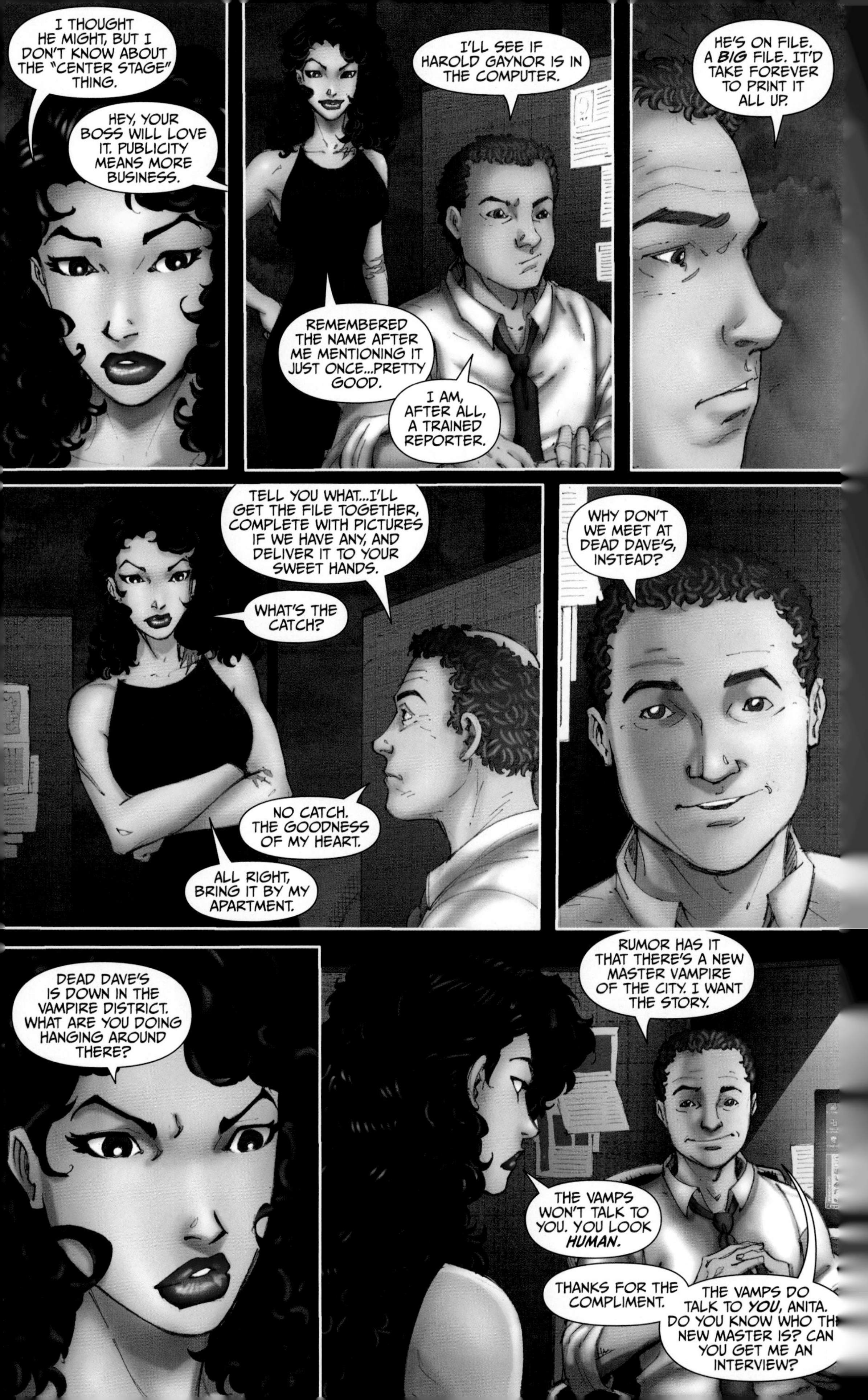
I THOUGHT HE MIGHT, BUT I DON'T KNOW ABOUT THE "CENTER STAGE" THING.
HEY, YOUR BOSS WILL LOVE IT. PUBLICITY MEANS MORE BUSINESS.
I'LL SEE IF HAROLD GAYNOR IS IN THE COMPUTER.
REMEMBERED THE NAME AFTER ME MENTIONING IT JUST ONCE...PRETTY GOOD.
I AM, AFTER ALL, A TRAINED REPORTER.
HE'S ON FILE. A BIG FILE. IT'D TAKE FOREVER TO PRINT IT ALL UP.
TELL YOU WHAT...I'LL GET THE FILE TOGETHER, COMPLETE WITH PICTURES IF WE HAVE ANY, AND DELIVER IT TO YOUR SWEET HANDS.
WHAT'S THE CATCH?
NO CATCH. THE GOODNESS OF MY HEART.
ALL RIGHT, BRING IT BY MY APARTMENT.
WHY DON'T WE MEET AT DEAD DAVE'S, INSTEAD?
DEAD DAVE'S IS DOWN IN THE VAMPIRE DISTRICT. WHAT ARE YOU DOING HANGING AROUND THERE?
RUMOR HAS IT THAT THERE'S A NEW MASTER VAMPIRE OF THE CITY. I WANT THE STORY.
THE VAMPS WON'T TALK TO YOU. YOU LOOK HUMAN.
THANKS FOR THE COMPLIMENT.
THE VAMPS DO TALK TO YOU, ANITA. DO YOU KNOW WHO THE NEW MASTER IS? CAN YOU GET ME AN INTERVIEW?

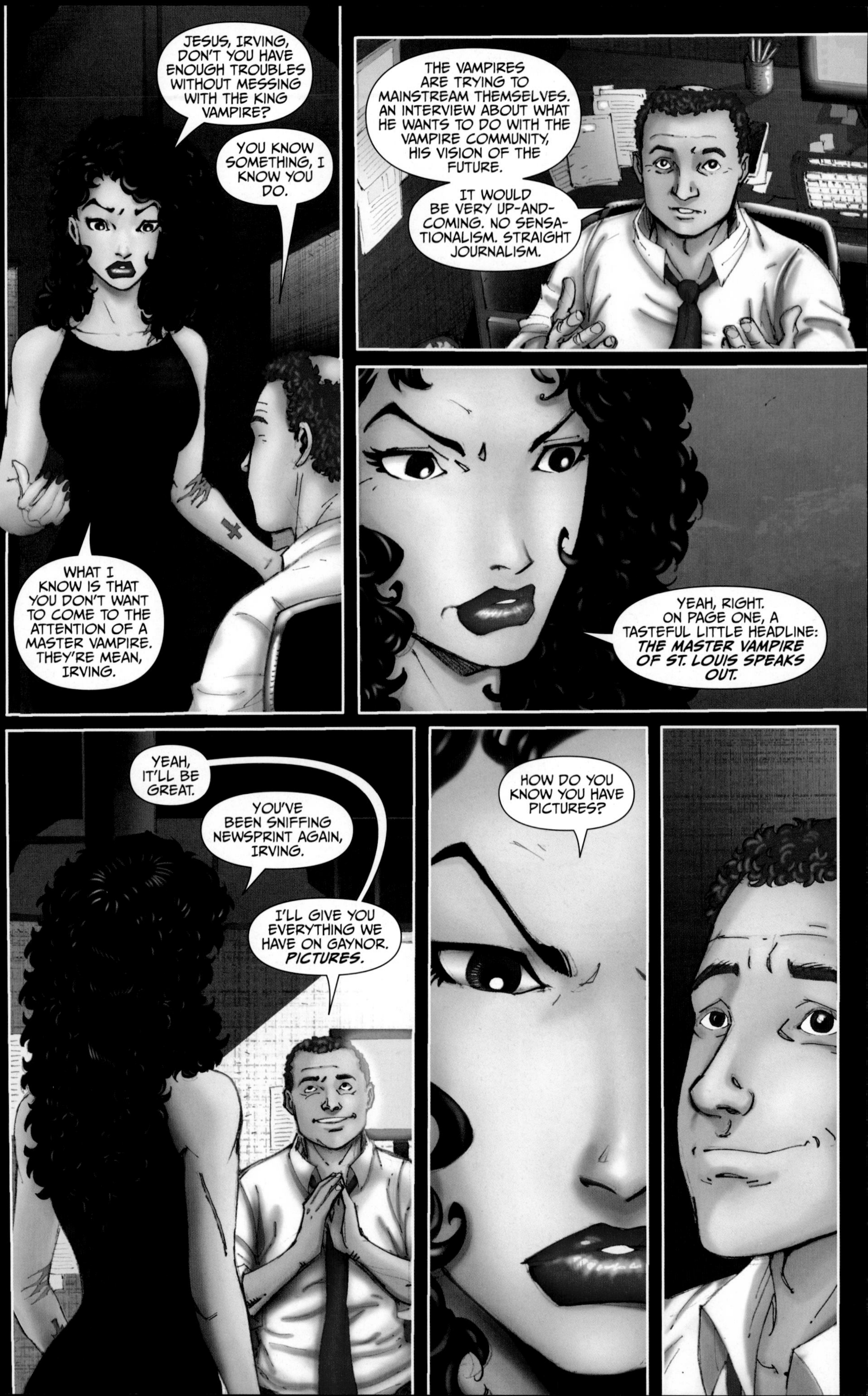
JESUS, IRVING, DON'T YOU HAVE ENOUGH TROUBLES WITHOUT MESSING WITH THE KING VAMPIRE?
YOU KNOW SOMETHING, I KNOW YOU DO.
WHAT I KNOW IS THAT YOU DON'T WANT TO COME TO THE ATTENTION OF A MASTER VAMPIRE. THEY'RE MEAN, IRVING.
THE VAMPIRES ARE TRYING TO MAINSTREAM THEMSELVES. AN INTERVIEW ABOUT WHAT HE WANTS TO DO WITH THE VAMPIRE COMMUNITY, HIS VISION OF THE FUTURE.
IT WOULD BE VERY UP-AND-COMING. NO SENSATIONALISM. STRAIGHT JOURNALISM.
YEAH, RIGHT. ON PAGE ONE, A TASTEFUL LITTLE HEADLINE: *THE MASTER VAMPIRE OF ST. LOUIS SPEAKS OUT.*
YEAH, IT'LL BE GREAT.
YOU'VE BEEN SNIFFING NEWSPRINT AGAIN, IRVING.
I'LL GIVE YOU EVERYTHING WE HAVE ON GAYNOR. *PICTURES.*
HOW DO YOU KNOW YOU HAVE PICTURES?

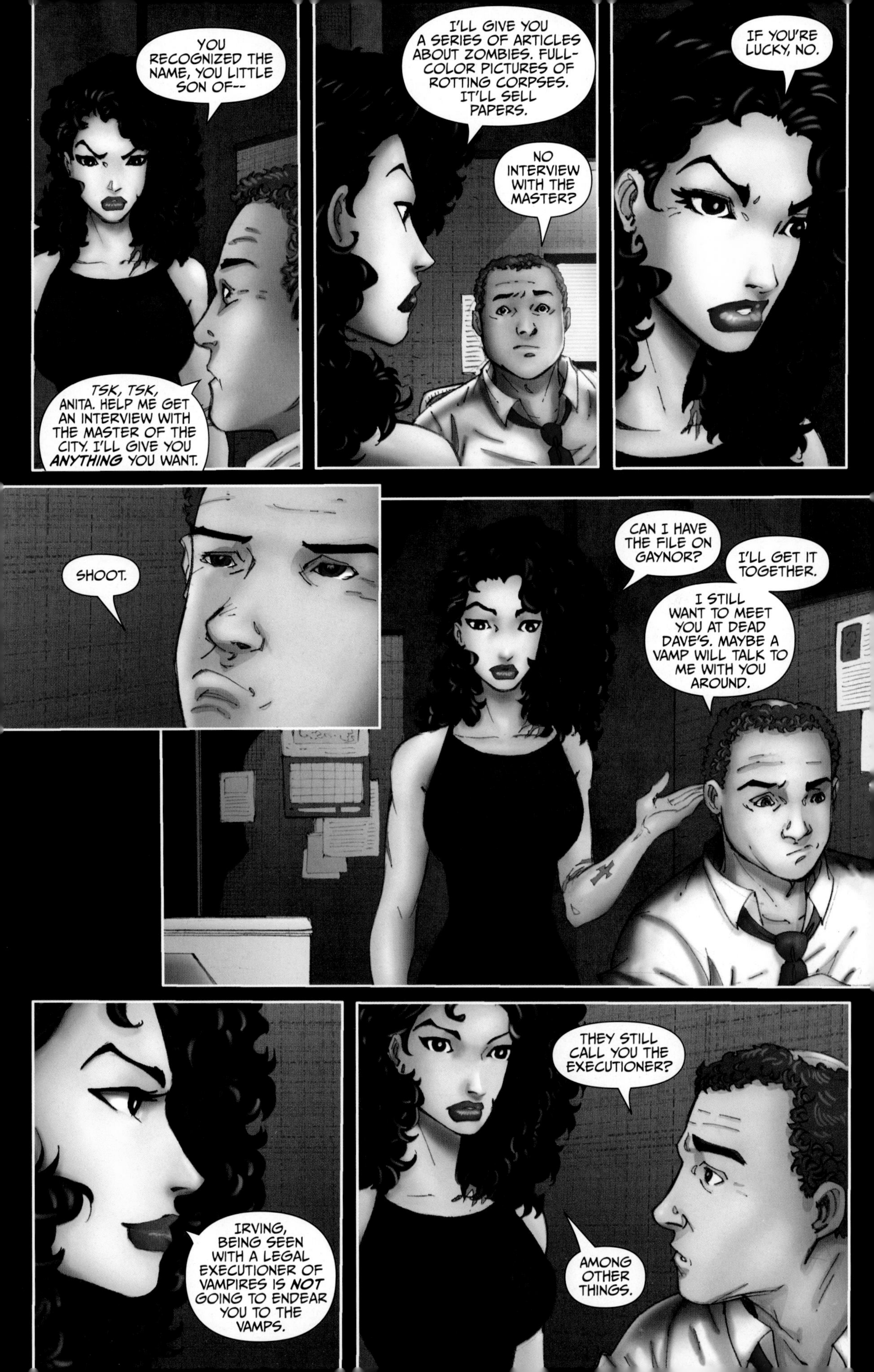

YOU RECOGNIZED THE NAME, YOU LITTLE SON OF--
TSK, TSK, ANITA. HELP ME GET AN INTERVIEW WITH THE MASTER OF THE CITY. I'LL GIVE YOU ***ANYTHING*** YOU WANT.
I'LL GIVE YOU A SERIES OF ARTICLES ABOUT ZOMBIES. FULL-COLOR PICTURES OF ROTTING CORPSES. IT'LL SELL PAPERS.
NO INTERVIEW WITH THE MASTER?
IF YOU'RE LUCKY, NO.
SHOOT.
CAN I HAVE THE FILE ON GAYNOR?
I'LL GET IT TOGETHER.
I STILL WANT TO MEET YOU AT DEAD DAVE'S. MAYBE A VAMP WILL TALK TO ME WITH YOU AROUND.
IRVING, BEING SEEN WITH A LEGAL EXECUTIONER OF VAMPIRES IS ***NOT*** GOING TO ENDEAR YOU TO THE VAMPS.
THEY STILL CALL YOU THE EXECUTIONER?
AMONG OTHER THINGS.

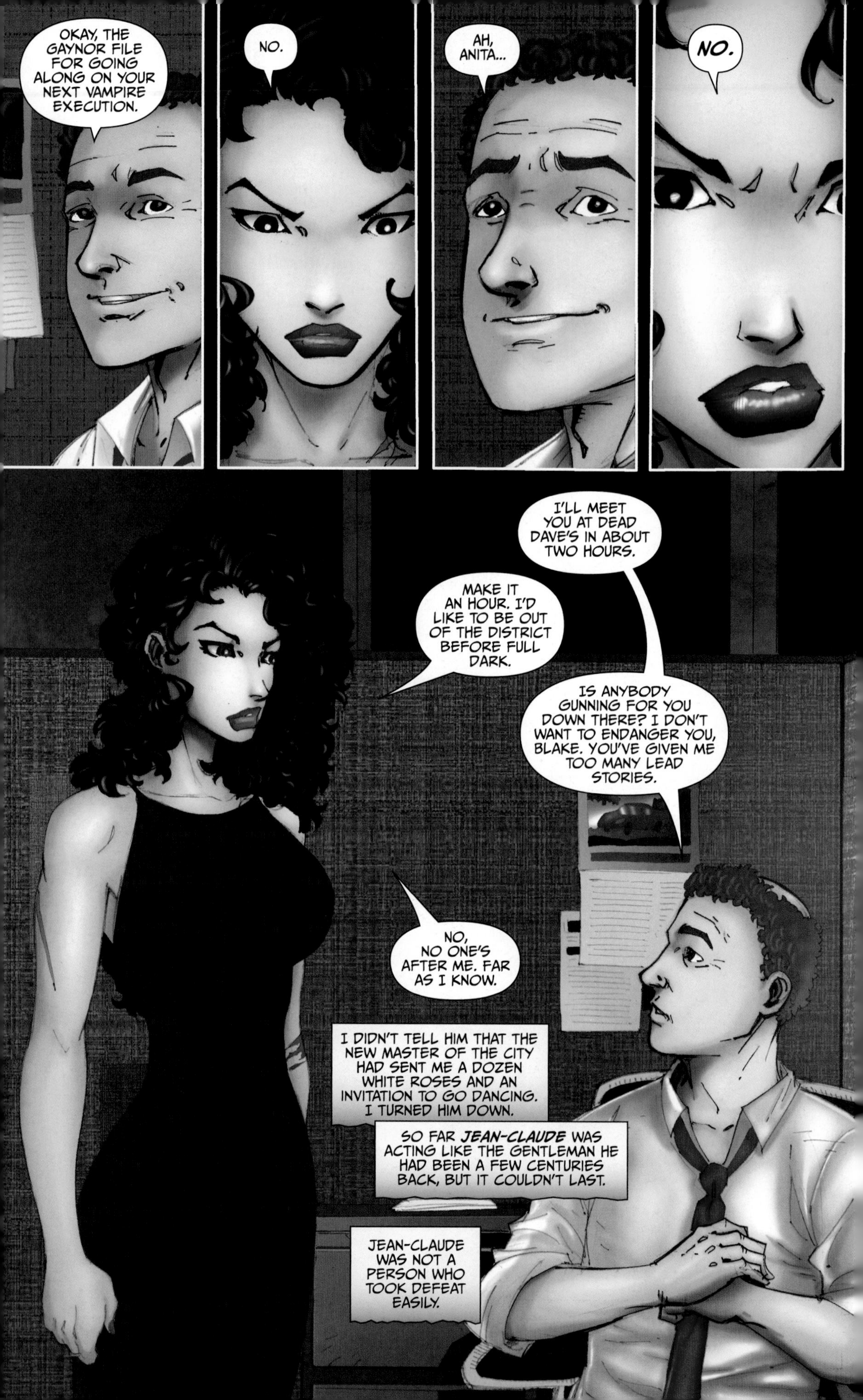

OKAY, THE GAYNOR FILE FOR GOING ALONG ON YOUR NEXT VAMPIRE EXECUTION.
NO.
AH, ANITA...
NO.
I'LL MEET YOU AT DEAD DAVE'S IN ABOUT TWO HOURS.
MAKE IT AN HOUR. I'D LIKE TO BE OUT OF THE DISTRICT BEFORE FULL DARK.
IS ANYBODY GUNNING FOR YOU DOWN THERE? I DON'T WANT TO ENDANGER YOU, BLAKE. YOU'VE GIVEN ME TOO MANY LEAD STORIES.
NO, NO ONE'S AFTER ME. FAR AS I KNOW.
I DIDN'T TELL HIM THAT THE NEW MASTER OF THE CITY HAD SENT ME A DOZEN WHITE ROSES AND AN INVITATION TO GO DANCING. I TURNED HIM DOWN.
SO FAR JEAN-CLAUDE WAS ACTING LIKE THE GENTLEMAN HE HAD BEEN A FEW CENTURIES BACK, BUT IT COULDN'T LAST.
JEAN-CLAUDE WAS NOT A PERSON WHO TOOK DEFEAT EASILY.

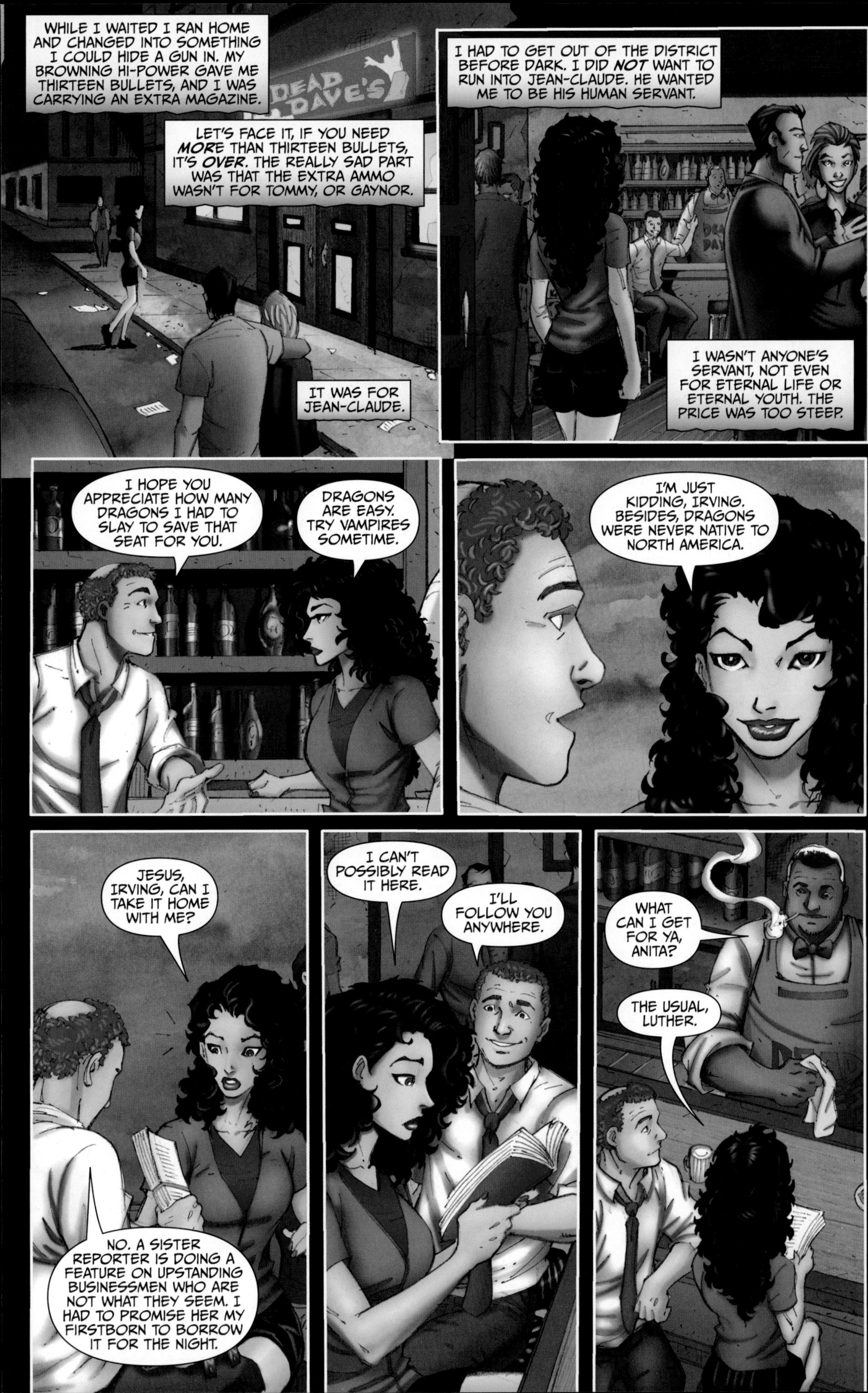
WHILE I WAITED I RAN HOME AND CHANGED INTO SOMETHING I COULD HIDE A GUN IN. MY BROWNING HI-POWER GAVE ME THIRTEEN BULLETS, AND I WAS CARRYING AN EXTRA MAGAZINE.
DEAD DAVE'S
LET'S FACE IT, IF YOU NEED MORE THAN THIRTEEN BULLETS, IT'S OVER. THE REALLY SAD PART WAS THAT THE EXTRA AMMO WASN'T FOR TOMMY, OR GAYNOR.
IT WAS FOR JEAN-CLAUDE.
I HAD TO GET OUT OF THE DISTRICT BEFORE DARK. I DID NOT WANT TO RUN INTO JEAN-CLAUDE. HE WANTED ME TO BE HIS HUMAN SERVANT.
I WASN'T ANYONE'S SERVANT, NOT EVEN FOR ETERNAL LIFE OR ETERNAL YOUTH. THE PRICE WAS TOO STEEP.
I HOPE YOU APPRECIATE HOW MANY DRAGONS I HAD TO SLAY TO SAVE THAT SEAT FOR YOU.
DRAGONS ARE EASY. TRY VAMPIRES SOMETIME.
I'M JUST KIDDING, IRVING. BESIDES, DRAGONS WERE NEVER NATIVE TO NORTH AMERICA.
JESUS, IRVING, CAN I TAKE IT HOME WITH ME?
NO. A SISTER REPORTER IS DOING A FEATURE ON UPSTANDING BUSINESSMEN WHO ARE NOT WHAT THEY SEEM. I HAD TO PROMISE HER MY FIRSTBORN TO BORROW IT FOR THE NIGHT.
I CAN'T POSSIBLY READ IT HERE.
I'LL FOLLOW YOU ANYWHERE.
WHAT CAN I GET FOR YA, ANITA?
THE USUAL, LUTHER.

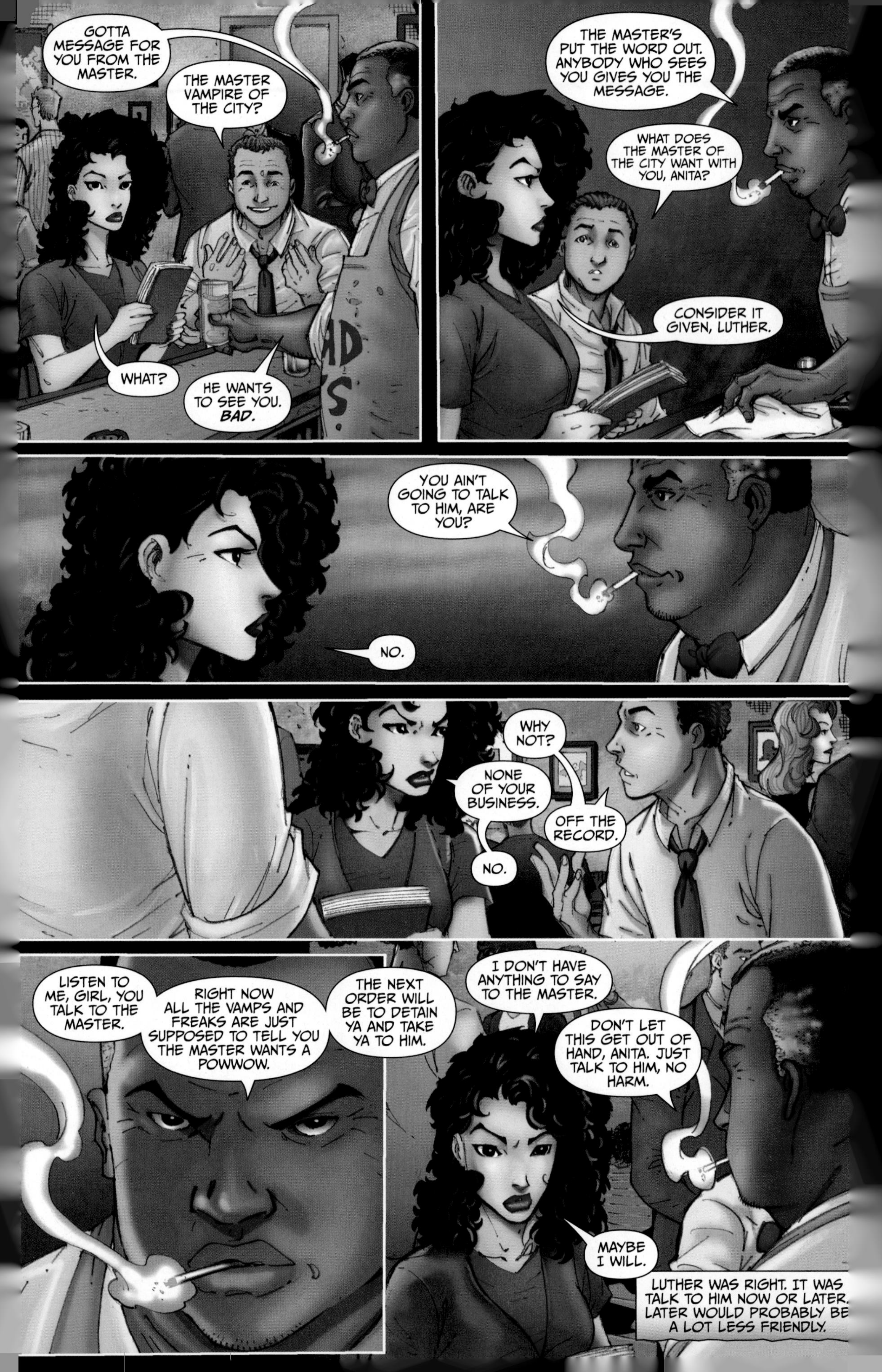
GOTTA MESSAGE FOR YOU FROM THE MASTER.
THE MASTER VAMPIRE OF THE CITY?
WHAT?
HE WANTS TO SEE YOU. *BAD.*
THE MASTER'S PUT THE WORD OUT. ANYBODY WHO SEES YOU GIVES YOU THE MESSAGE.
WHAT DOES THE MASTER OF THE CITY WANT WITH YOU, ANITA?
CONSIDER IT GIVEN, LUTHER.
YOU AIN'T GOING TO TALK TO HIM, ARE YOU?
NO.
WHY NOT?
NONE OF YOUR BUSINESS.
OFF THE RECORD.
NO.
LISTEN TO ME, GIRL, YOU TALK TO THE MASTER.
RIGHT NOW ALL THE VAMPS AND FREAKS ARE JUST SUPPOSED TO TELL YOU THE MASTER WANTS A POWWOW.
THE NEXT ORDER WILL BE TO DETAIN YA AND TAKE YA TO HIM.
I DON'T HAVE ANYTHING TO SAY TO THE MASTER.
DON'T LET THIS GET OUT OF HAND, ANITA. JUST TALK TO HIM, NO HARM.
MAYBE I WILL.
LUTHER WAS RIGHT. IT WAS TALK TO HIM NOW OR LATER. LATER WOULD PROBABLY BE A LOT LESS FRIENDLY.

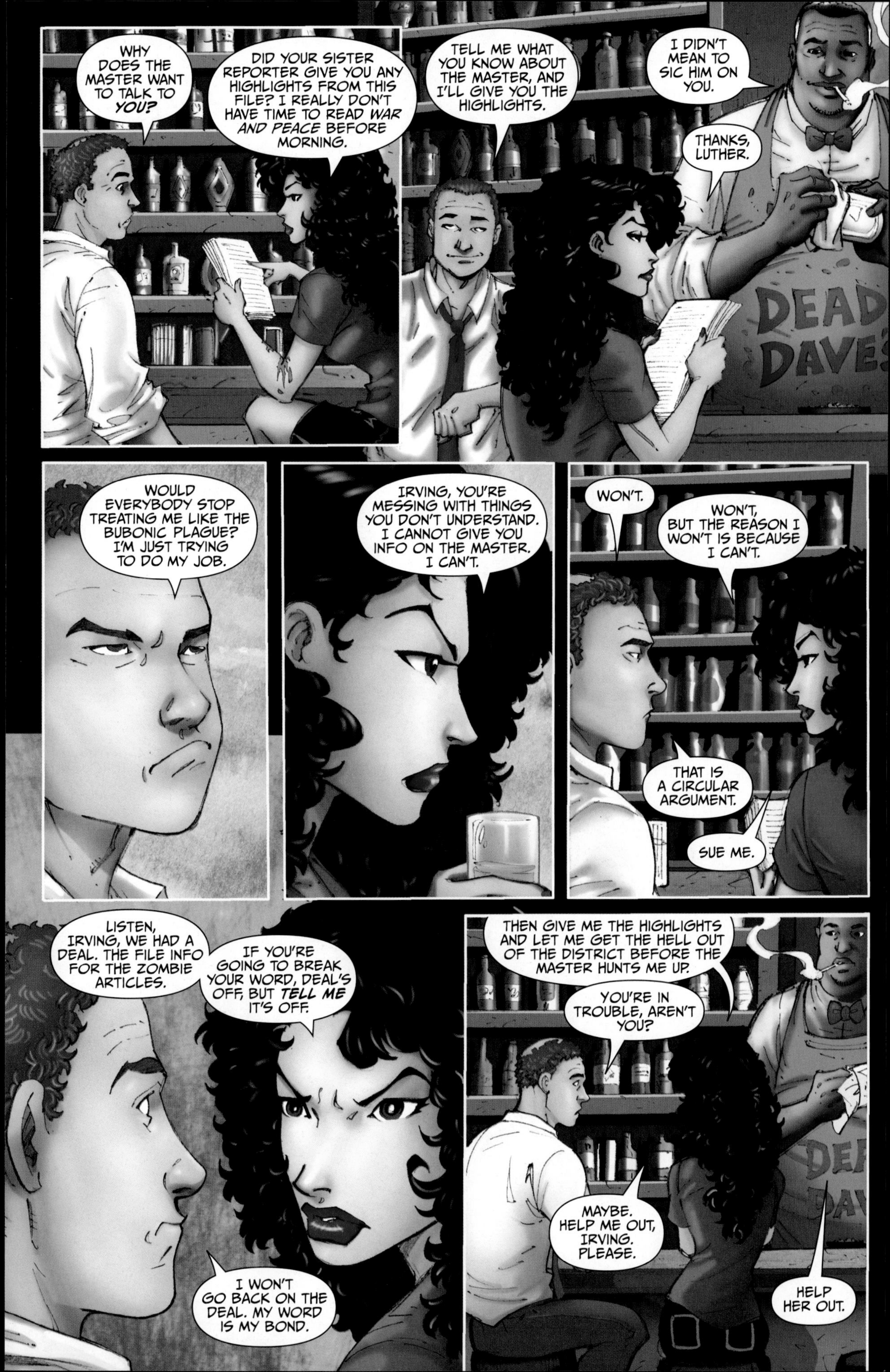
WHY DOES THE MASTER WANT TO TALK TO *YOU?*
DID YOUR SISTER REPORTER GIVE YOU ANY HIGHLIGHTS FROM THIS FILE? I REALLY DON'T HAVE TIME TO READ *WAR AND PEACE* BEFORE MORNING.
TELL ME WHAT YOU KNOW ABOUT THE MASTER, AND I'LL GIVE YOU THE HIGHLIGHTS.
I DIDN'T MEAN TO SIC HIM ON YOU.
THANKS, LUTHER.
DEAD DAVE'S
WOULD EVERYBODY STOP TREATING ME LIKE THE BUBONIC PLAGUE? I'M JUST TRYING TO DO MY JOB.
IRVING, YOU'RE MESSING WITH THINGS YOU DON'T UNDERSTAND. I CANNOT GIVE YOU INFO ON THE MASTER. I CAN'T.
WON'T.
WON'T, BUT THE REASON I WON'T IS BECAUSE I CAN'T.
THAT IS A CIRCULAR ARGUMENT.
SUE ME.
LISTEN, IRVING, WE HAD A DEAL. THE FILE INFO FOR THE ZOMBIE ARTICLES.
IF YOU'RE GOING TO BREAK YOUR WORD, DEAL'S OFF, BUT *TELL ME* IT'S OFF.
I WON'T GO BACK ON THE DEAL. MY WORD IS MY BOND.
THEN GIVE ME THE HIGHLIGHTS AND LET ME GET THE HELL OUT OF THE DISTRICT BEFORE THE MASTER HUNTS ME UP.
YOU'RE IN TROUBLE, AREN'T YOU?
MAYBE. HELP ME OUT, IRVING. PLEASE.
HELP HER OUT.

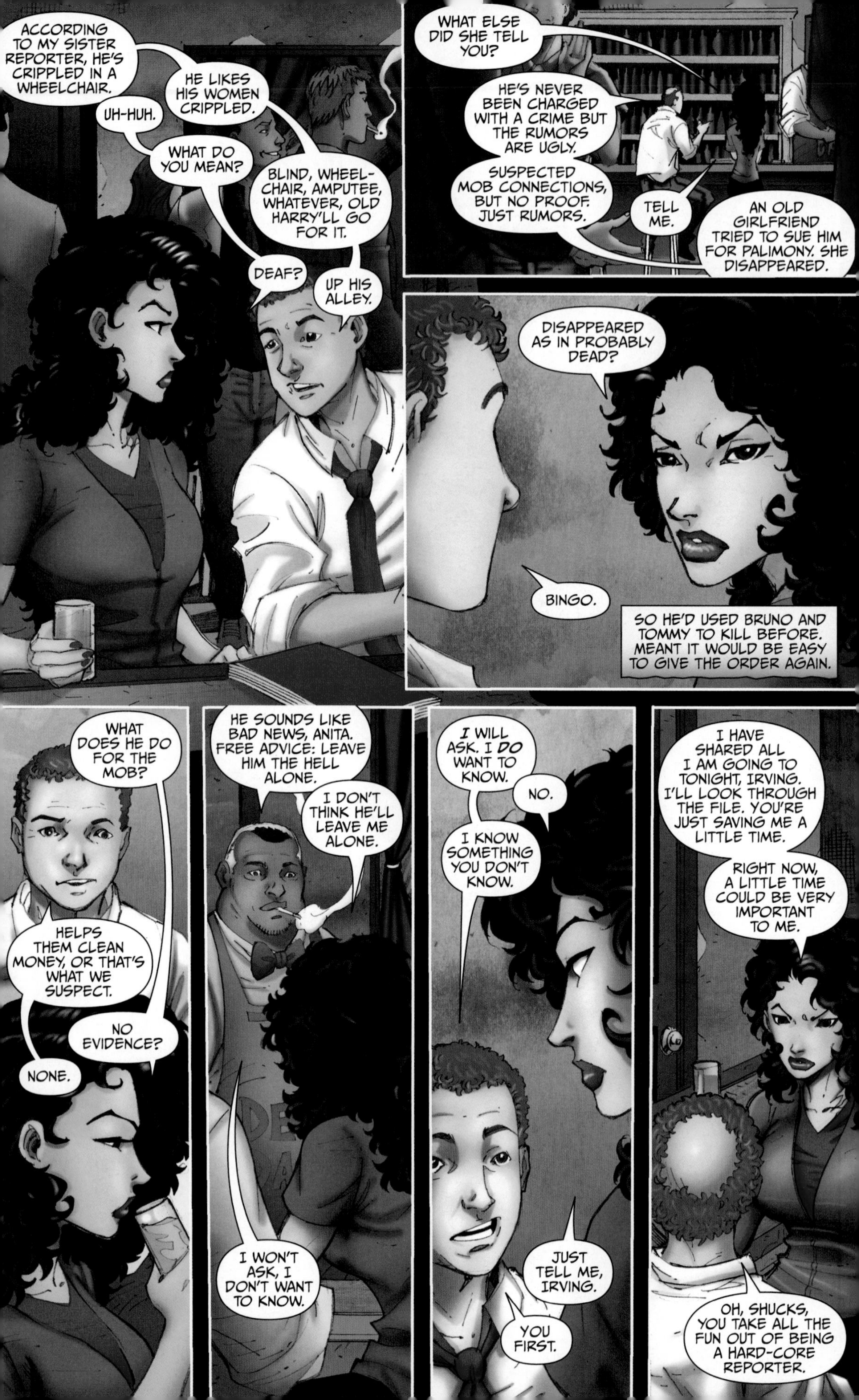
ACCORDING TO MY SISTER REPORTER, HE'S CRIPPLED IN A WHEELCHAIR.
HE LIKES HIS WOMEN CRIPPLED.
UH-HUH.
WHAT DO YOU MEAN?
BLIND, WHEEL-CHAIR, AMPUTEE, WHATEVER, OLD HARRY'LL GO FOR IT.
DEAF?
UP HIS ALLEY.
WHAT ELSE DID SHE TELL YOU?
HE'S NEVER BEEN CHARGED WITH A CRIME BUT THE RUMORS ARE UGLY.
SUSPECTED MOB CONNECTIONS, BUT NO PROOF. JUST RUMORS.
TELL ME.
AN OLD GIRLFRIEND TRIED TO SUE HIM FOR PALIMONY. SHE DISAPPEARED.
DISAPPEARED AS IN PROBABLY DEAD?
BINGO.
SO HE'D USED BRUNO AND TOMMY TO KILL BEFORE. MEANT IT WOULD BE EASY TO GIVE THE ORDER AGAIN.
WHAT DOES HE DO FOR THE MOB?
HELPS THEM CLEAN MONEY, OR THAT'S WHAT WE SUSPECT.
NO EVIDENCE?
NONE.
HE SOUNDS LIKE BAD NEWS, ANITA. FREE ADVICE: LEAVE HIM THE HELL ALONE.
I DON'T THINK HE'LL LEAVE ME ALONE.
I WON'T ASK, I DON'T WANT TO KNOW.
I WILL ASK. I *DO* WANT TO KNOW.
NO.
I KNOW SOMETHING YOU DON'T KNOW.
JUST TELL ME, IRVING.
YOU FIRST.
I HAVE SHARED ALL I AM GOING TO TONIGHT, IRVING. I'LL LOOK THROUGH THE FILE. YOU'RE JUST SAVING ME A LITTLE TIME.
RIGHT NOW, A LITTLE TIME COULD BE VERY IMPORTANT TO ME.
OH, SHUCKS, YOU TAKE ALL THE FUN OUT OF BEING A HARD-CORE REPORTER.

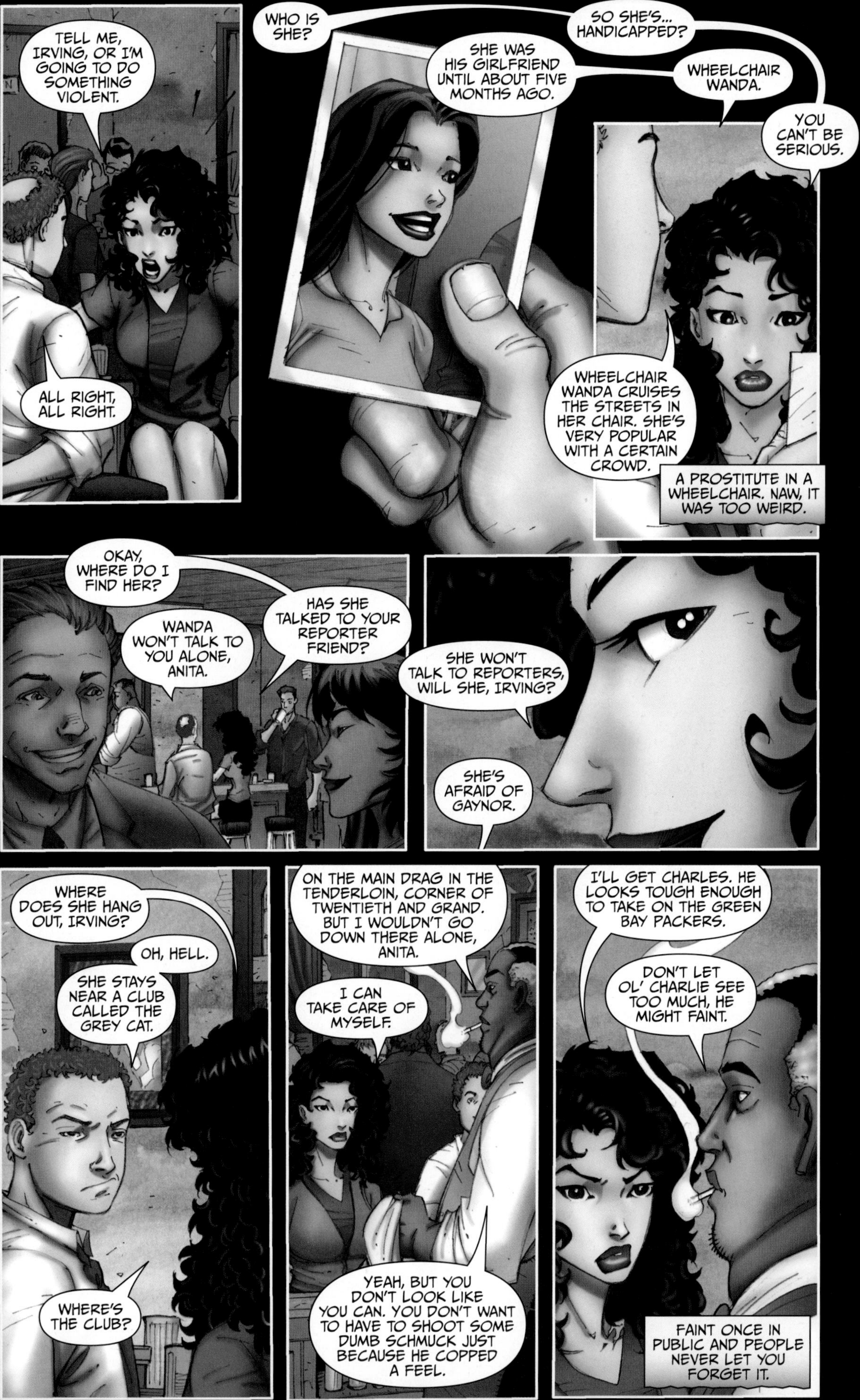
TELL ME, IRVING, OR I'M GOING TO DO SOMETHING VIOLENT.
ALL RIGHT, ALL RIGHT.
WHO IS SHE?
SHE WAS HIS GIRLFRIEND UNTIL ABOUT FIVE MONTHS AGO.
SO SHE'S... HANDICAPPED?
WHEELCHAIR WANDA.
YOU CAN'T BE SERIOUS.
WHEELCHAIR WANDA CRUISES THE STREETS IN HER CHAIR. SHE'S VERY POPULAR WITH A CERTAIN CROWD.
A PROSTITUTE IN A WHEELCHAIR. NAW, IT WAS TOO WEIRD.
OKAY, WHERE DO I FIND HER?
WANDA WON'T TALK TO YOU ALONE, ANITA.
HAS SHE TALKED TO YOUR REPORTER FRIEND?
SHE WON'T TALK TO REPORTERS, WILL SHE, IRVING?
SHE'S AFRAID OF GAYNOR.
WHERE DOES SHE HANG OUT, IRVING?
OH, HELL.
SHE STAYS NEAR A CLUB CALLED THE GREY CAT.
WHERE'S THE CLUB?
ON THE MAIN DRAG IN THE TENDERLOIN, CORNER OF TWENTIETH AND GRAND. BUT I WOULDN'T GO DOWN THERE ALONE, ANITA.
I CAN TAKE CARE OF MYSELF.
YEAH, BUT YOU DON'T LOOK LIKE YOU CAN. YOU DON'T WANT TO HAVE TO SHOOT SOME DUMB SCHMUCK JUST BECAUSE HE COPPED A FEEL.
I'LL GET CHARLES. HE LOOKS TOUGH ENOUGH TO TAKE ON THE GREEN BAY PACKERS.
DON'T LET OL' CHARLIE SEE TOO MUCH, HE MIGHT FAINT.
FAINT ONCE IN PUBLIC AND PEOPLE NEVER LET YOU FORGET IT.

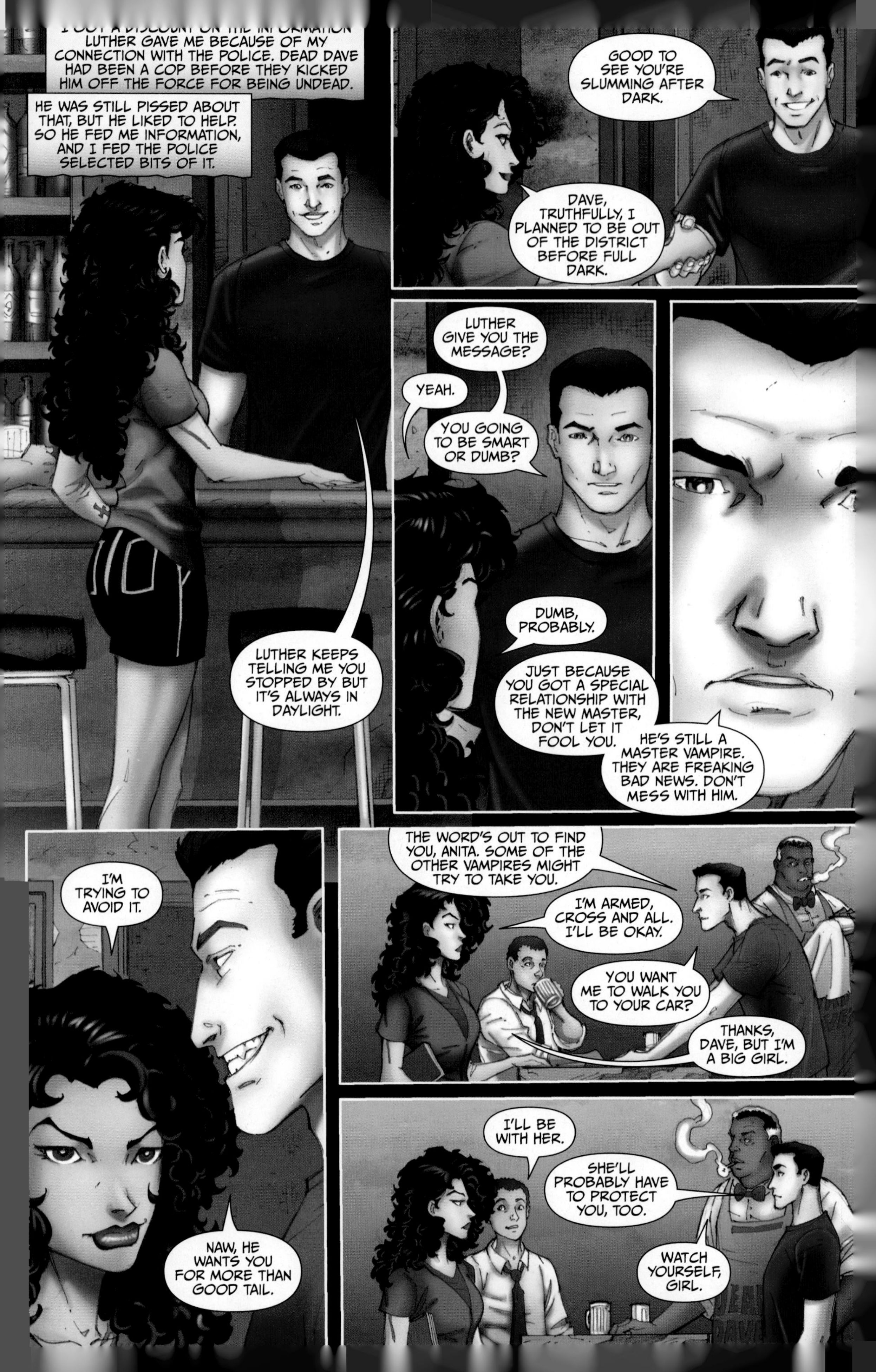
I GOT A DISCOUNT ON THE INFORMATION LUTHER GAVE ME BECAUSE OF MY CONNECTION WITH THE POLICE. DEAD DAVE HAD BEEN A COP BEFORE THEY KICKED HIM OFF THE FORCE FOR BEING UNDEAD.
HE WAS STILL PISSED ABOUT THAT, BUT HE LIKED TO HELP. SO HE FED ME INFORMATION, AND I FED THE POLICE SELECTED BITS OF IT.
LUTHER KEEPS TELLING ME YOU STOPPED BY BUT IT'S ALWAYS IN DAYLIGHT.
GOOD TO SEE YOU'RE SLUMMING AFTER DARK.
DAVE, TRUTHFULLY, I PLANNED TO BE OUT OF THE DISTRICT BEFORE FULL DARK.
LUTHER GIVE YOU THE MESSAGE?
YEAH.
YOU GOING TO BE SMART OR DUMB?
DUMB, PROBABLY.
JUST BECAUSE YOU GOT A SPECIAL RELATIONSHIP WITH THE NEW MASTER, DON'T LET IT FOOL YOU.
HE'S STILL A MASTER VAMPIRE. THEY ARE FREAKING BAD NEWS. DON'T MESS WITH HIM.
I'M TRYING TO AVOID IT.
NAW, HE WANTS YOU FOR MORE THAN GOOD TAIL.
THE WORD'S OUT TO FIND YOU, ANITA. SOME OF THE OTHER VAMPIRES MIGHT TRY TO TAKE YOU.
I'M ARMED, CROSS AND ALL. I'LL BE OKAY.
YOU WANT ME TO WALK YOU TO YOUR CAR?
THANKS, DAVE, BUT I'M A BIG GIRL.
I'LL BE WITH HER.
SHE'LL PROBABLY HAVE TO PROTECT YOU, TOO.
WATCH YOURSELF, GIRL.

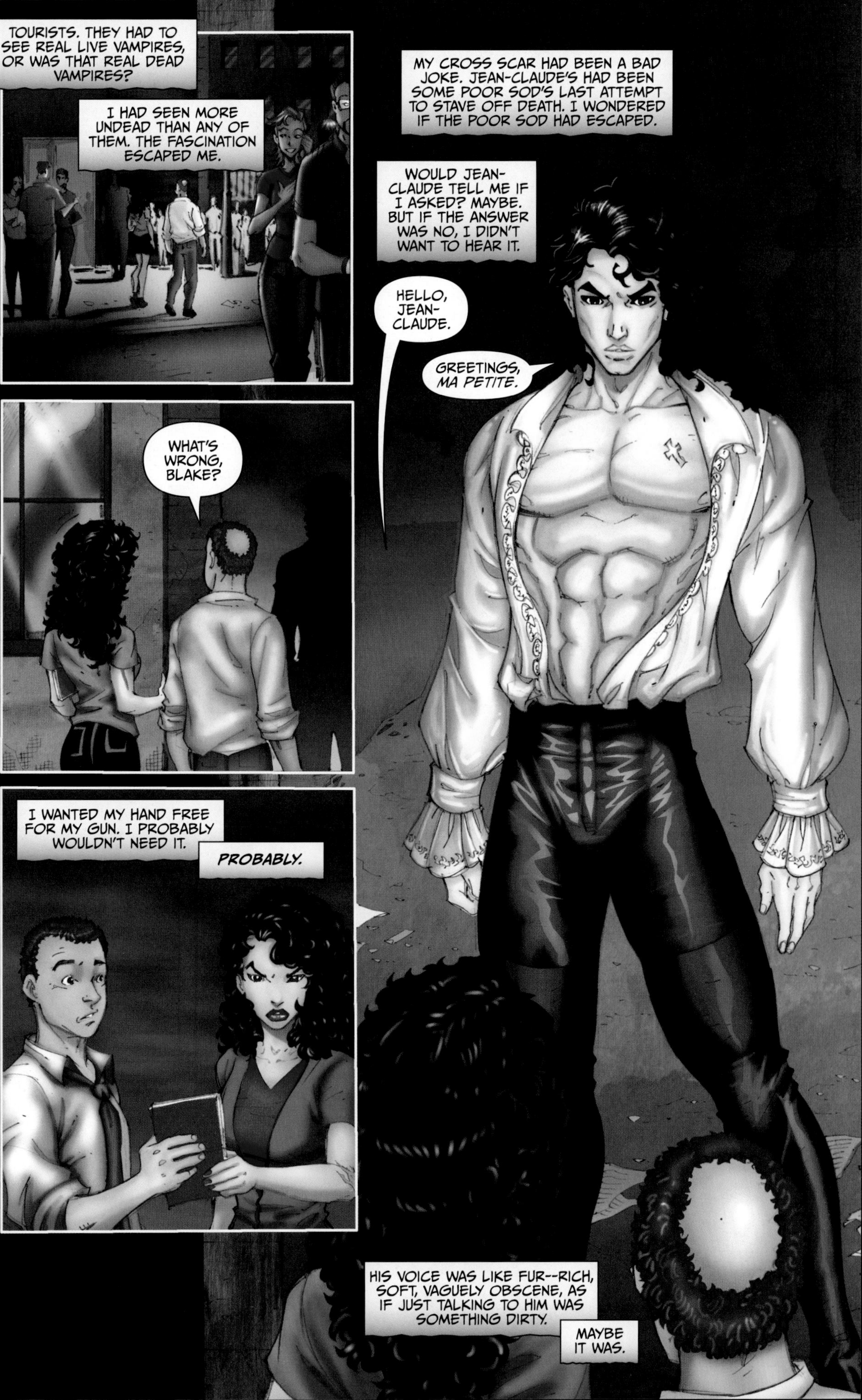
TOURISTS. THEY HAD TO SEE REAL LIVE VAMPIRES, OR WAS THAT REAL DEAD VAMPIRES?
I HAD SEEN MORE UNDEAD THAN ANY OF THEM. THE FASCINATION ESCAPED ME.
WHAT'S WRONG, BLAKE?
I WANTED MY HAND FREE FOR MY GUN. I PROBABLY WOULDN'T NEED IT.
PROBABLY.
MY CROSS SCAR HAD BEEN A BAD JOKE. JEAN-CLAUDE'S HAD BEEN SOME POOR SOD'S LAST ATTEMPT TO STAVE OFF DEATH. I WONDERED IF THE POOR SOD HAD ESCAPED.
WOULD JEAN-CLAUDE TELL ME IF I ASKED? MAYBE. BUT IF THE ANSWER WAS NO, I DIDN'T WANT TO HEAR IT.
HELLO, JEAN-CLAUDE.
GREETINGS, MA PETITE.
HIS VOICE WAS LIKE FUR--RICH, SOFT, VAGUELY OBSCENE, AS IF JUST TALKING TO HIM WAS SOMETHING DIRTY.
MAYBE IT WAS.

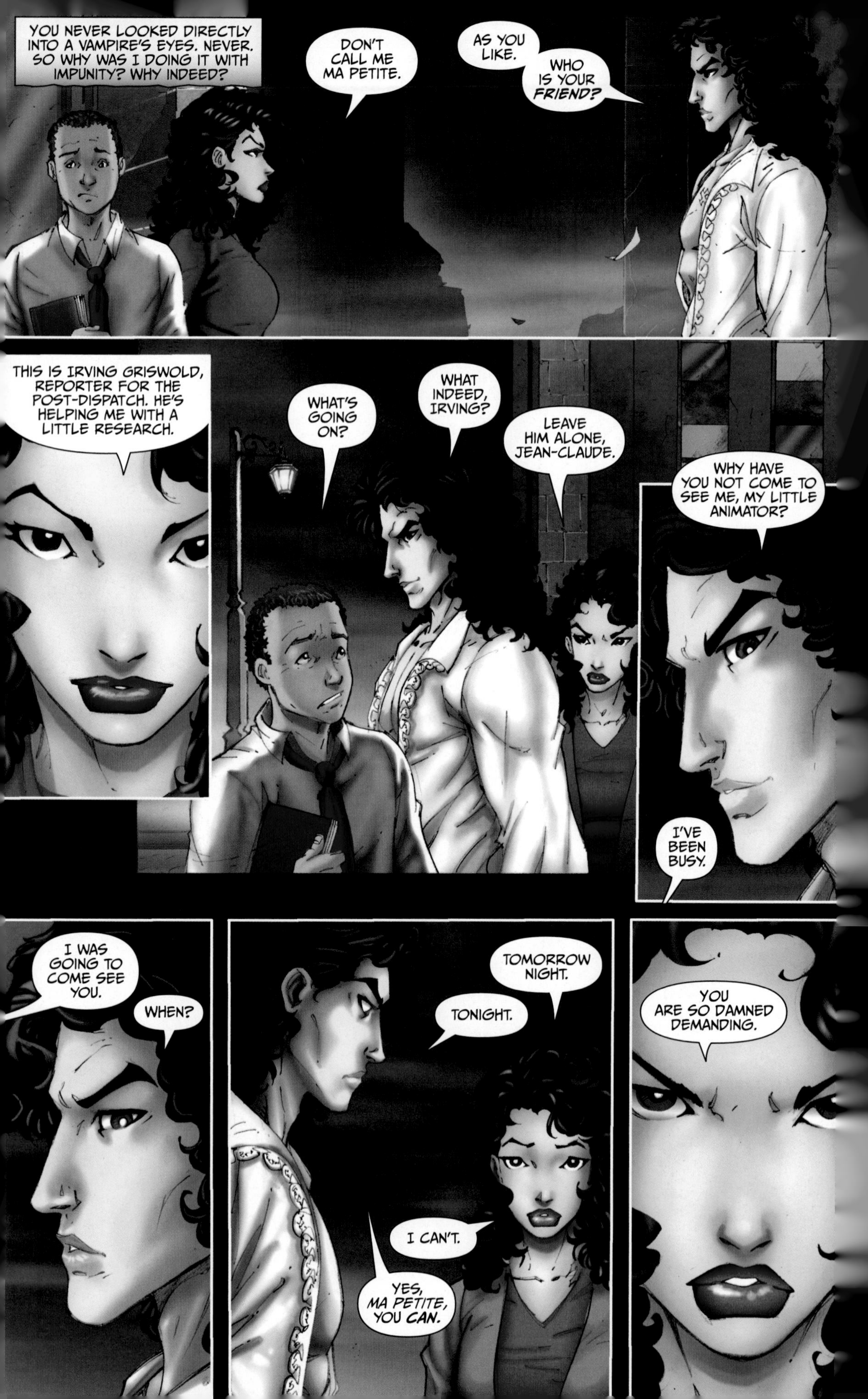
YOU NEVER LOOKED DIRECTLY INTO A VAMPIRE'S EYES. NEVER. SO WHY WAS I DOING IT WITH IMPUNITY? WHY INDEED?
DON'T CALL ME MA PETITE.
AS YOU LIKE.
WHO IS YOUR FRIEND?
THIS IS IRVING GRISWOLD, REPORTER FOR THE POST-DISPATCH. HE'S HELPING ME WITH A LITTLE RESEARCH.
WHAT'S GOING ON?
WHAT INDEED, IRVING?
LEAVE HIM ALONE, JEAN-CLAUDE.
WHY HAVE YOU NOT COME TO SEE ME, MY LITTLE ANIMATOR?
I'VE BEEN BUSY.
I WAS GOING TO COME SEE YOU.
WHEN?
TOMORROW NIGHT.
TONIGHT.
I CAN'T.
YES, MA PETITE, YOU CAN.
YOU ARE SO DAMNED DEMANDING.

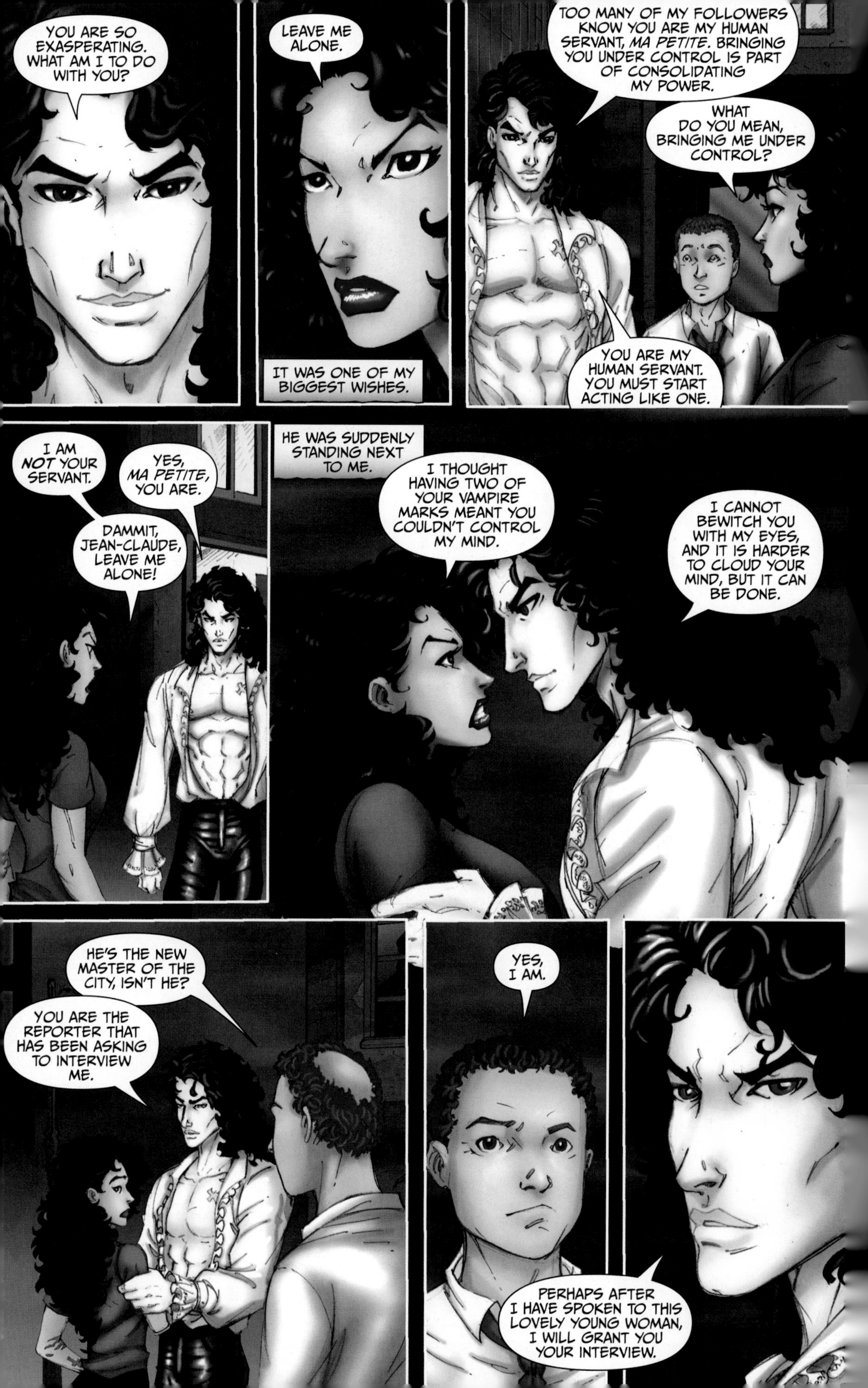
YOU ARE SO EXASPERATING. WHAT AM I TO DO WITH YOU?
LEAVE ME ALONE.
IT WAS ONE OF MY BIGGEST WISHES.
TOO MANY OF MY FOLLOWERS KNOW YOU ARE MY HUMAN SERVANT, MA PETITE. BRINGING YOU UNDER CONTROL IS PART OF CONSOLIDATING MY POWER.
WHAT DO YOU MEAN, BRINGING ME UNDER CONTROL?
YOU ARE MY HUMAN SERVANT. YOU MUST START ACTING LIKE ONE.
I AM NOT YOUR SERVANT.
YES, MA PETITE, YOU ARE.
DAMMIT, JEAN-CLAUDE, LEAVE ME ALONE!
HE WAS SUDDENLY STANDING NEXT TO ME.
I THOUGHT HAVING TWO OF YOUR VAMPIRE MARKS MEANT YOU COULDN'T CONTROL MY MIND.
I CANNOT BEWITCH YOU WITH MY EYES, AND IT IS HARDER TO CLOUD YOUR MIND, BUT IT CAN BE DONE.
HE'S THE NEW MASTER OF THE CITY, ISN'T HE?
YOU ARE THE REPORTER THAT HAS BEEN ASKING TO INTERVIEW ME.
YES, I AM.
PERHAPS AFTER I HAVE SPOKEN TO THIS LOVELY YOUNG WOMAN, I WILL GRANT YOU YOUR INTERVIEW.

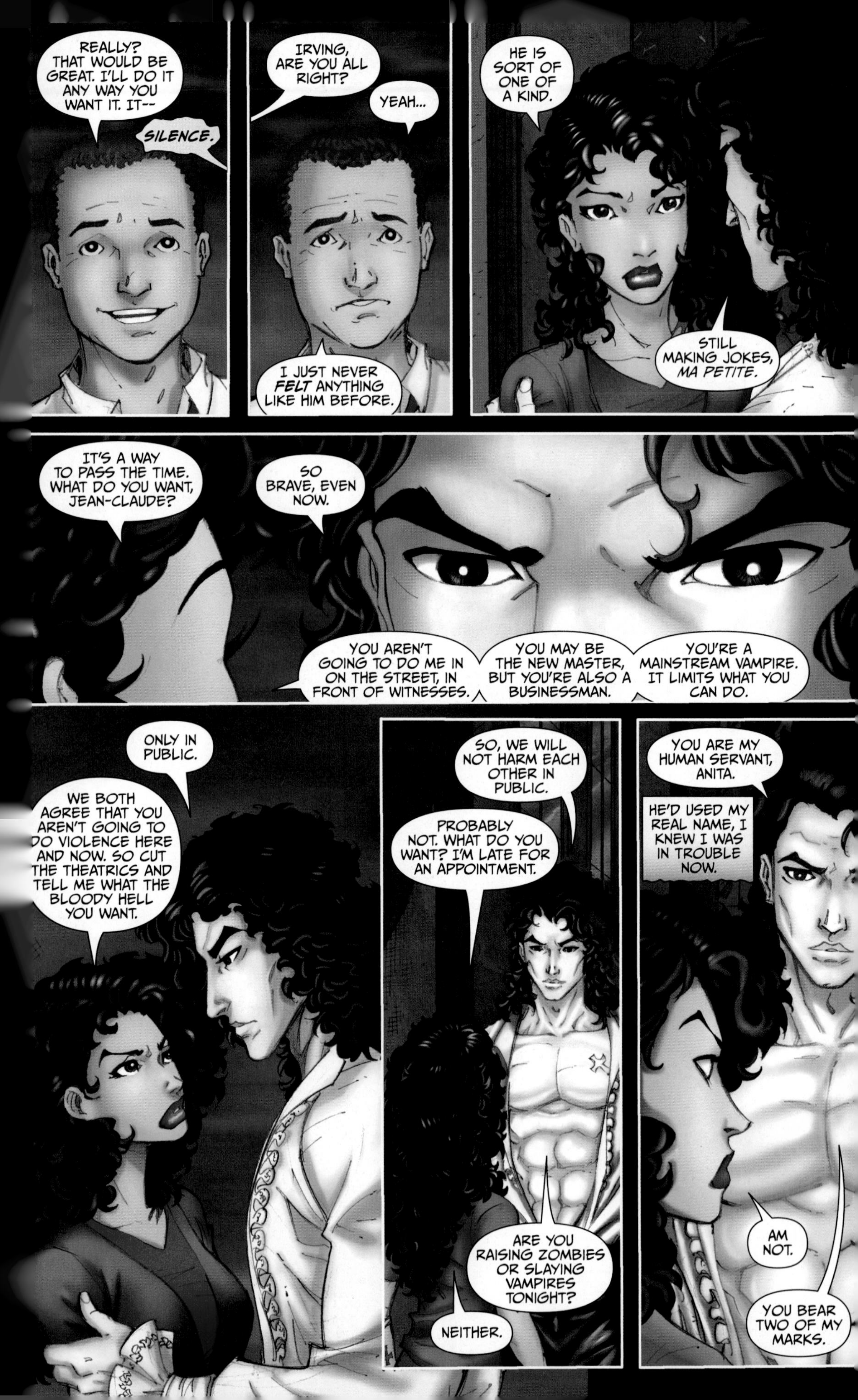
REALLY? THAT WOULD BE GREAT. I'LL DO IT ANY WAY YOU WANT IT. IT--
SILENCE.
IRVING, ARE YOU ALL RIGHT?
YEAH...
I JUST NEVER FELT ANYTHING LIKE HIM BEFORE.
HE IS SORT OF ONE OF A KIND.
STILL MAKING JOKES, MA PETITE.
IT'S A WAY TO PASS THE TIME. WHAT DO YOU WANT, JEAN-CLAUDE?
SO BRAVE, EVEN NOW.
YOU AREN'T GOING TO DO ME IN ON THE STREET, IN FRONT OF WITNESSES.
YOU MAY BE THE NEW MASTER, BUT YOU'RE ALSO A BUSINESSMAN.
YOU'RE A MAINSTREAM VAMPIRE. IT LIMITS WHAT YOU CAN DO.
ONLY IN PUBLIC.
WE BOTH AGREE THAT YOU AREN'T GOING TO DO VIOLENCE HERE AND NOW. SO CUT THE THEATRICS AND TELL ME WHAT THE BLOODY HELL YOU WANT.
SO, WE WILL NOT HARM EACH OTHER IN PUBLIC.
PROBABLY NOT. WHAT DO YOU WANT? I'M LATE FOR AN APPOINTMENT.
ARE YOU RAISING ZOMBIES OR SLAYING VAMPIRES TONIGHT?
NEITHER.
YOU ARE MY HUMAN SERVANT, ANITA.
HE'D USED MY REAL NAME, I KNEW I WAS IN TROUBLE NOW.
AM NOT.
YOU BEAR TWO OF MY MARKS.

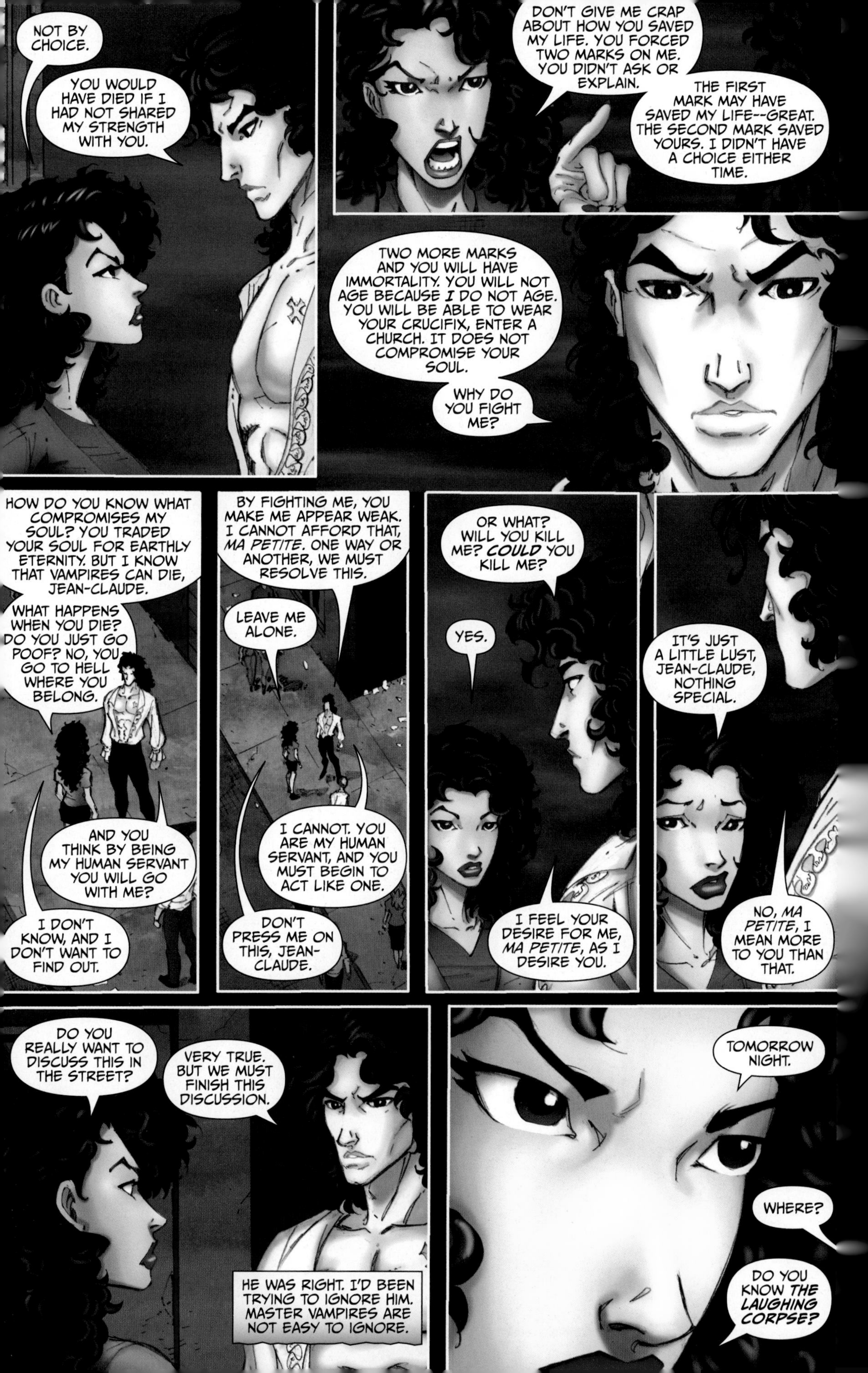
NOT BY CHOICE.
YOU WOULD HAVE DIED IF I HAD NOT SHARED MY STRENGTH WITH YOU.
DON'T GIVE ME CRAP ABOUT HOW YOU SAVED MY LIFE. YOU FORCED TWO MARKS ON ME. YOU DIDN'T ASK OR EXPLAIN.
THE FIRST MARK MAY HAVE SAVED MY LIFE--GREAT. THE SECOND MARK SAVED YOURS. I DIDN'T HAVE A CHOICE EITHER TIME.
TWO MORE MARKS AND YOU WILL HAVE IMMORTALITY. YOU WILL NOT AGE BECAUSE *I* DO NOT AGE. YOU WILL BE ABLE TO WEAR YOUR CRUCIFIX, ENTER A CHURCH. IT DOES NOT COMPROMISE YOUR SOUL.
WHY DO YOU FIGHT ME?
HOW DO YOU KNOW WHAT COMPROMISES MY SOUL? YOU TRADED YOUR SOUL FOR EARTHLY ETERNITY. BUT I KNOW THAT VAMPIRES CAN DIE, JEAN-CLAUDE.
WHAT HAPPENS WHEN YOU DIE? DO YOU JUST GO POOF? NO, YOU GO TO HELL WHERE YOU BELONG.
AND YOU THINK BY BEING MY HUMAN SERVANT YOU WILL GO WITH ME?
I DON'T KNOW, AND I DON'T WANT TO FIND OUT.
BY FIGHTING ME, YOU MAKE ME APPEAR WEAK. I CANNOT AFFORD THAT, *MA PETITE*. ONE WAY OR ANOTHER, WE MUST RESOLVE THIS.
LEAVE ME ALONE.
I CANNOT. YOU ARE MY HUMAN SERVANT, AND YOU MUST BEGIN TO ACT LIKE ONE.
DON'T PRESS ME ON THIS, JEAN-CLAUDE.
OR WHAT? WILL YOU KILL ME? ***COULD*** YOU KILL ME?
YES.
I FEEL YOUR DESIRE FOR ME, *MA PETITE*, AS I DESIRE YOU.
IT'S JUST A LITTLE LUST, JEAN-CLAUDE, NOTHING SPECIAL.
NO, *MA PETITE*, I MEAN MORE TO YOU THAN THAT.
DO YOU REALLY WANT TO DISCUSS THIS IN THE STREET?
VERY TRUE. BUT WE MUST FINISH THIS DISCUSSION.
HE WAS RIGHT. I'D BEEN TRYING TO IGNORE HIM. MASTER VAMPIRES ARE NOT EASY TO IGNORE.
TOMORROW NIGHT.
WHERE?
DO YOU KNOW ***THE LAUGHING CORPSE?***

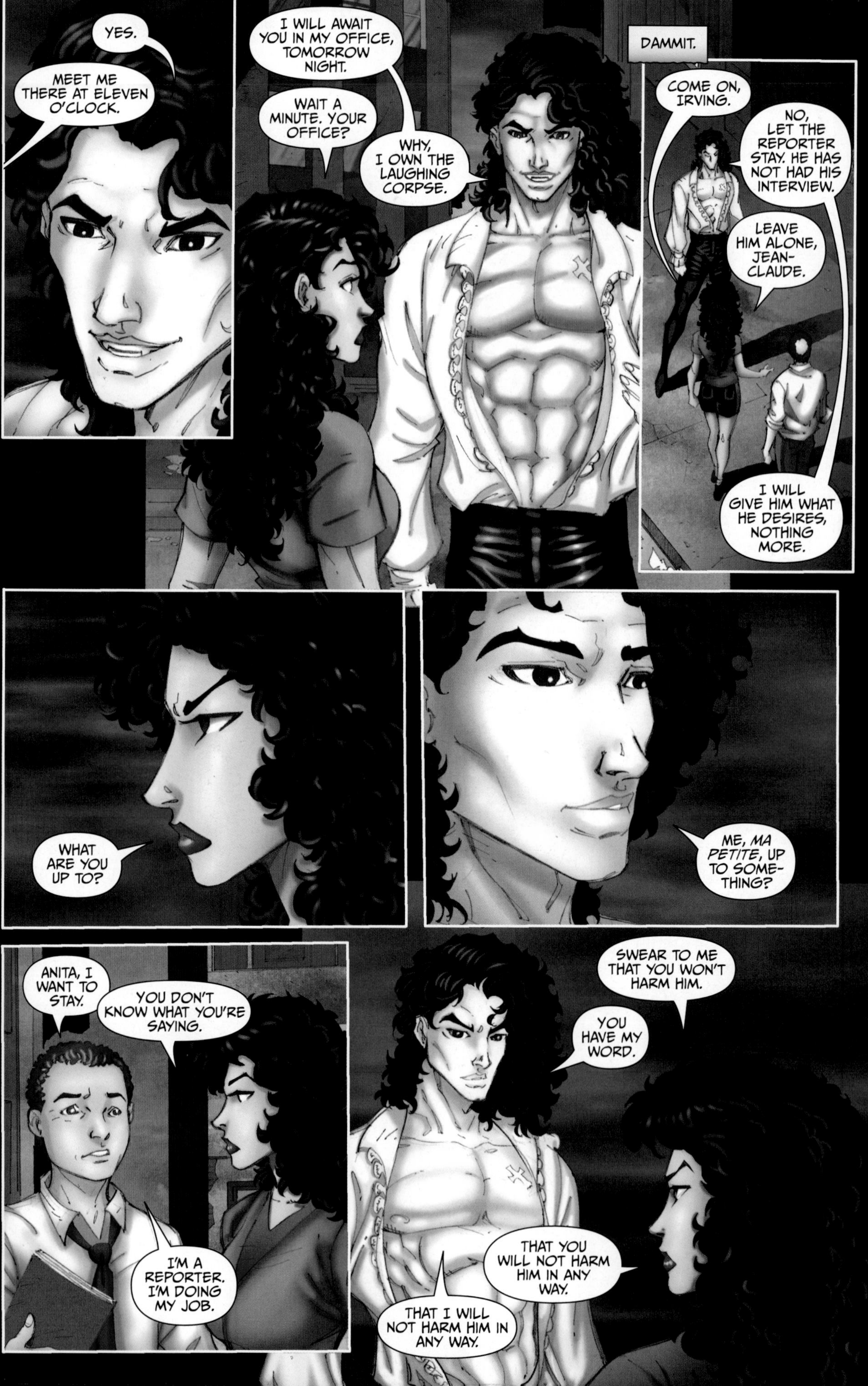
YES.
MEET ME THERE AT ELEVEN O'CLOCK.
I WILL AWAIT YOU IN MY OFFICE, TOMORROW NIGHT.
WAIT A MINUTE. YOUR OFFICE?
WHY, I OWN THE LAUGHING CORPSE.
DAMMIT.
COME ON, IRVING.
NO, LET THE REPORTER STAY. HE HAS NOT HAD HIS INTERVIEW.
LEAVE HIM ALONE, JEAN-CLAUDE.
I WILL GIVE HIM WHAT HE DESIRES, NOTHING MORE.
WHAT ARE YOU UP TO?
ME, *MA PETITE*, UP TO SOMETHING?
ANITA, I WANT TO STAY.
YOU DON'T KNOW WHAT YOU'RE SAYING.
I'M A REPORTER. I'M DOING MY JOB.
SWEAR TO ME THAT YOU WON'T HARM HIM.
YOU HAVE MY WORD.
THAT YOU WILL NOT HARM HIM IN ANY WAY.
THAT I WILL NOT HARM HIM IN ANY WAY.

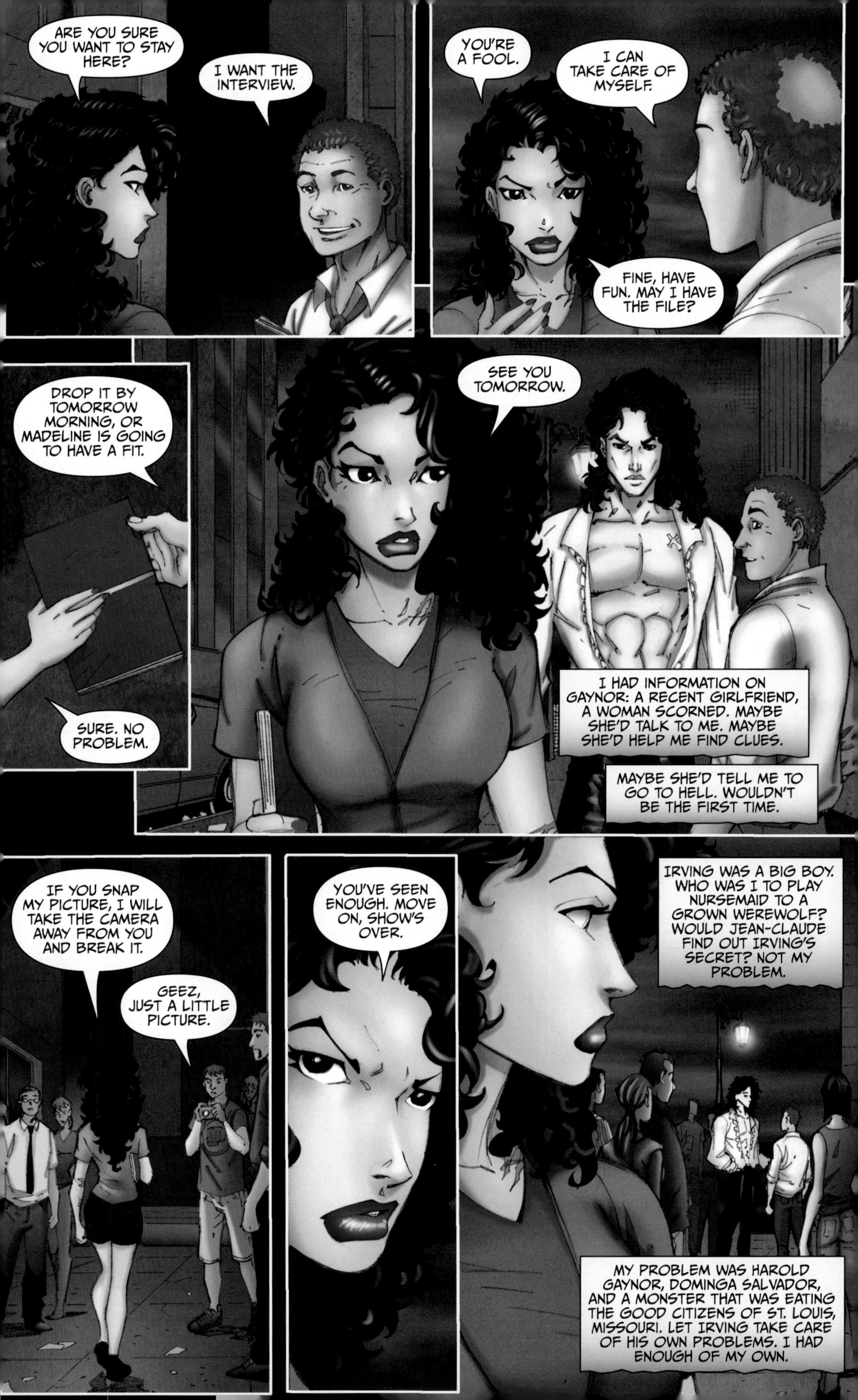
ARE YOU SURE YOU WANT TO STAY HERE?
I WANT THE INTERVIEW.
YOU'RE A FOOL.
I CAN TAKE CARE OF MYSELF.
FINE, HAVE FUN. MAY I HAVE THE FILE?
DROP IT BY TOMORROW MORNING, OR MADELINE IS GOING TO HAVE A FIT.
SURE. NO PROBLEM.
SEE YOU TOMORROW.
I HAD INFORMATION ON GAYNOR: A RECENT GIRLFRIEND, A WOMAN SCORNED. MAYBE SHE'D TALK TO ME. MAYBE SHE'D HELP ME FIND CLUES.
MAYBE SHE'D TELL ME TO GO TO HELL. WOULDN'T BE THE FIRST TIME.
IF YOU SNAP MY PICTURE, I WILL TAKE THE CAMERA AWAY FROM YOU AND BREAK IT.
GEEZ, JUST A LITTLE PICTURE.
YOU'VE SEEN ENOUGH. MOVE ON, SHOW'S OVER.
IRVING WAS A BIG BOY. WHO WAS I TO PLAY NURSEMAID TO A GROWN WEREWOLF? WOULD JEAN-CLAUDE FIND OUT IRVING'S SECRET? NOT MY PROBLEM.
MY PROBLEM WAS HAROLD GAYNOR, DOMINGA SALVADOR, AND A MONSTER THAT WAS EATING THE GOOD CITIZENS OF ST. LOUIS, MISSOURI. LET IRVING TAKE CARE OF HIS OWN PROBLEMS. I HAD ENOUGH OF MY OWN.

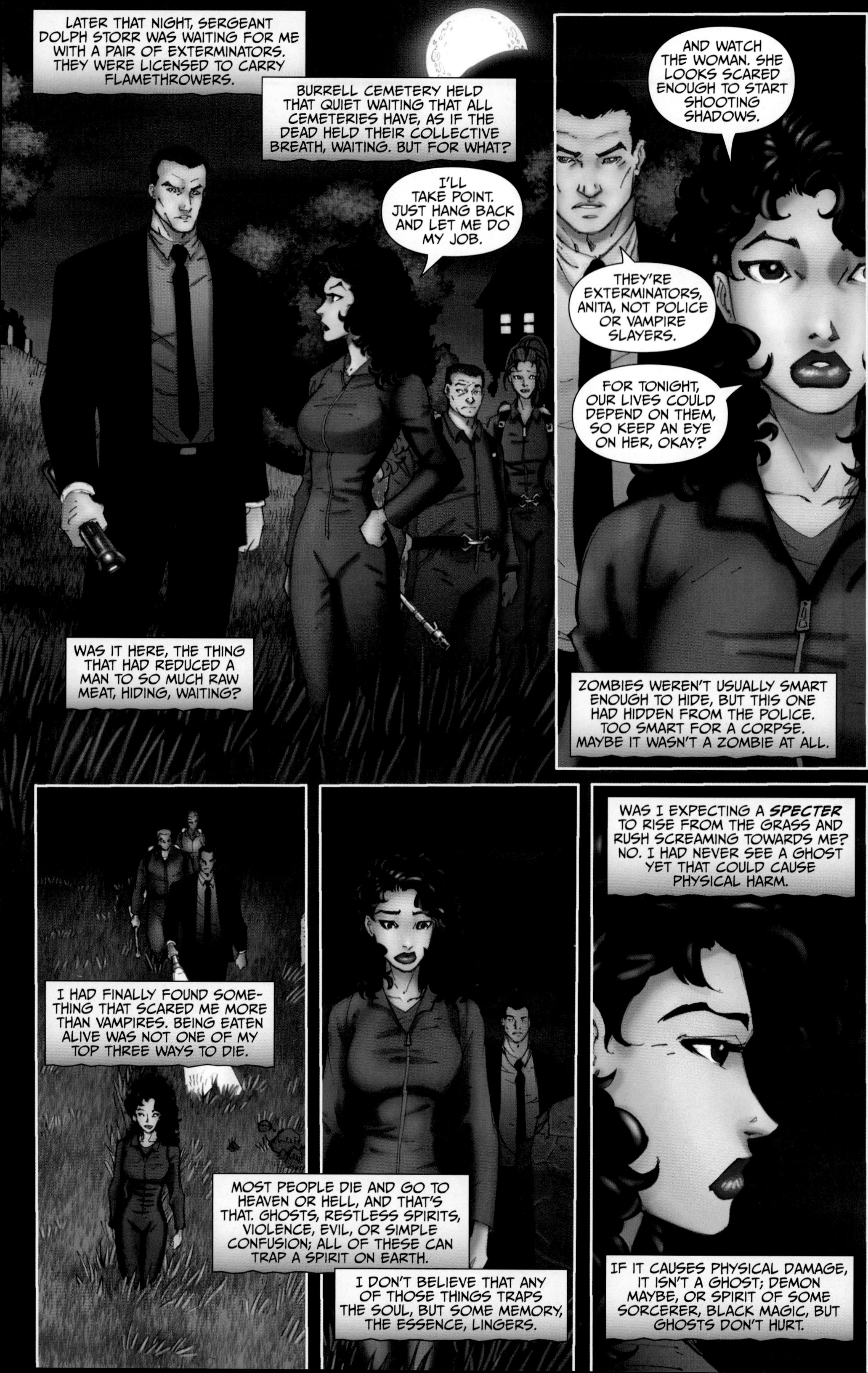
LATER THAT NIGHT, SERGEANT DOLPH STORR WAS WAITING FOR ME WITH A PAIR OF EXTERMINATORS. THEY WERE LICENSED TO CARRY FLAMETHROWERS.
BURRELL CEMETERY HELD THAT QUIET WAITING THAT ALL CEMETERIES HAVE, AS IF THE DEAD HELD THEIR COLLECTIVE BREATH, WAITING. BUT FOR WHAT?
I'LL TAKE POINT. JUST HANG BACK AND LET ME DO MY JOB.
WAS IT HERE, THE THING THAT HAD REDUCED A MAN TO SO MUCH RAW MEAT, HIDING, WAITING?
AND WATCH THE WOMAN. SHE LOOKS SCARED ENOUGH TO START SHOOTING SHADOWS.
THEY'RE EXTERMINATORS, ANITA, NOT POLICE OR VAMPIRE SLAYERS.
FOR TONIGHT, OUR LIVES COULD DEPEND ON THEM, SO KEEP AN EYE ON HER, OKAY?
ZOMBIES WEREN'T USUALLY SMART ENOUGH TO HIDE, BUT THIS ONE HAD HIDDEN FROM THE POLICE. TOO SMART FOR A CORPSE. MAYBE IT WASN'T A ZOMBIE AT ALL.
I HAD FINALLY FOUND SOME-THING THAT SCARED ME MORE THAN VAMPIRES. BEING EATEN ALIVE WAS NOT ONE OF MY TOP THREE WAYS TO DIE.
MOST PEOPLE DIE AND GO TO HEAVEN OR HELL, AND THAT'S THAT. GHOSTS, RESTLESS SPIRITS, VIOLENCE, EVIL, OR SIMPLE CONFUSION; ALL OF THESE CAN TRAP A SPIRIT ON EARTH.
I DON'T BELIEVE THAT ANY OF THOSE THINGS TRAPS THE SOUL, BUT SOME MEMORY, THE ESSENCE, LINGERS.
WAS I EXPECTING A *SPECTER* TO RISE FROM THE GRASS AND RUSH SCREAMING TOWARDS ME? NO. I HAD NEVER SEE A GHOST YET THAT COULD CAUSE PHYSICAL HARM.
IF IT CAUSES PHYSICAL DAMAGE, IT ISN'T A GHOST; DEMON MAYBE, OR SPIRIT OF SOME SORCERER, BLACK MAGIC, BUT GHOSTS DON'T HURT.

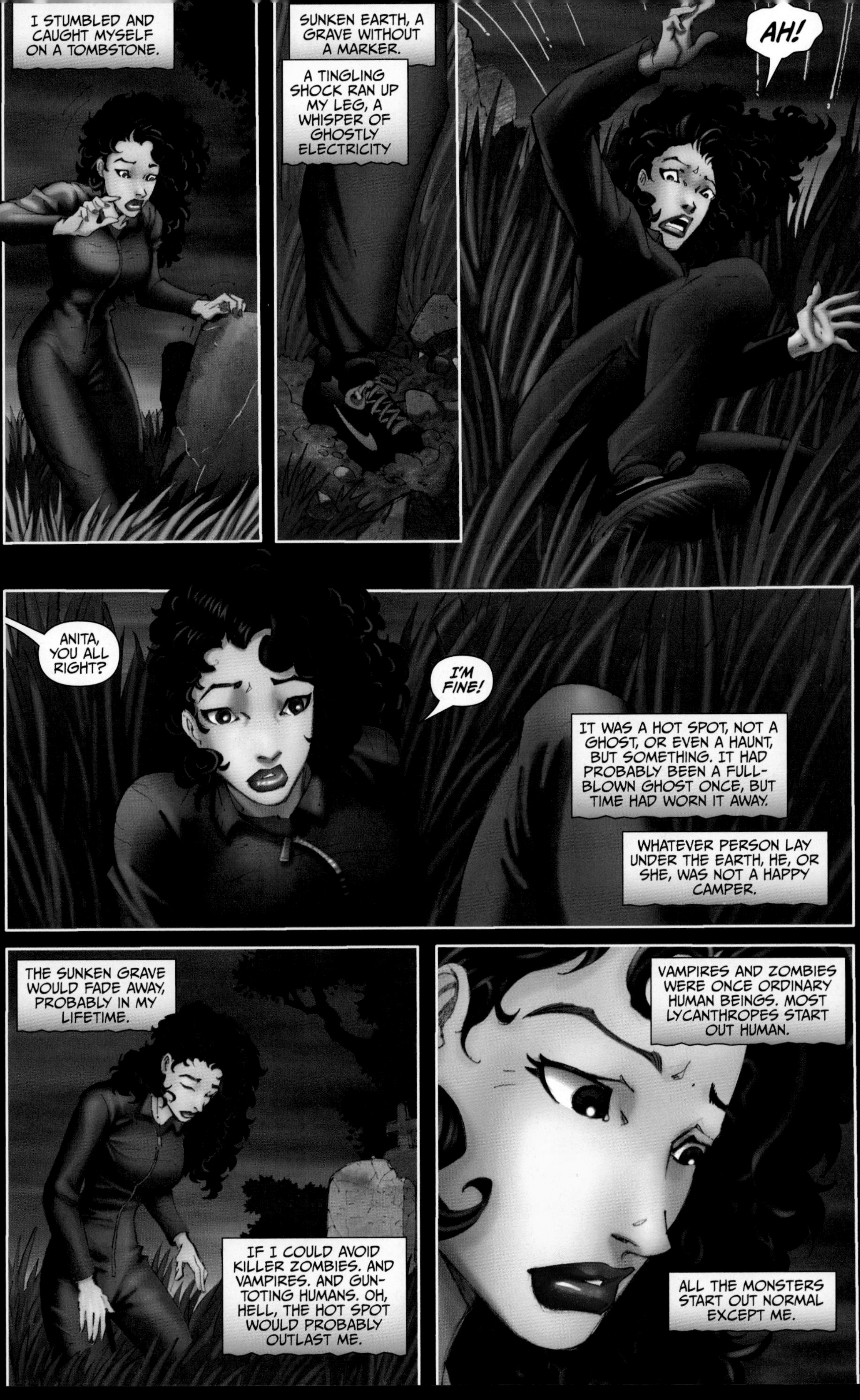
I STUMBLED AND CAUGHT MYSELF ON A TOMBSTONE.
SUNKEN EARTH, A GRAVE WITHOUT A MARKER.
A TINGLING SHOCK RAN UP MY LEG, A WHISPER OF GHOSTLY ELECTRICITY
AH!
ANITA, YOU ALL RIGHT?
I'M FINE!
IT WAS A HOT SPOT, NOT A GHOST, OR EVEN A HAUNT, BUT SOMETHING. IT HAD PROBABLY BEEN A FULL-BLOWN GHOST ONCE, BUT TIME HAD WORN IT AWAY.
WHATEVER PERSON LAY UNDER THE EARTH, HE, OR SHE, WAS NOT A HAPPY CAMPER.
THE SUNKEN GRAVE WOULD FADE AWAY, PROBABLY IN MY LIFETIME.
IF I COULD AVOID KILLER ZOMBIES. AND VAMPIRES. AND GUN-TOTING HUMANS. OH, HELL, THE HOT SPOT WOULD PROBABLY OUTLAST ME.
VAMPIRES AND ZOMBIES WERE ONCE ORDINARY HUMAN BEINGS. MOST LYCANTHROPES START OUT HUMAN.
ALL THE MONSTERS START OUT NORMAL EXCEPT ME.

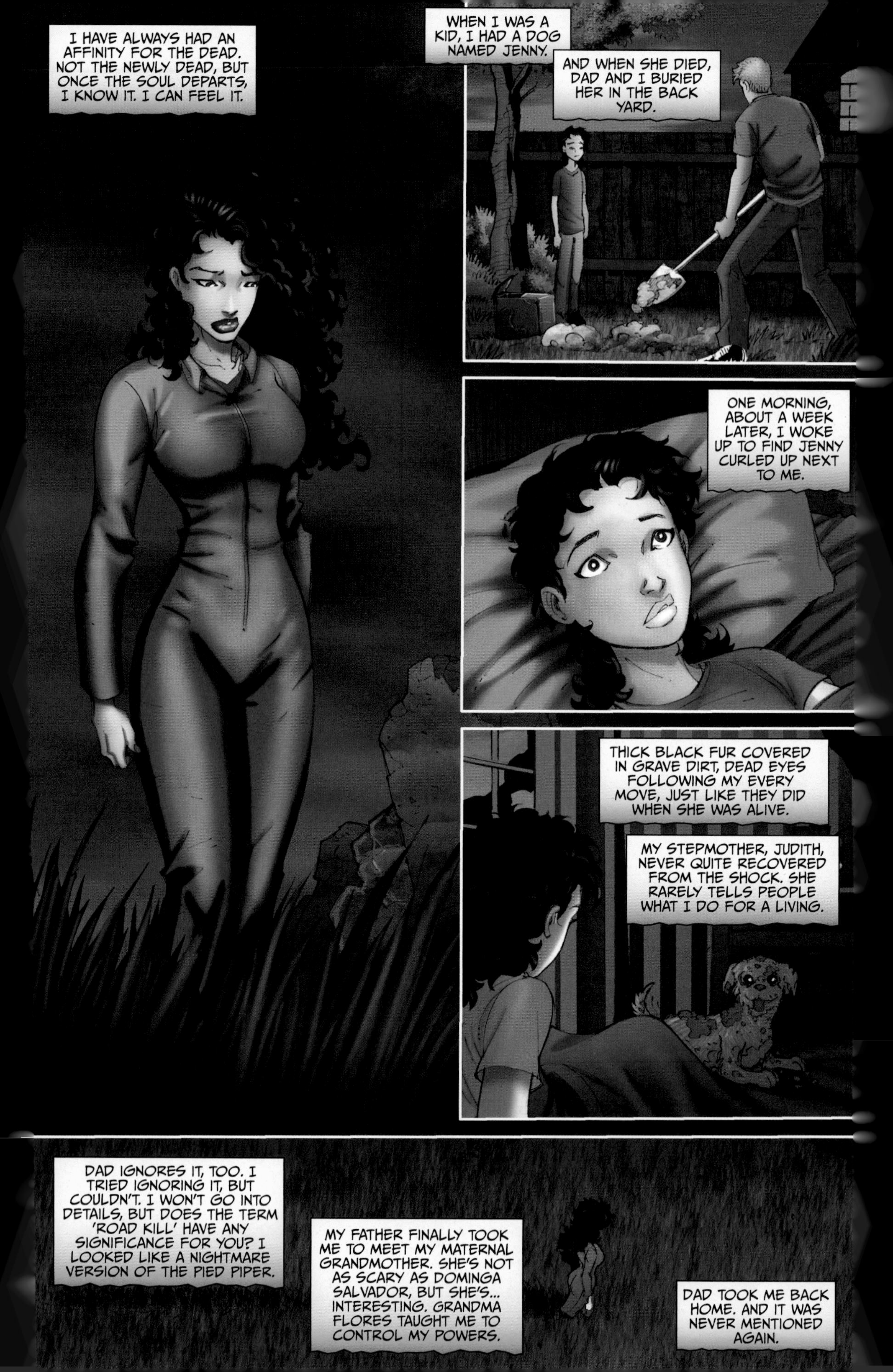
I HAVE ALWAYS HAD AN AFFINITY FOR THE DEAD. NOT THE NEWLY DEAD, BUT ONCE THE SOUL DEPARTS, I KNOW IT. I CAN FEEL IT.
WHEN I WAS A KID, I HAD A DOG NAMED JENNY.
AND WHEN SHE DIED, DAD AND I BURIED HER IN THE BACK YARD.
ONE MORNING, ABOUT A WEEK LATER, I WOKE UP TO FIND JENNY CURLED UP NEXT TO ME.
THICK BLACK FUR COVERED IN GRAVE DIRT, DEAD EYES FOLLOWING MY EVERY MOVE, JUST LIKE THEY DID WHEN SHE WAS ALIVE.
MY STEPMOTHER, JUDITH, NEVER QUITE RECOVERED FROM THE SHOCK. SHE RARELY TELLS PEOPLE WHAT I DO FOR A LIVING.
DAD IGNORES IT, TOO. I TRIED IGNORING IT, BUT COULDN'T. I WON'T GO INTO DETAILS, BUT DOES THE TERM 'ROAD KILL' HAVE ANY SIGNIFICANCE FOR YOU? I LOOKED LIKE A NIGHTMARE VERSION OF THE PIED PIPER.
MY FATHER FINALLY TOOK ME TO MEET MY MATERNAL GRANDMOTHER. SHE'S NOT AS SCARY AS DOMINGA SALVADOR, BUT SHE'S... INTERESTING. GRANDMA FLORES TAUGHT ME TO CONTROL MY POWERS.
DAD TOOK ME BACK HOME. AND IT WAS NEVER MENTIONED AGAIN.

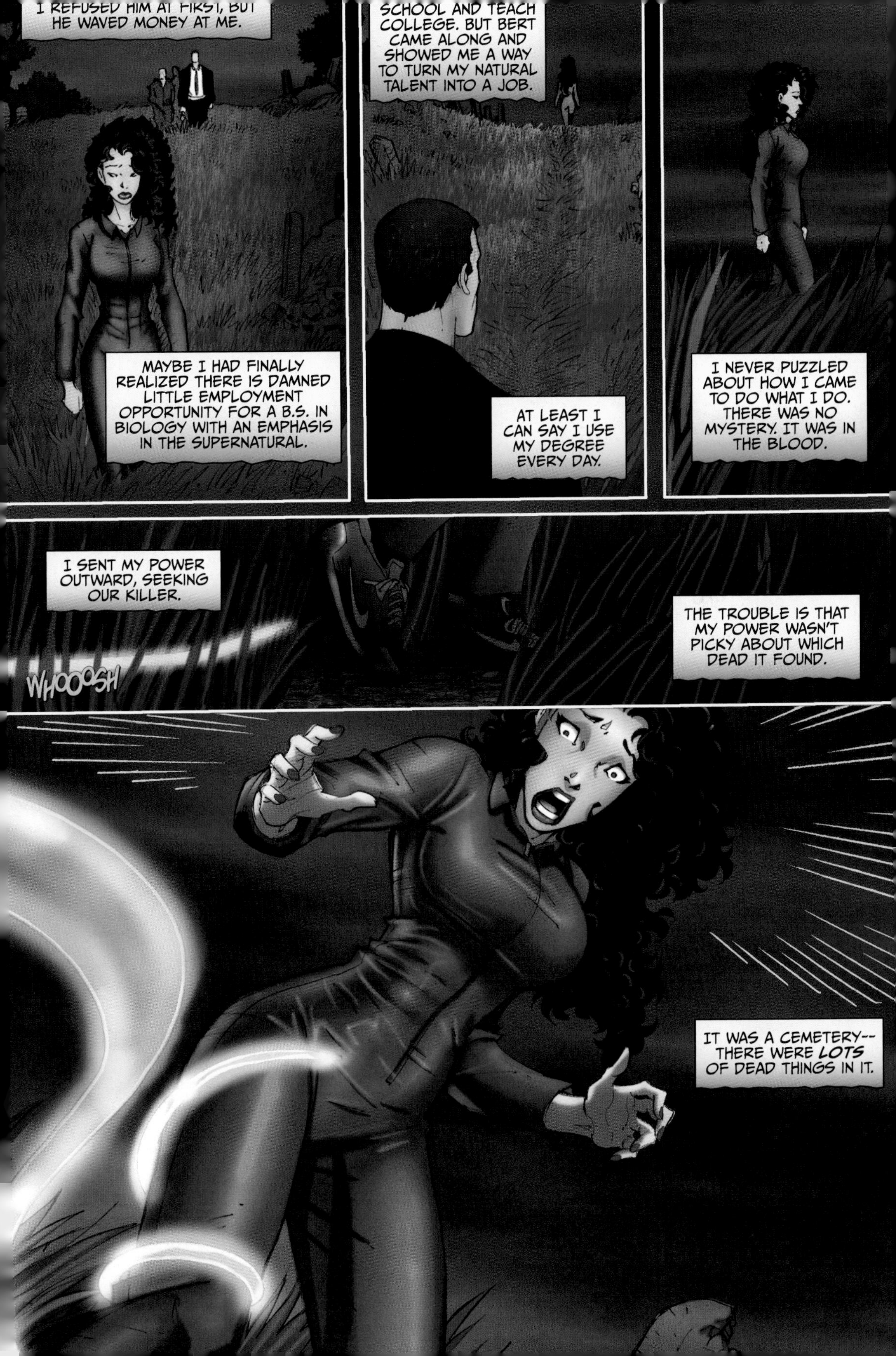
I REFUSED HIM AT FIRST, BUT HE WAVED MONEY AT ME.
MAYBE I HAD FINALLY REALIZED THERE IS DAMNED LITTLE EMPLOYMENT OPPORTUNITY FOR A B.S. IN BIOLOGY WITH AN EMPHASIS IN THE SUPERNATURAL.
SCHOOL AND TEACH COLLEGE. BUT BERT CAME ALONG AND SHOWED ME A WAY TO TURN MY NATURAL TALENT INTO A JOB.
AT LEAST I CAN SAY I USE MY DEGREE EVERY DAY.
I NEVER PUZZLED ABOUT HOW I CAME TO DO WHAT I DO. THERE WAS NO MYSTERY. IT WAS IN THE BLOOD.
I SENT MY POWER OUTWARD, SEEKING OUR KILLER.
WHOOOSH
THE TROUBLE IS THAT MY POWER WASN'T PICKY ABOUT WHICH DEAD IT FOUND.
IT WAS A CEMETERY-- THERE WERE *LOTS* OF DEAD THINGS IN IT.

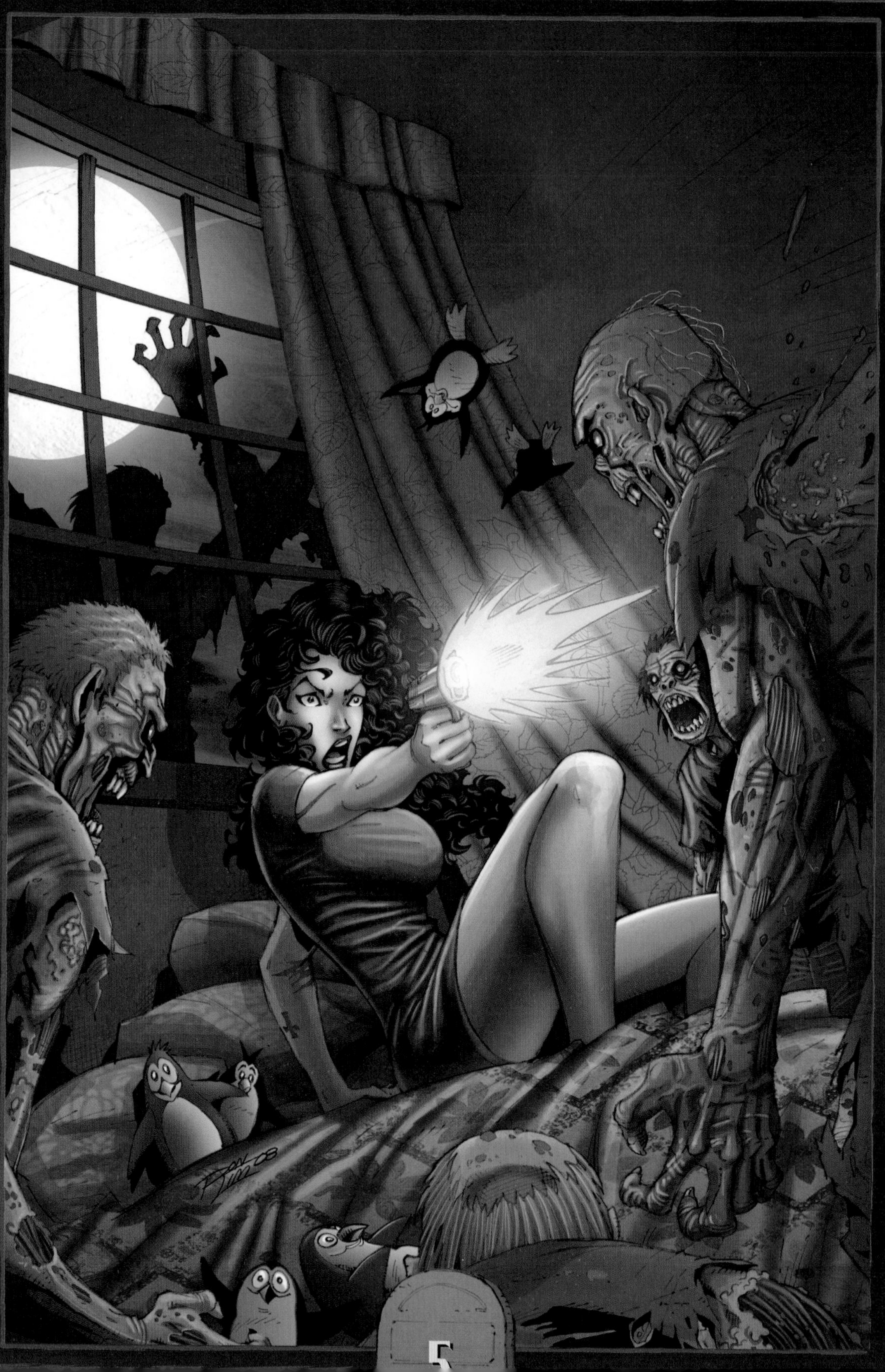

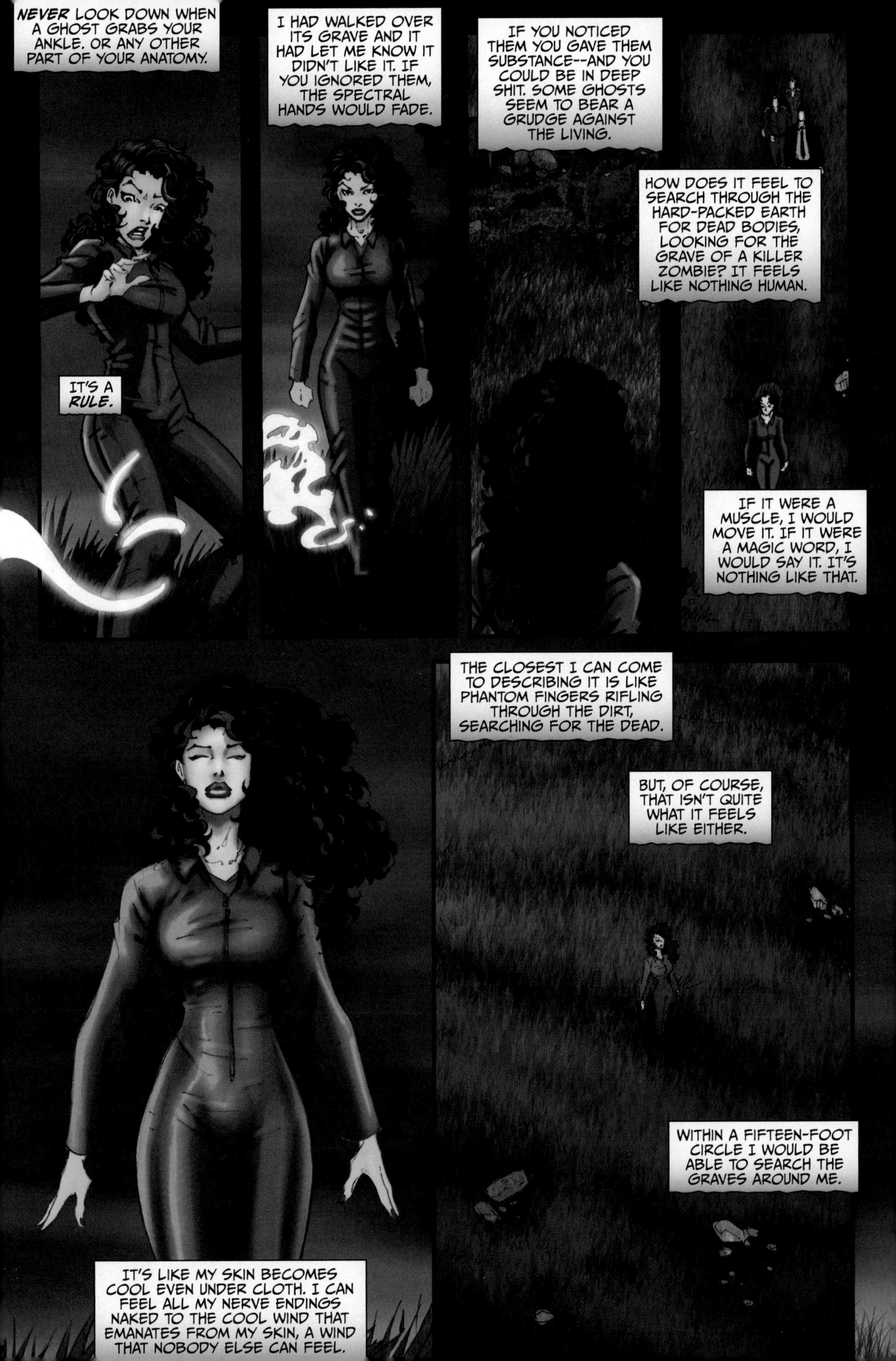
NEVER LOOK DOWN WHEN A GHOST GRABS YOUR ANKLE. OR ANY OTHER PART OF YOUR ANATOMY.
IT'S A ***RULE***.
I HAD WALKED OVER ITS GRAVE AND IT HAD LET ME KNOW IT DIDN'T LIKE IT. IF YOU IGNORED THEM, THE SPECTRAL HANDS WOULD FADE.
IF YOU NOTICED THEM YOU GAVE THEM SUBSTANCE--AND YOU COULD BE IN DEEP SHIT. SOME GHOSTS SEEM TO BEAR A GRUDGE AGAINST THE LIVING.
HOW DOES IT FEEL TO SEARCH THROUGH THE HARD-PACKED EARTH FOR DEAD BODIES, LOOKING FOR THE GRAVE OF A KILLER ZOMBIE? IT FEELS LIKE NOTHING HUMAN.
IF IT WERE A MUSCLE, I WOULD MOVE IT. IF IT WERE A MAGIC WORD, I WOULD SAY IT. IT'S NOTHING LIKE THAT.
IT'S LIKE MY SKIN BECOMES COOL EVEN UNDER CLOTH. I CAN FEEL ALL MY NERVE ENDINGS NAKED TO THE COOL WIND THAT EMANATES FROM MY SKIN, A WIND THAT NOBODY ELSE CAN FEEL.
THE CLOSEST I CAN COME TO DESCRIBING IT IS LIKE PHANTOM FINGERS RIFLING THROUGH THE DIRT, SEARCHING FOR THE DEAD.
BUT, OF COURSE, THAT ISN'T QUITE WHAT IT FEELS LIKE EITHER.
WITHIN A FIFTEEN-FOOT CIRCLE I WOULD BE ABLE TO SEARCH THE GRAVES AROUND ME.

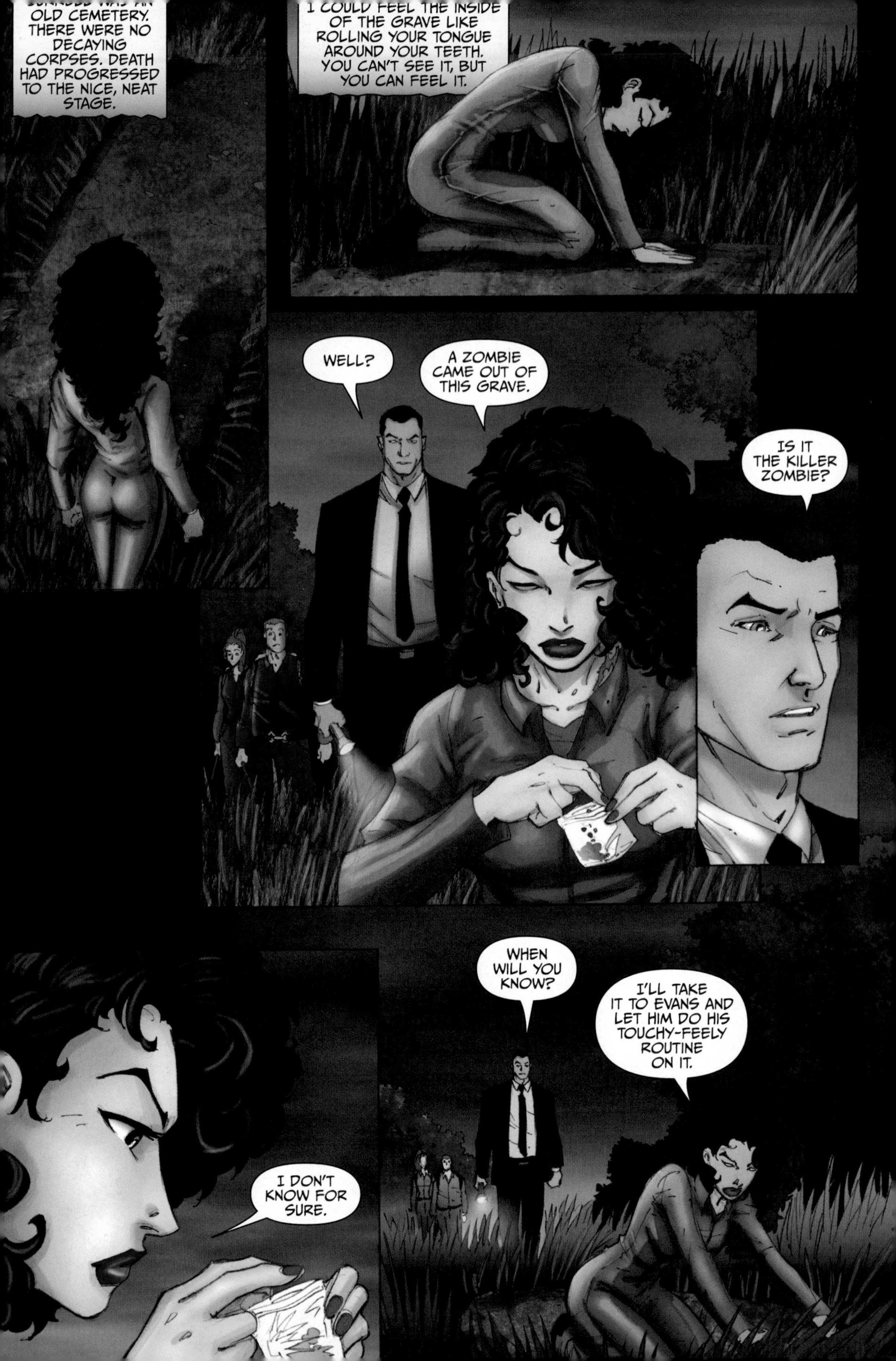
OLD CEMETERY. THERE WERE NO DECAYING CORPSES. DEATH HAD PROGRESSED TO THE NICE, NEAT STAGE.
I COULD FEEL THE INSIDE OF THE GRAVE LIKE ROLLING YOUR TONGUE AROUND YOUR TEETH. YOU CAN'T SEE IT, BUT YOU CAN FEEL IT.
WELL?
A ZOMBIE CAME OUT OF THIS GRAVE.
IS IT THE KILLER ZOMBIE?
I DON'T KNOW FOR SURE.
WHEN WILL YOU KNOW?
I'LL TAKE IT TO EVANS AND LET HIM DO HIS TOUCHY-FEELY ROUTINE ON IT.

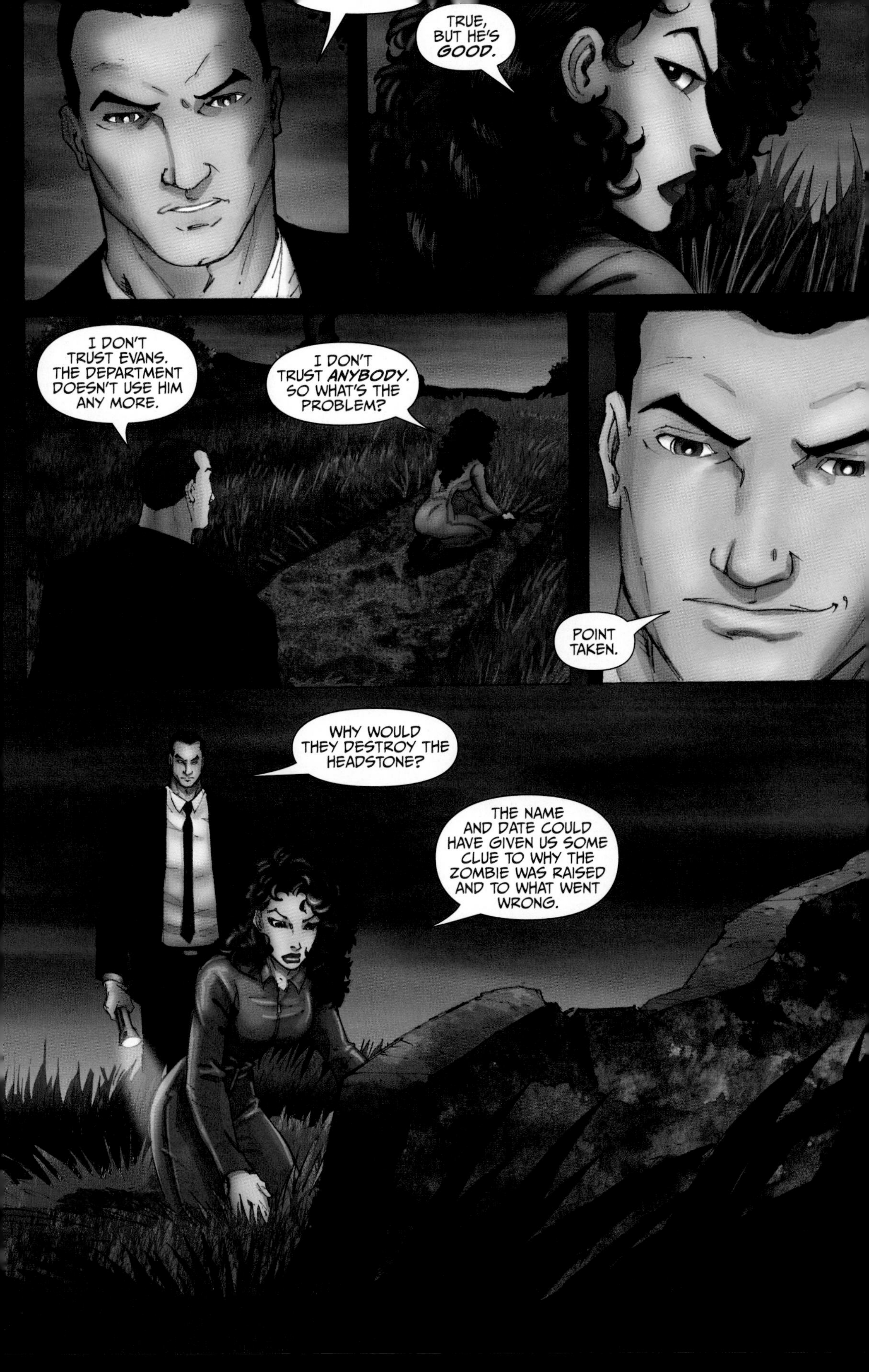
TRUE, BUT HE'S *GOOD*.
I DON'T TRUST EVANS. THE DEPARTMENT DOESN'T USE HIM ANY MORE.
I DON'T TRUST *ANYBODY*. SO WHAT'S THE PROBLEM?
POINT TAKEN.
WHY WOULD THEY DESTROY THE HEADSTONE?
THE NAME AND DATE COULD HAVE GIVEN US SOME CLUE TO WHY THE ZOMBIE WAS RAISED AND TO WHAT WENT WRONG.

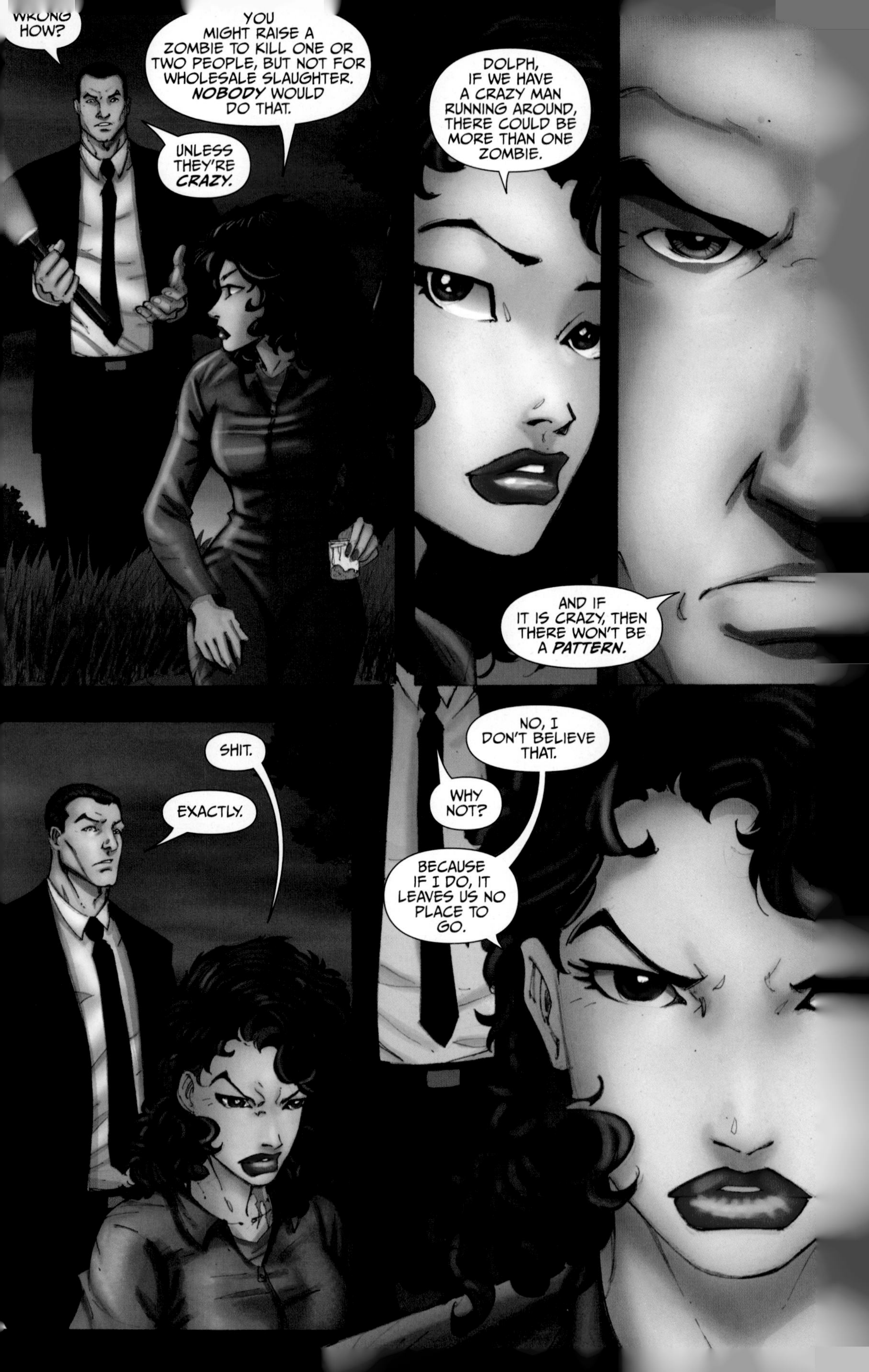

WRONG HOW?
YOU MIGHT RAISE A ZOMBIE TO KILL ONE OR TWO PEOPLE, BUT NOT FOR WHOLESALE SLAUGHTER. NOBODY WOULD DO THAT.
UNLESS THEY'RE CRAZY.
DOLPH, IF WE HAVE A CRAZY MAN RUNNING AROUND, THERE COULD BE MORE THAN ONE ZOMBIE.
AND IF IT IS CRAZY, THEN THERE WON'T BE A PATTERN.
SHIT.
EXACTLY.
NO, I DON'T BELIEVE THAT.
WHY NOT?
BECAUSE IF I DO, IT LEAVES US NO PLACE TO GO.

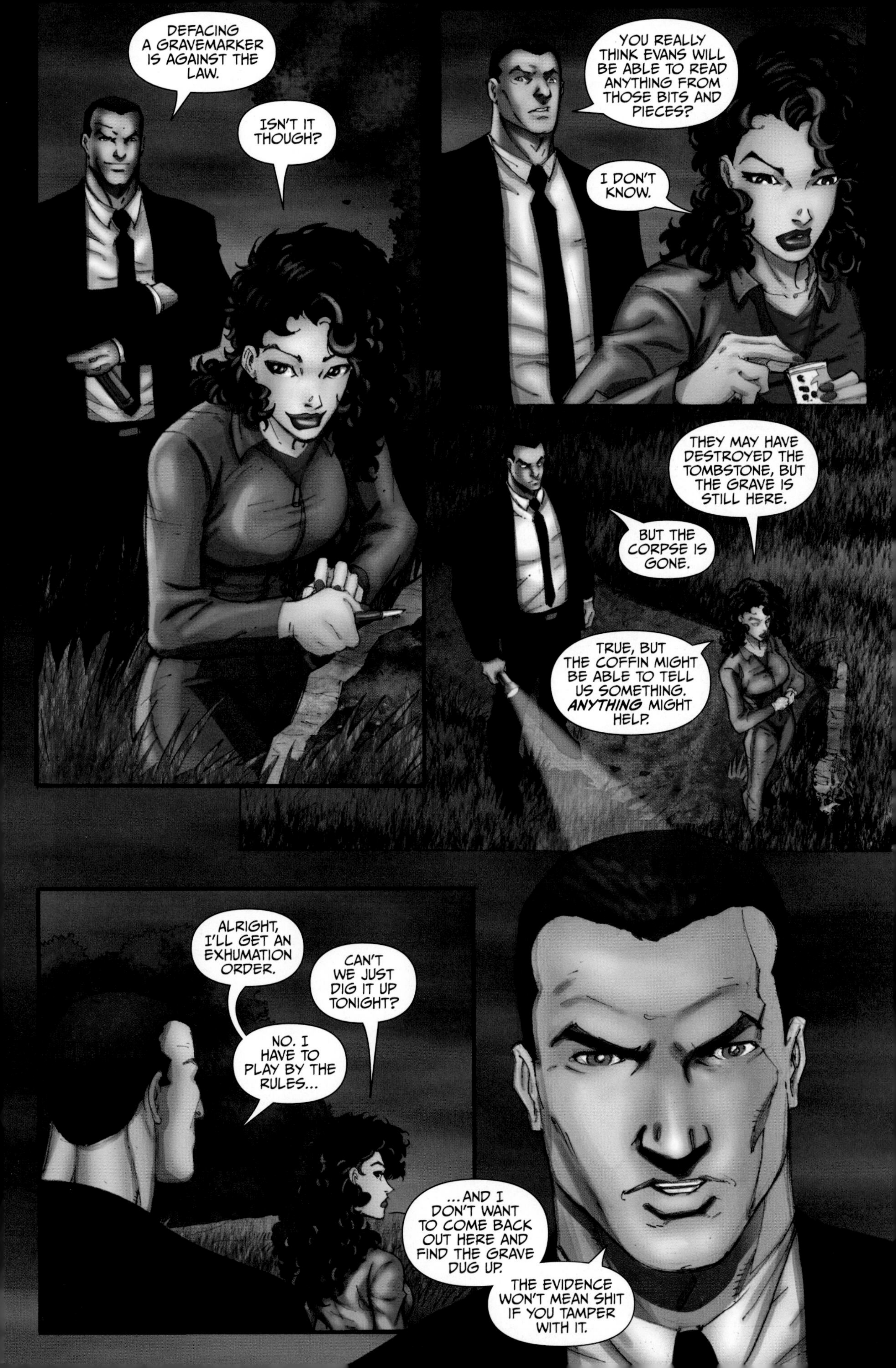
DEFACING A GRAVEMARKER IS AGAINST THE LAW.
ISN'T IT THOUGH?
YOU REALLY THINK EVANS WILL BE ABLE TO READ ANYTHING FROM THOSE BITS AND PIECES?
I DON'T KNOW.
THEY MAY HAVE DESTROYED THE TOMBSTONE, BUT THE GRAVE IS STILL HERE.
BUT THE CORPSE IS GONE.
TRUE, BUT THE COFFIN MIGHT BE ABLE TO TELL US SOMETHING. *ANYTHING* MIGHT HELP.
ALRIGHT, I'LL GET AN EXHUMATION ORDER.
CAN'T WE JUST DIG IT UP TONIGHT?
NO. I HAVE TO PLAY BY THE RULES...
...AND I DON'T WANT TO COME BACK OUT HERE AND FIND THE GRAVE DUG UP.
THE EVIDENCE WON'T MEAN SHIT IF YOU TAMPER WITH IT.

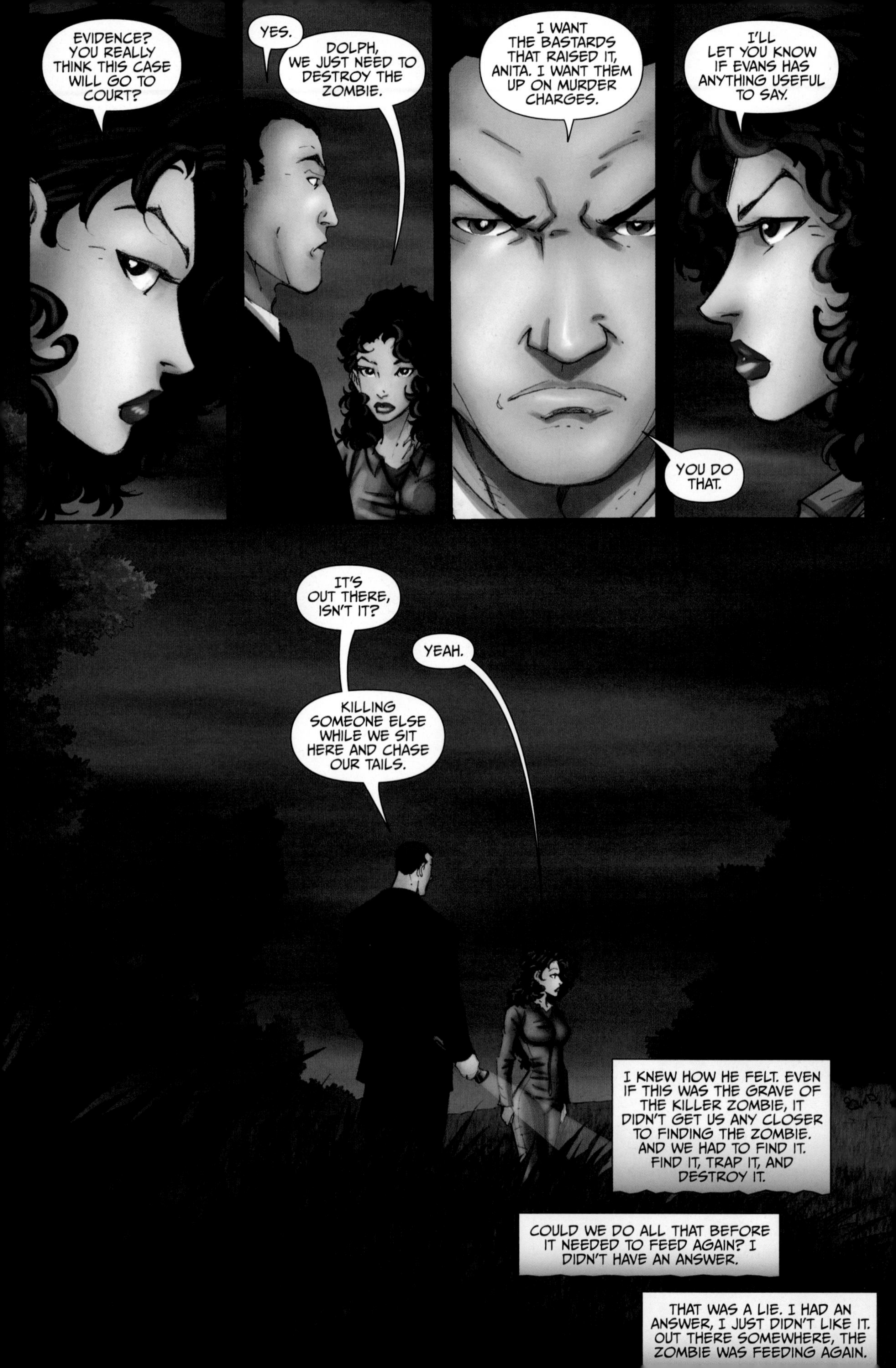
EVIDENCE? YOU REALLY THINK THIS CASE WILL GO TO COURT?
YES.
DOLPH, WE JUST NEED TO DESTROY THE ZOMBIE.
I WANT THE BASTARDS THAT RAISED IT, ANITA. I WANT THEM UP ON MURDER CHARGES.
I'LL LET YOU KNOW IF EVANS HAS ANYTHING USEFUL TO SAY.
YOU DO THAT.
IT'S OUT THERE, ISN'T IT?
YEAH.
KILLING SOMEONE ELSE WHILE WE SIT HERE AND CHASE OUR TAILS.
I KNEW HOW HE FELT. EVEN IF THIS WAS THE GRAVE OF THE KILLER ZOMBIE, IT DIDN'T GET US ANY CLOSER TO FINDING THE ZOMBIE. AND WE HAD TO FIND IT. FIND IT, TRAP IT, AND DESTROY IT.
COULD WE DO ALL THAT BEFORE IT NEEDED TO FEED AGAIN? I DIDN'T HAVE AN ANSWER.
THAT WAS A LIE. I HAD AN ANSWER, I JUST DIDN'T LIKE IT. OUT THERE SOMEWHERE, THE ZOMBIE WAS FEEDING AGAIN.

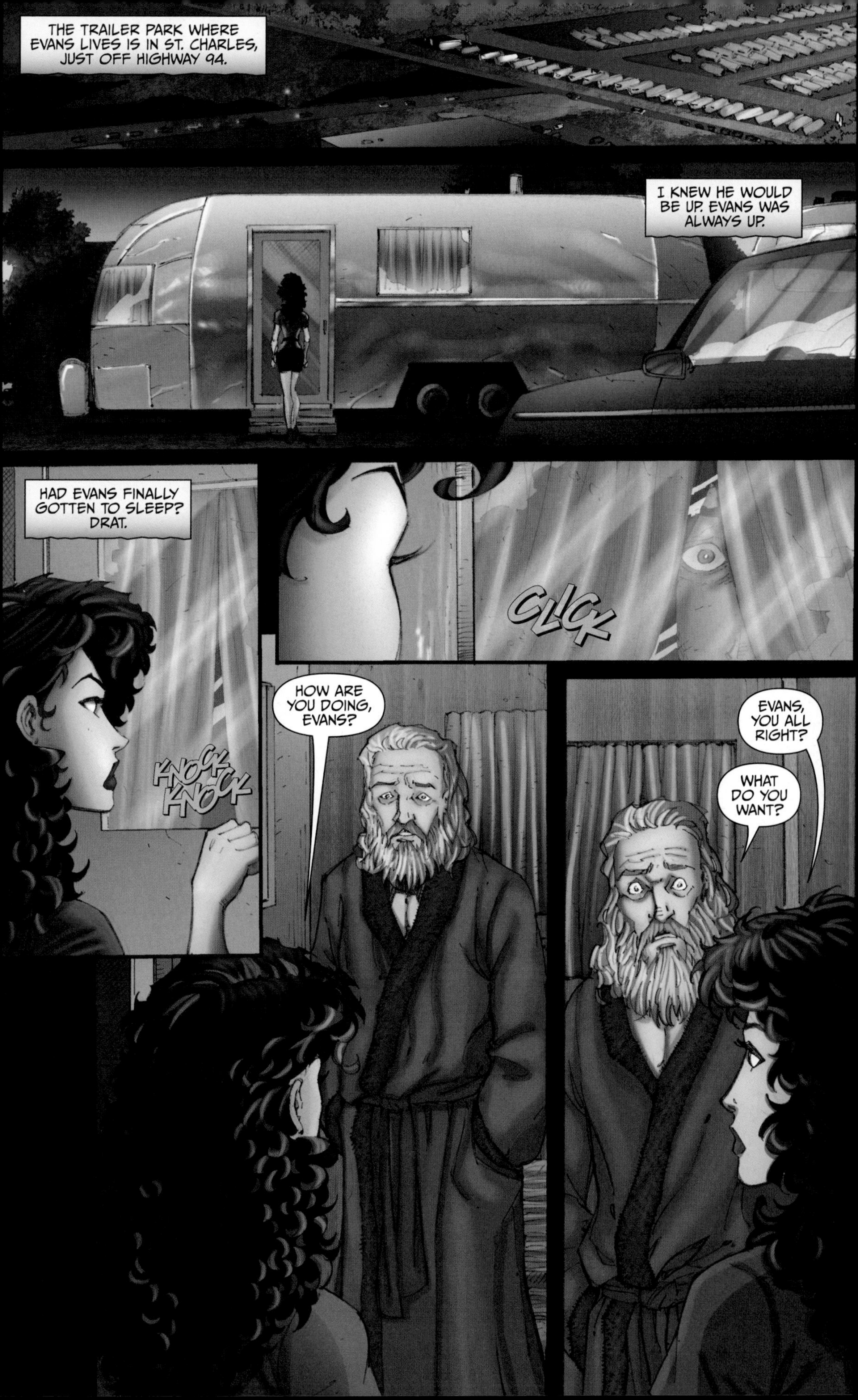
THE TRAILER PARK WHERE EVANS LIVES IS IN ST. CHARLES, JUST OFF HIGHWAY 94.
I KNEW HE WOULD BE UP. EVANS WAS ALWAYS UP.
HAD EVANS FINALLY GOTTEN TO SLEEP? DRAT.
KNOCK KNOCK
CLICK
HOW ARE YOU DOING, EVANS?
EVANS, YOU ALL RIGHT?
WHAT DO YOU WANT?

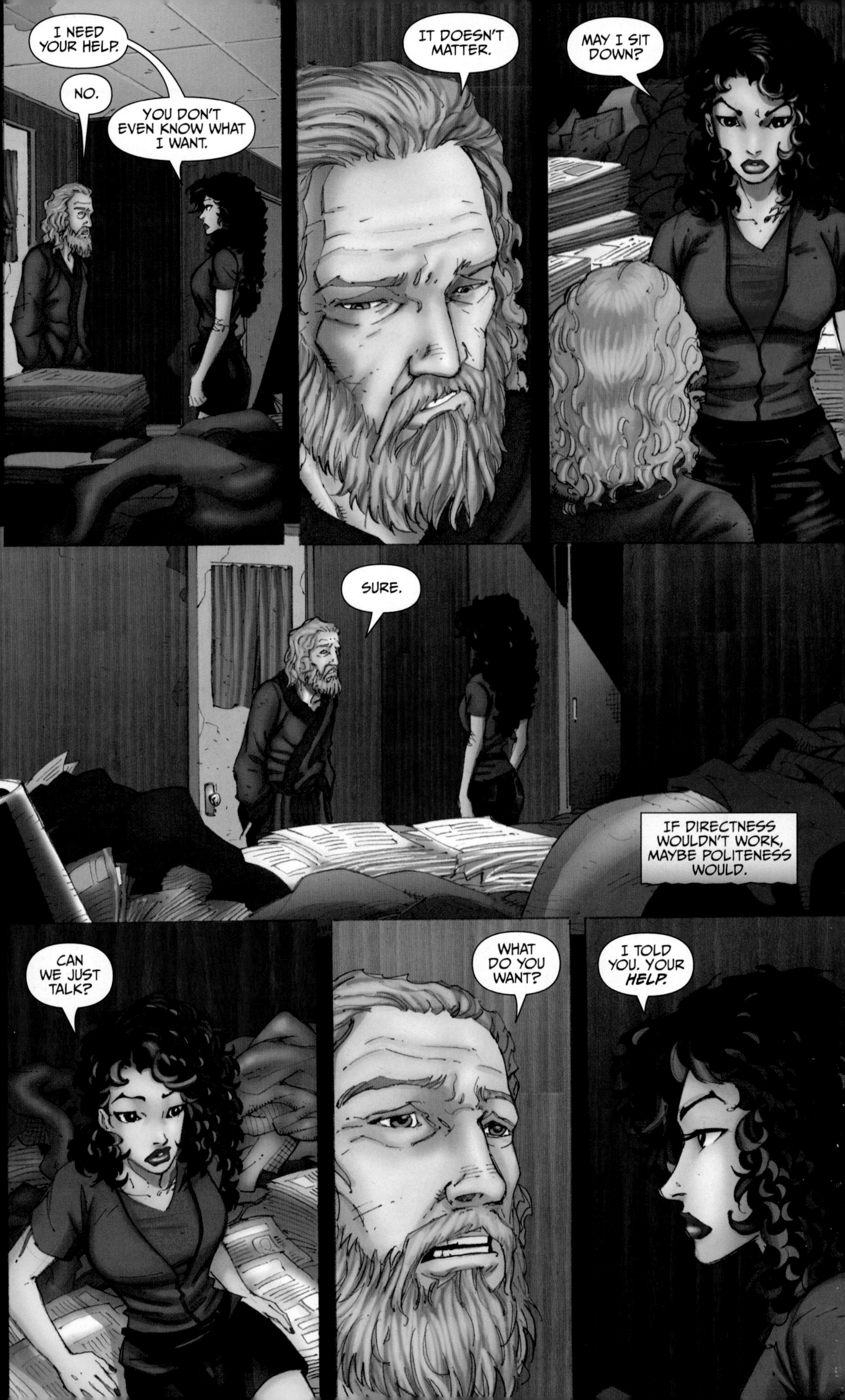
I NEED YOUR HELP.
NO.
YOU DON'T EVEN KNOW WHAT I WANT.
IT DOESN'T MATTER.
MAY I SIT DOWN?
SURE.
IF DIRECTNESS WOULDN'T WORK, MAYBE POLITENESS WOULD.
CAN WE JUST TALK?
WHAT DO YOU WANT?
I TOLD YOU. YOUR *HELP.*

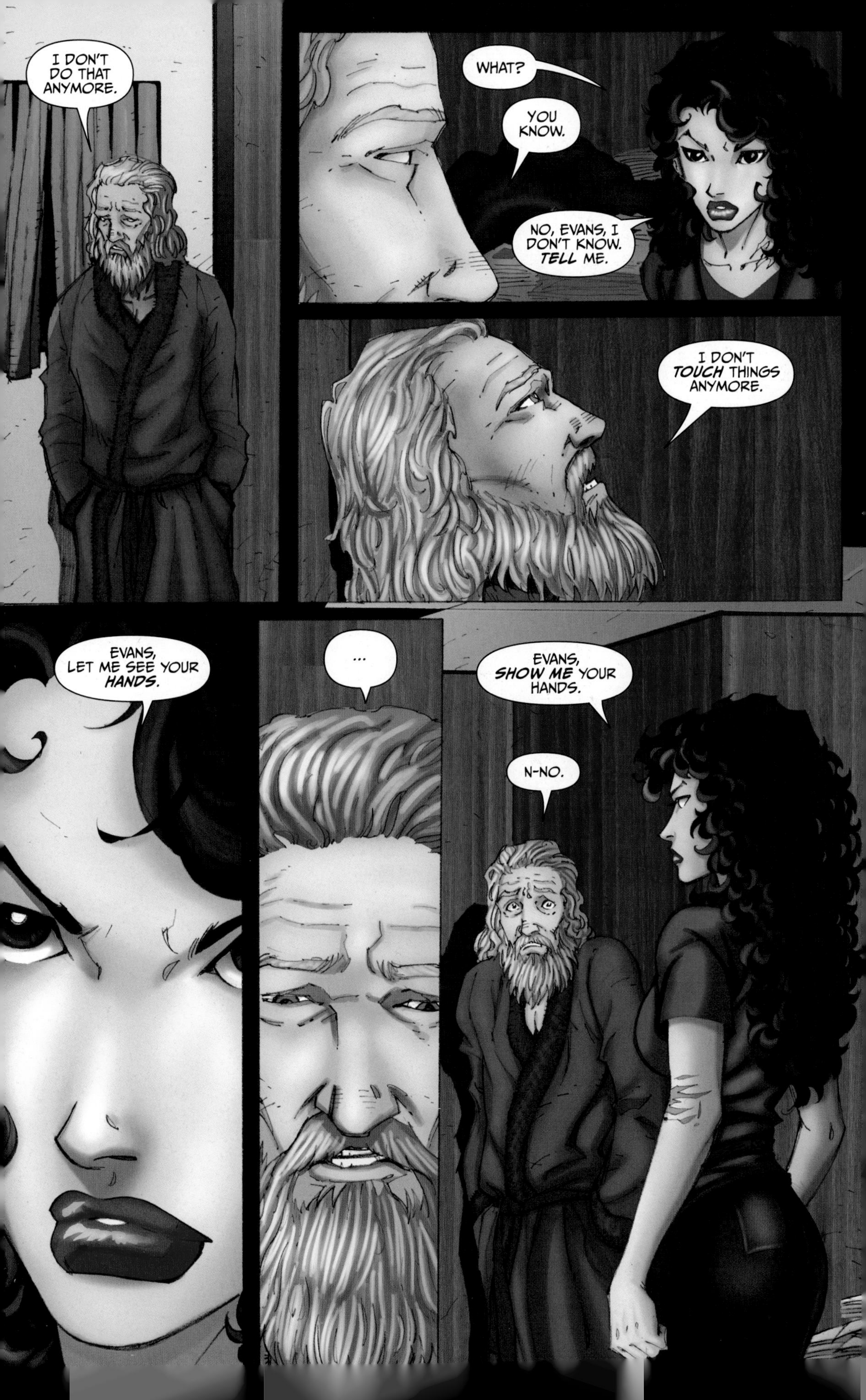
I DON'T DO THAT ANYMORE.
WHAT?
YOU KNOW.
NO, EVANS, I DON'T KNOW. TELL ME.
I DON'T TOUCH THINGS ANYMORE.
EVANS, LET ME SEE YOUR HANDS.
...
EVANS, SHOW ME YOUR HANDS.
N-NO.

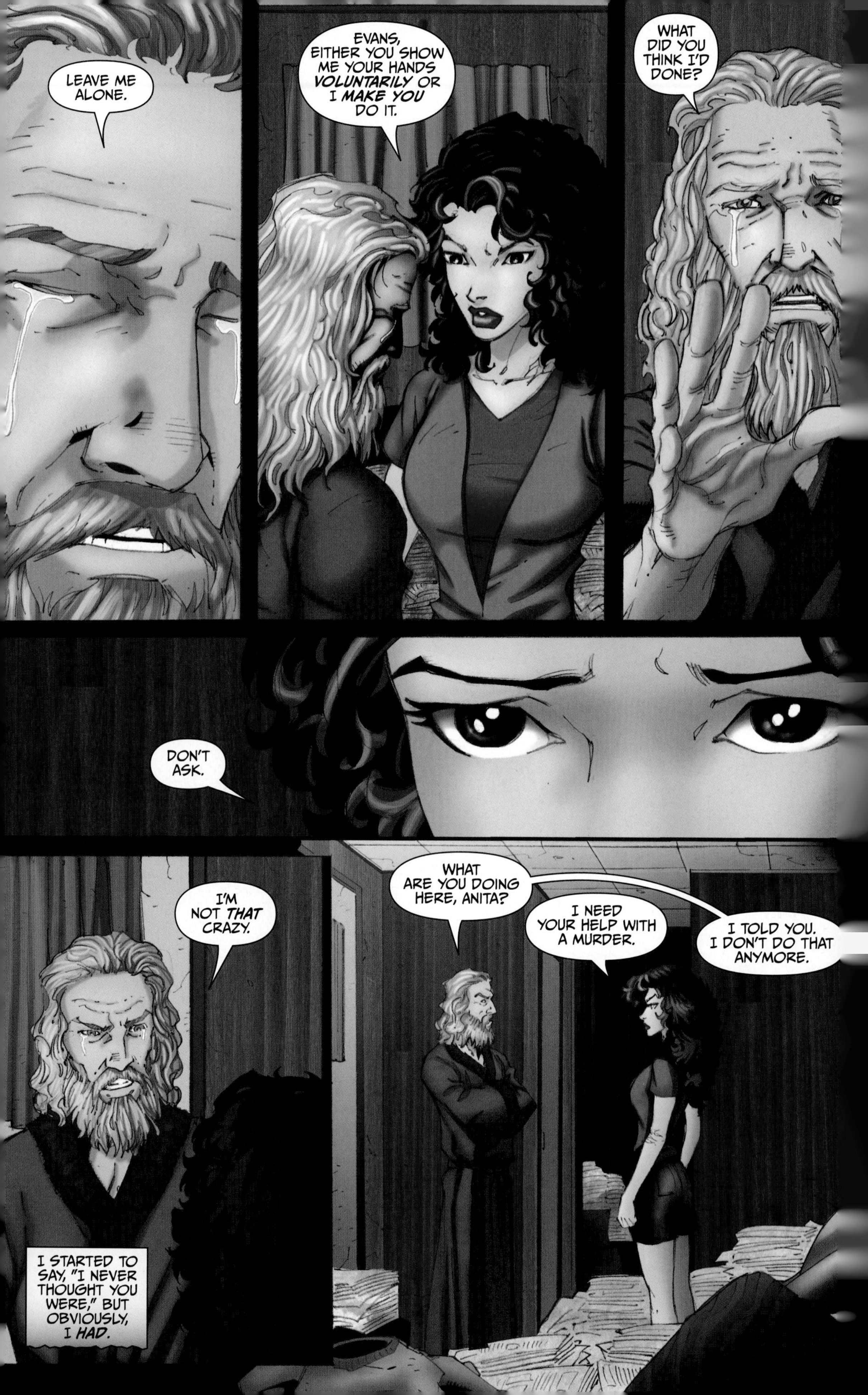
LEAVE ME ALONE.
EVANS, EITHER YOU SHOW ME YOUR HANDS *VOLUNTARILY* OR I *MAKE YOU* DO IT.
WHAT DID YOU THINK I'D DONE?
DON'T ASK.
I'M NOT *THAT* CRAZY.
I STARTED TO SAY, "I NEVER THOUGHT YOU WERE," BUT OBVIOUSLY, I *HAD*.
WHAT ARE YOU DOING HERE, ANITA?
I NEED YOUR HELP WITH A MURDER.
I TOLD YOU. I DON'T DO THAT ANYMORE.

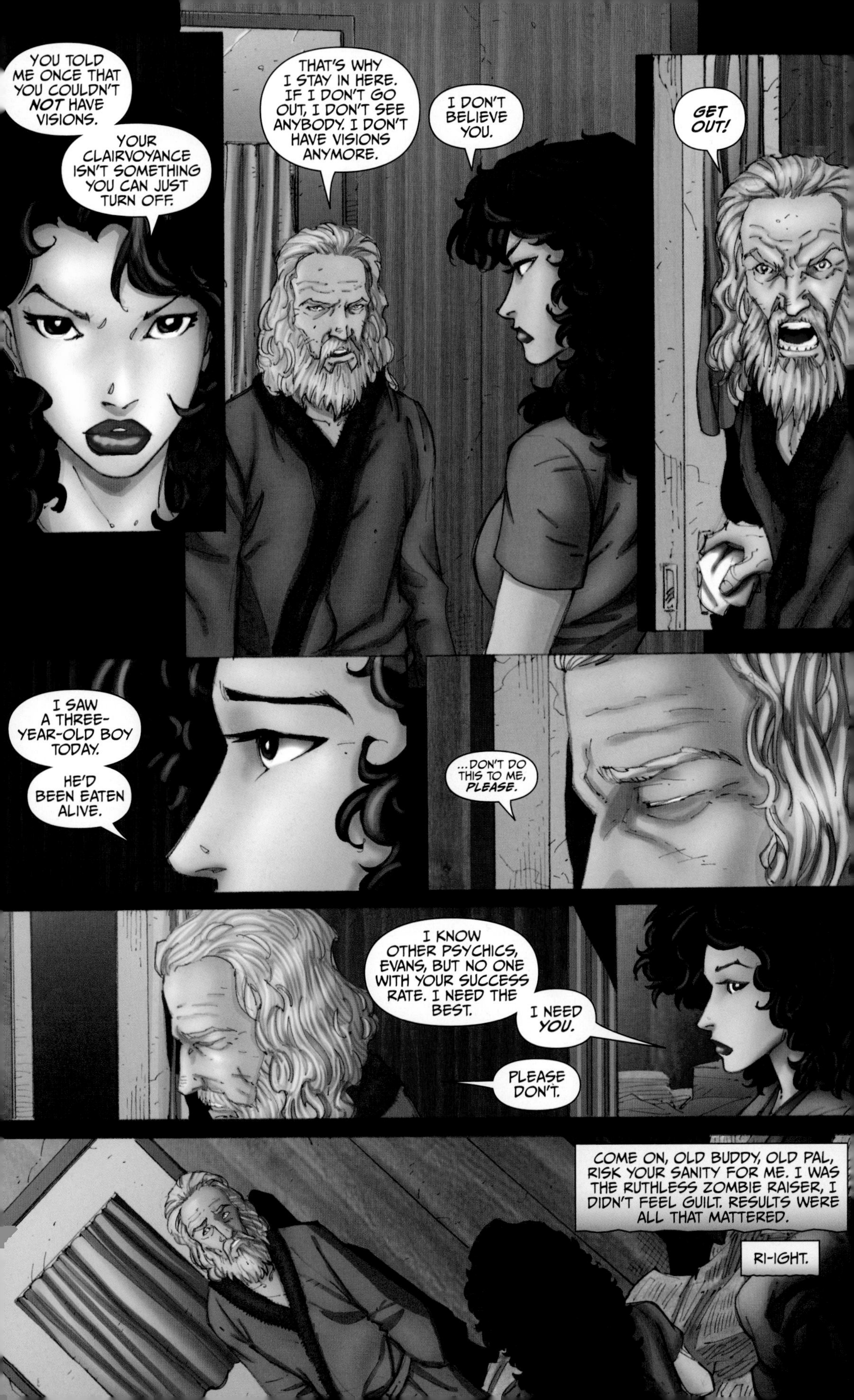
YOU TOLD ME ONCE THAT YOU COULDN'T NOT HAVE VISIONS.
YOUR CLAIRVOYANCE ISN'T SOMETHING YOU CAN JUST TURN OFF.
THAT'S WHY I STAY IN HERE. IF I DON'T GO OUT, I DON'T SEE ANYBODY. I DON'T HAVE VISIONS ANYMORE.
I DON'T BELIEVE YOU.
GET OUT!
I SAW A THREE-YEAR-OLD BOY TODAY.
HE'D BEEN EATEN ALIVE.
...DON'T DO THIS TO ME, PLEASE.
I KNOW OTHER PSYCHICS, EVANS, BUT NO ONE WITH YOUR SUCCESS RATE. I NEED THE BEST.
I NEED YOU.
PLEASE DON'T.
COME ON, OLD BUDDY, OLD PAL, RISK YOUR SANITY FOR ME. I WAS THE RUTHLESS ZOMBIE RAISER, I DIDN'T FEEL GUILT. RESULTS WERE ALL THAT MATTERED.
RI-IGHT.

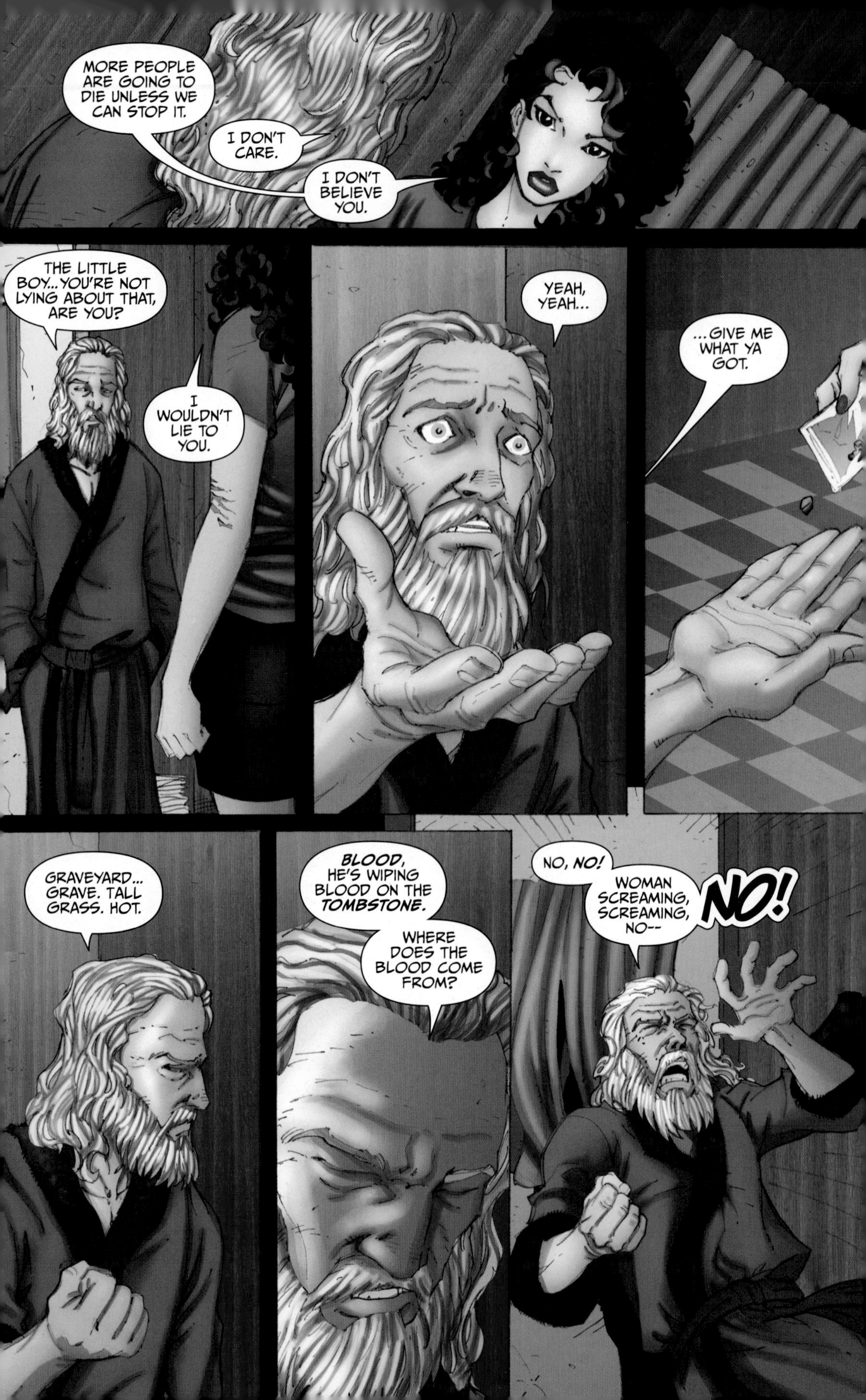
MORE PEOPLE ARE GOING TO DIE UNLESS WE CAN STOP IT.
I DON'T CARE.
I DON'T BELIEVE YOU.
THE LITTLE BOY... YOU'RE NOT LYING ABOUT THAT, ARE YOU?
I WOULDN'T LIE TO YOU.
YEAH, YEAH...
...GIVE ME WHAT YA GOT.
GRAVEYARD... GRAVE. TALL GRASS. HOT.
BLOOD, HE'S WIPING BLOOD ON THE *TOMBSTONE*.
WHERE DOES THE BLOOD COME FROM?
NO, *NO!*
WOMAN SCREAMING, SCREAMING, NO--
NO!

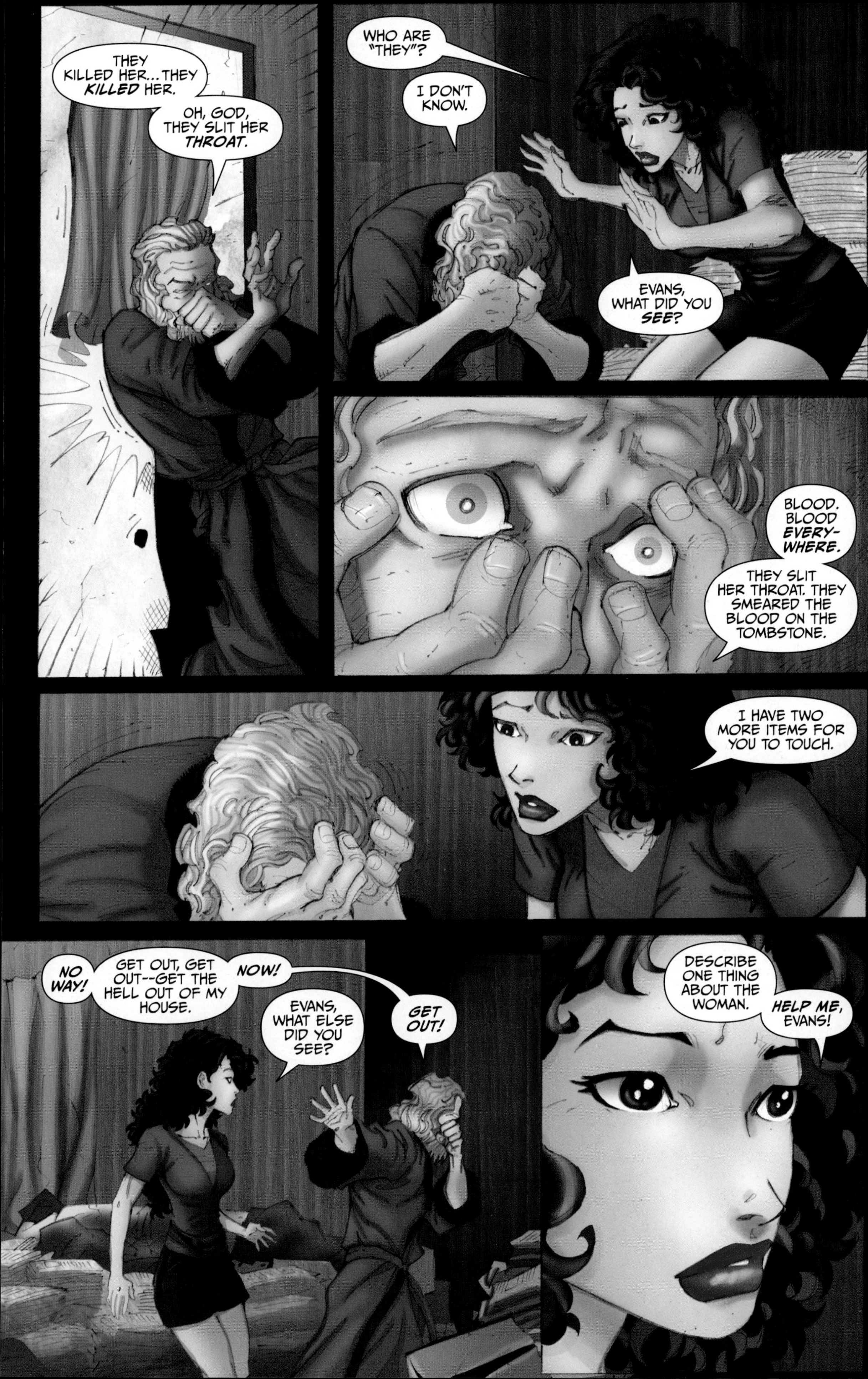
THEY KILLED HER... THEY KILLED HER.
OH, GOD, THEY SLIT HER THROAT.
WHO ARE "THEY"?
I DON'T KNOW.
EVANS, WHAT DID YOU SEE?
BLOOD. BLOOD EVERY-WHERE.
THEY SLIT HER THROAT. THEY SMEARED THE BLOOD ON THE TOMBSTONE.
I HAVE TWO MORE ITEMS FOR YOU TO TOUCH.
NO WAY!
GET OUT, GET OUT--GET THE HELL OUT OF MY HOUSE.
NOW!
EVANS, WHAT ELSE DID YOU SEE?
GET OUT!
DESCRIBE ONE THING ABOUT THE WOMAN.
HELP ME, EVANS!

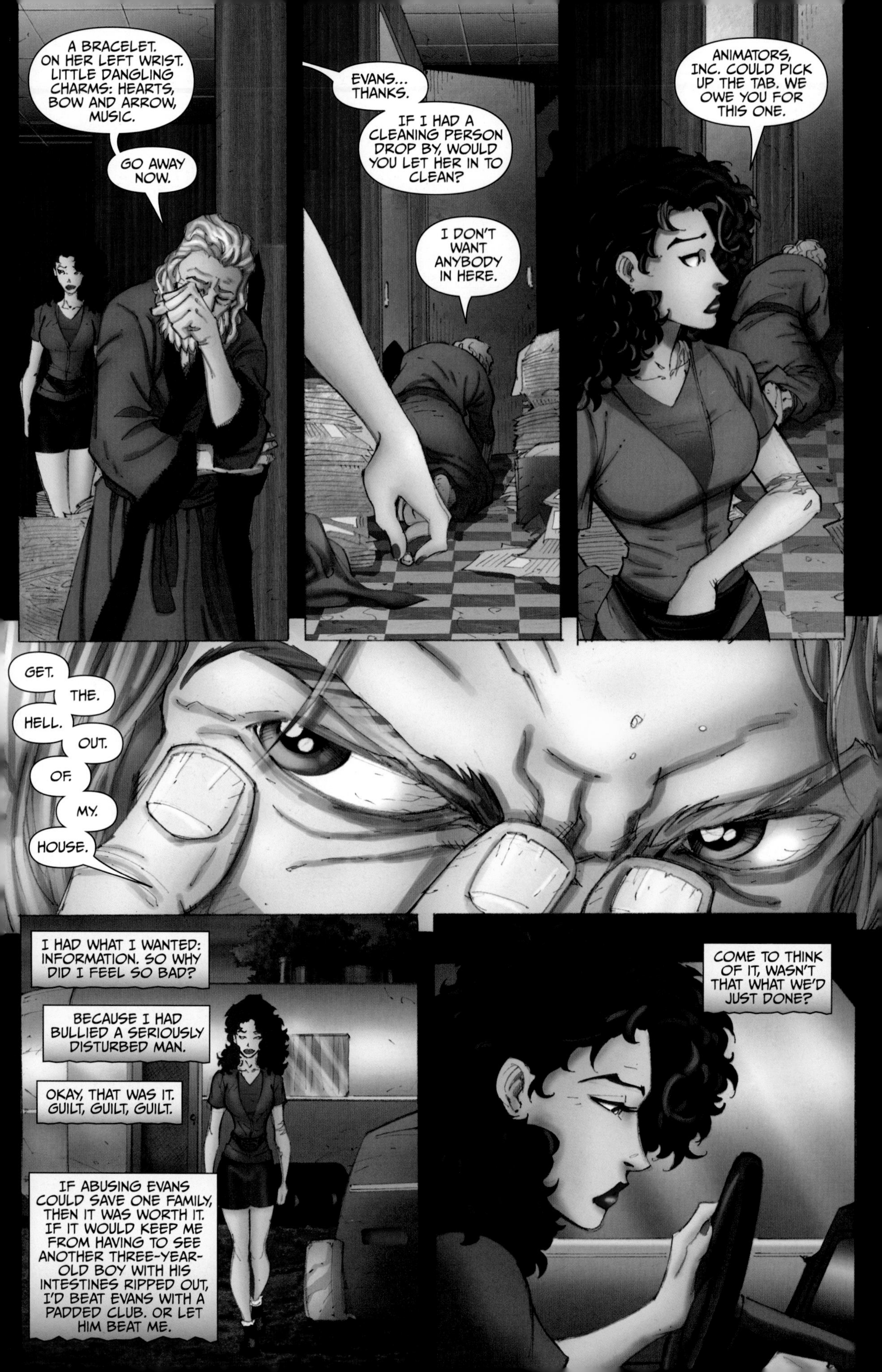
A BRACELET. ON HER LEFT WRIST. LITTLE DANGLING CHARMS: HEARTS, BOW AND ARROW, MUSIC.
GO AWAY NOW.
EVANS... THANKS.
IF I HAD A CLEANING PERSON DROP BY, WOULD YOU LET HER IN TO CLEAN?
I DON'T WANT ANYBODY IN HERE.
ANIMATORS, INC. COULD PICK UP THE TAB. WE OWE YOU FOR THIS ONE.
GET.
THE.
HELL.
OUT.
OF.
MY.
HOUSE.
I HAD WHAT I WANTED: INFORMATION. SO WHY DID I FEEL SO BAD?
BECAUSE I HAD BULLIED A SERIOUSLY DISTURBED MAN.
OKAY, THAT WAS IT. GUILT, GUILT, GUILT.
IF ABUSING EVANS COULD SAVE ONE FAMILY, THEN IT WAS WORTH IT. IF IT WOULD KEEP ME FROM HAVING TO SEE ANOTHER THREE-YEAR-OLD BOY WITH HIS INTESTINES RIPPED OUT, I'D BEAT EVANS WITH A PADDED CLUB. OR LET HIM BEAT ME.
COME TO THINK OF IT, WASN'T THAT WHAT WE'D JUST DONE?

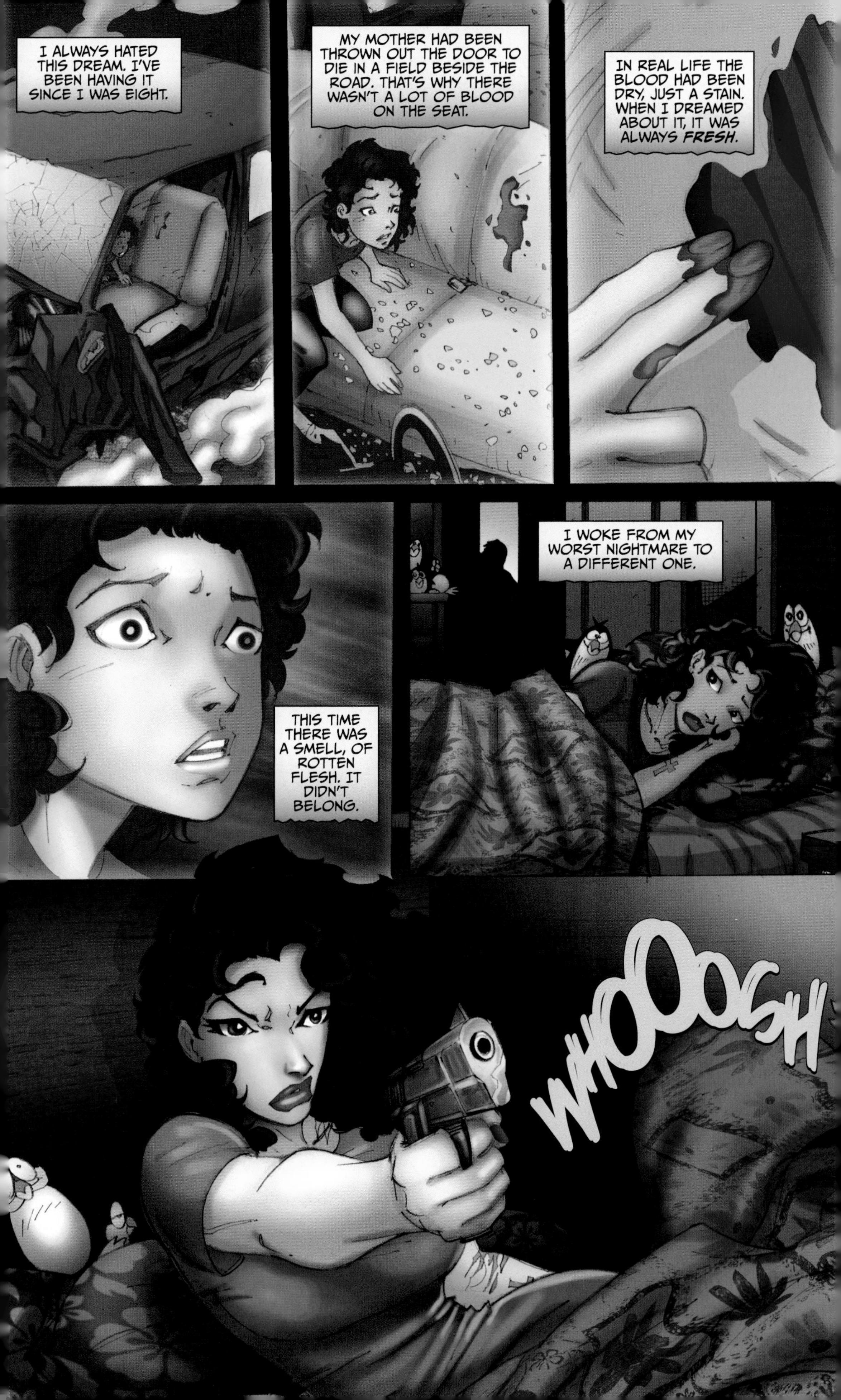
I ALWAYS HATED THIS DREAM. I'VE BEEN HAVING IT SINCE I WAS EIGHT.
MY MOTHER HAD BEEN THROWN OUT THE DOOR TO DIE IN A FIELD BESIDE THE ROAD. THAT'S WHY THERE WASN'T A LOT OF BLOOD ON THE SEAT.
IN REAL LIFE THE BLOOD HAD BEEN DRY, JUST A STAIN. WHEN I DREAMED ABOUT IT, IT WAS ALWAYS *FRESH*.
THIS TIME THERE WAS A SMELL, OF ROTTEN FLESH. IT DIDN'T BELONG.
I WOKE FROM MY WORST NIGHTMARE TO A DIFFERENT ONE.
WHOOOSH

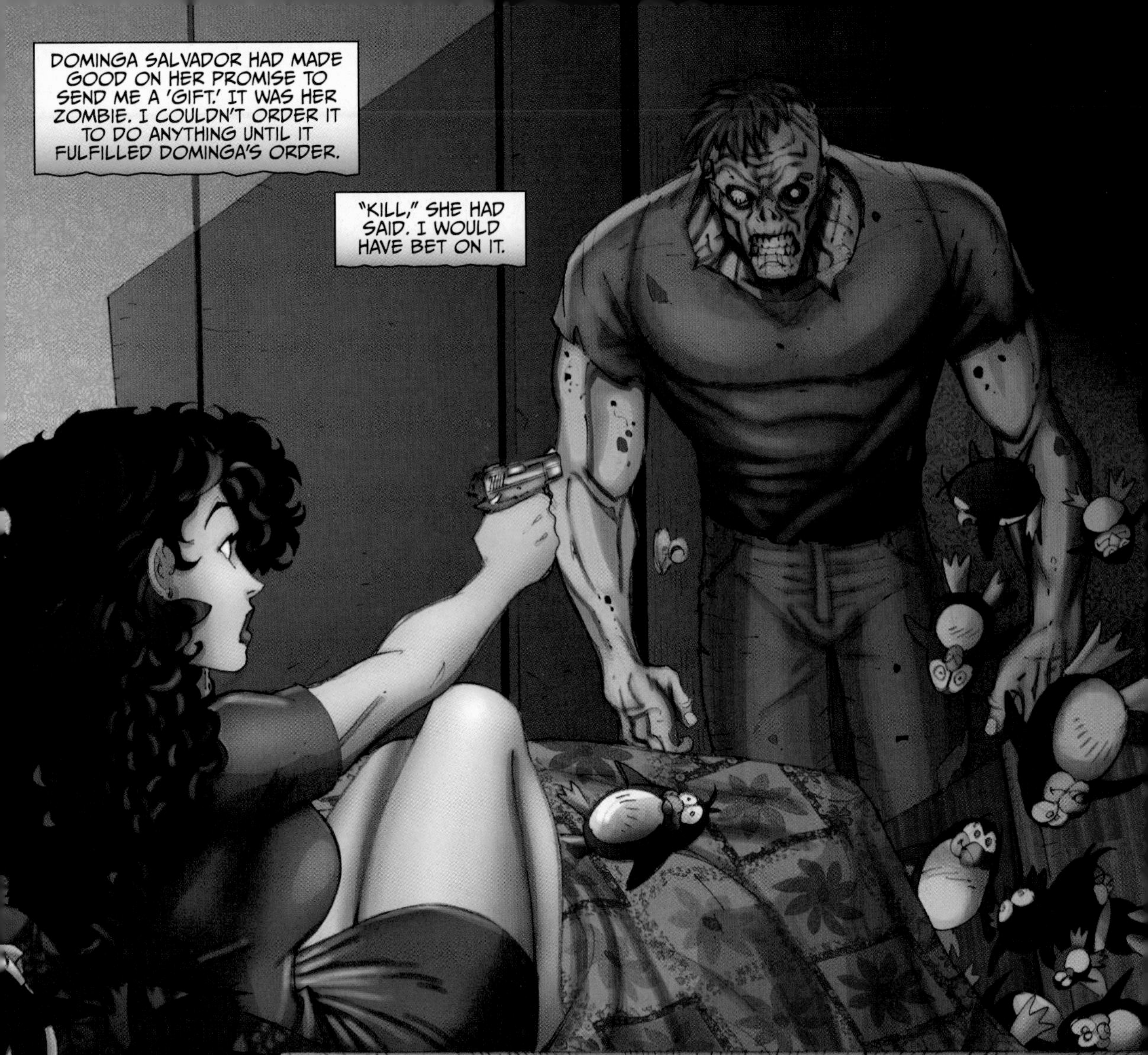
DOMINGA SALVADOR HAD MADE GOOD ON HER PROMISE TO SEND ME A 'GIFT.' IT WAS HER ZOMBIE. I COULDN'T ORDER IT TO DO ANYTHING UNTIL IT FULFILLED DOMINGA'S ORDER.
"KILL," SHE HAD SAID. I WOULD HAVE BET ON IT.

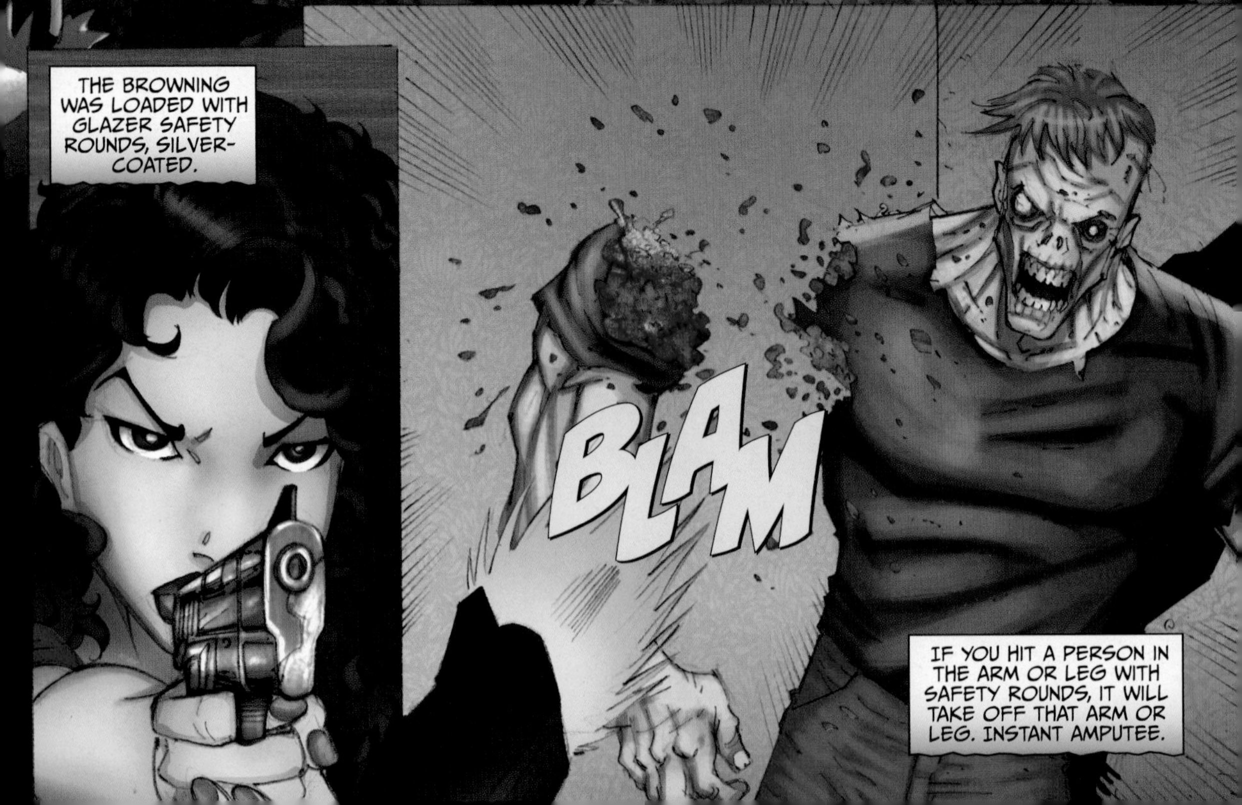
THE BROWNING WAS LOADED WITH GLAZER SAFETY ROUNDS, SILVER-COATED.
BLAM
IF YOU HIT A PERSON IN THE ARM OR LEG WITH SAFETY ROUNDS, IT WILL TAKE OFF THAT ARM OR LEG. INSTANT AMPUTEE.

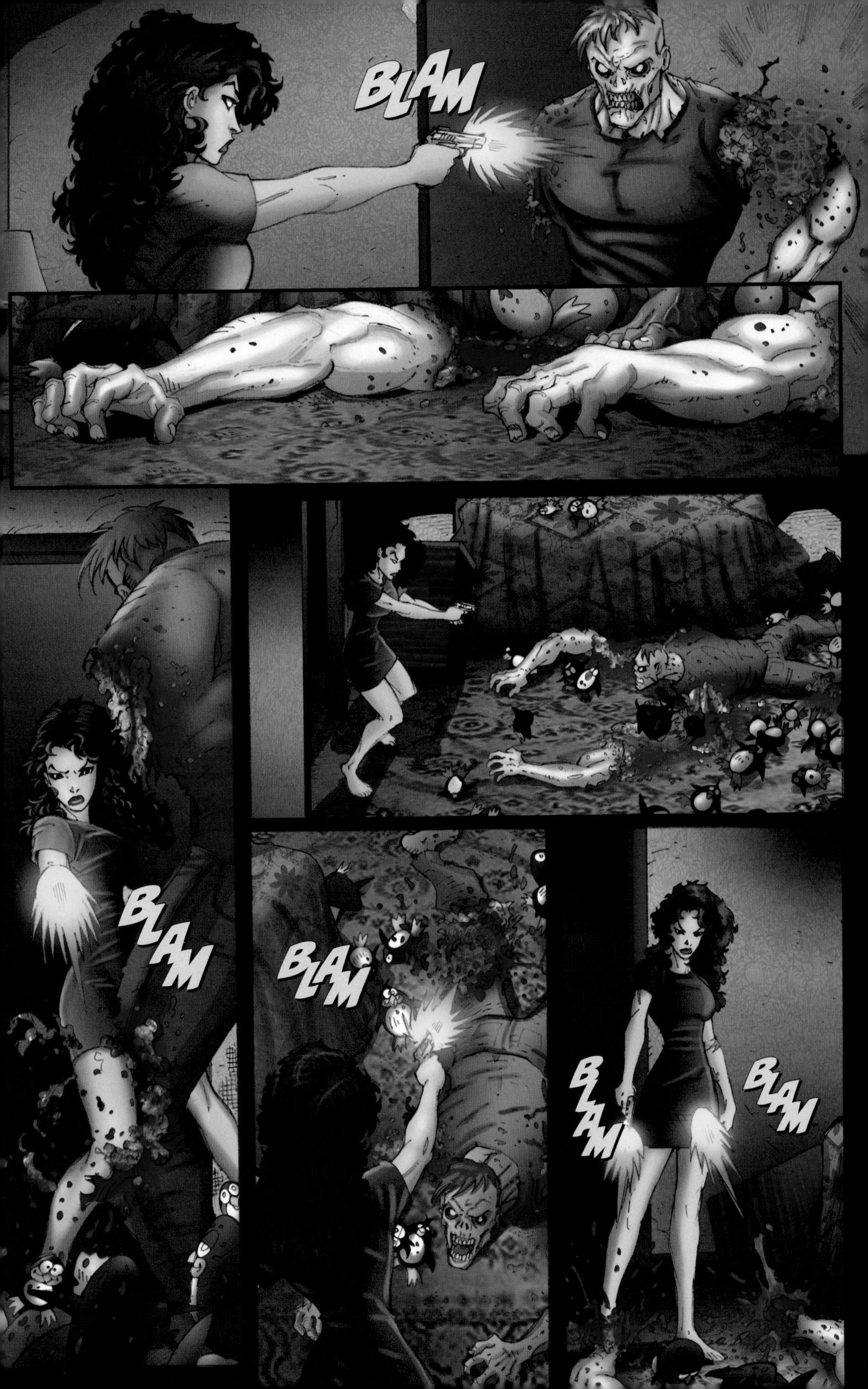
BLAM
BLAM
BLAM
BLAM
BLAM

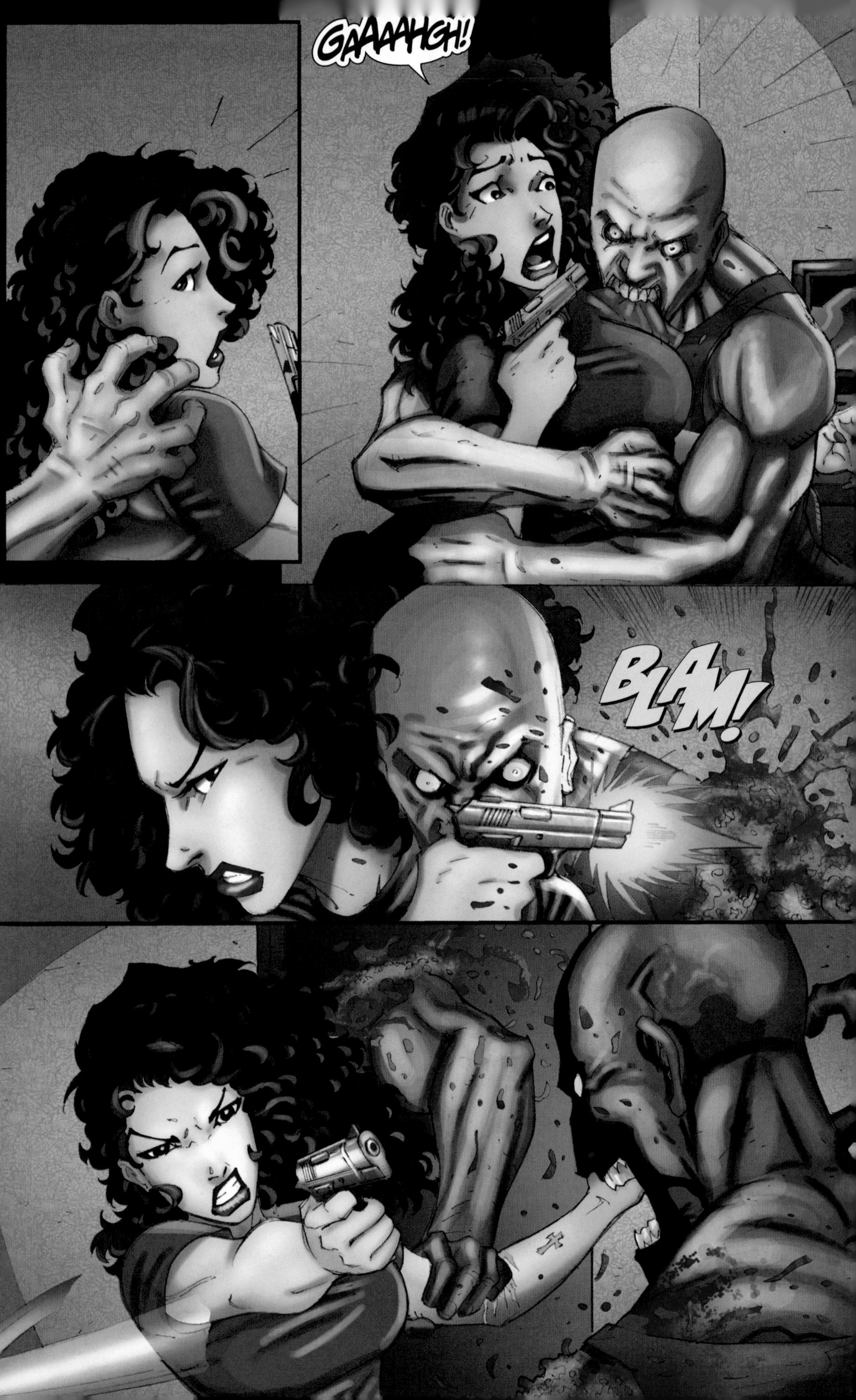
GAAAAHGH!
BLAM!

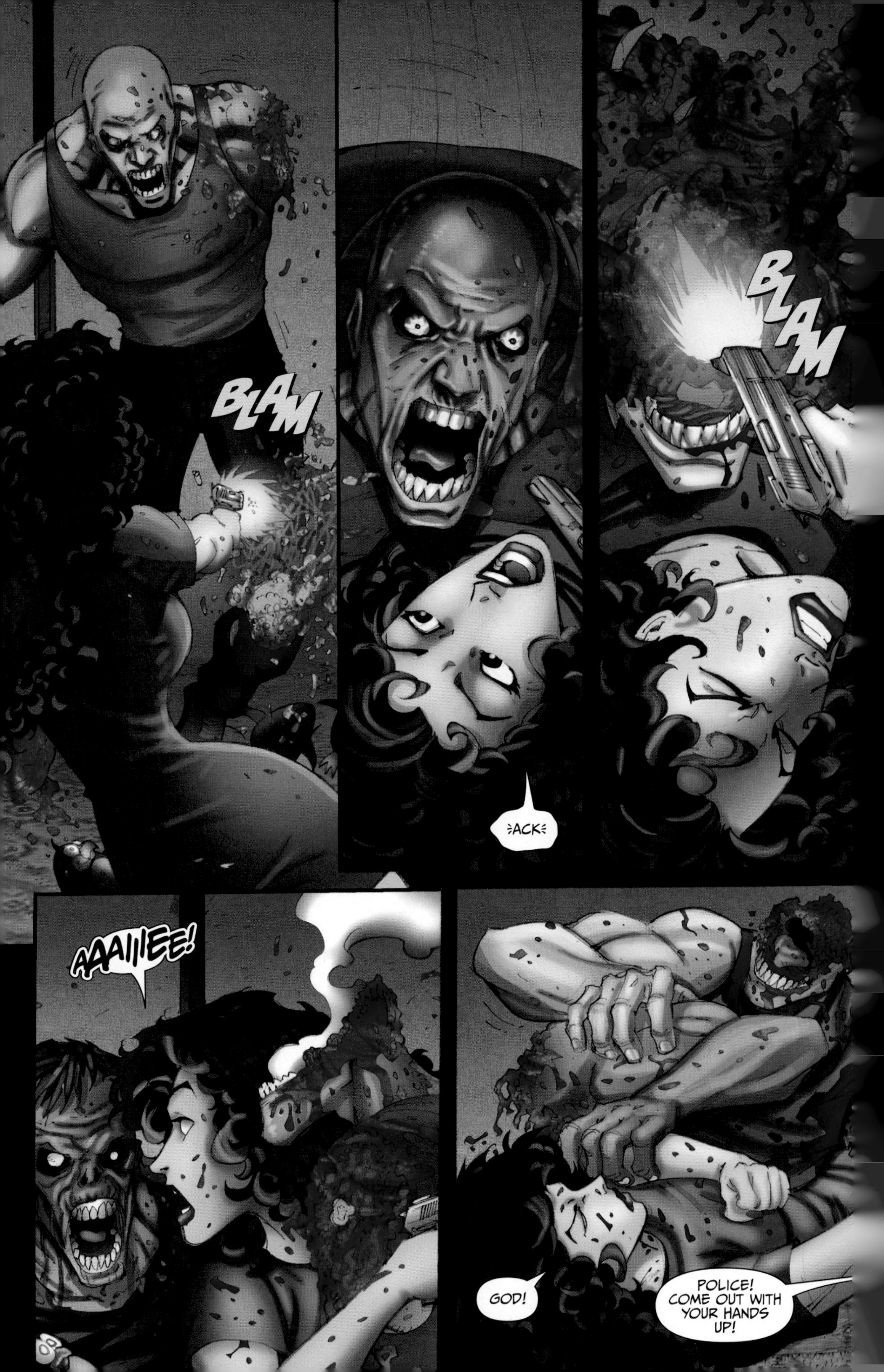
BLAM
ACK
BLAM BLAM
AAAIIIEE!
GOD!
POLICE! COME OUT WITH YOUR HANDS UP!

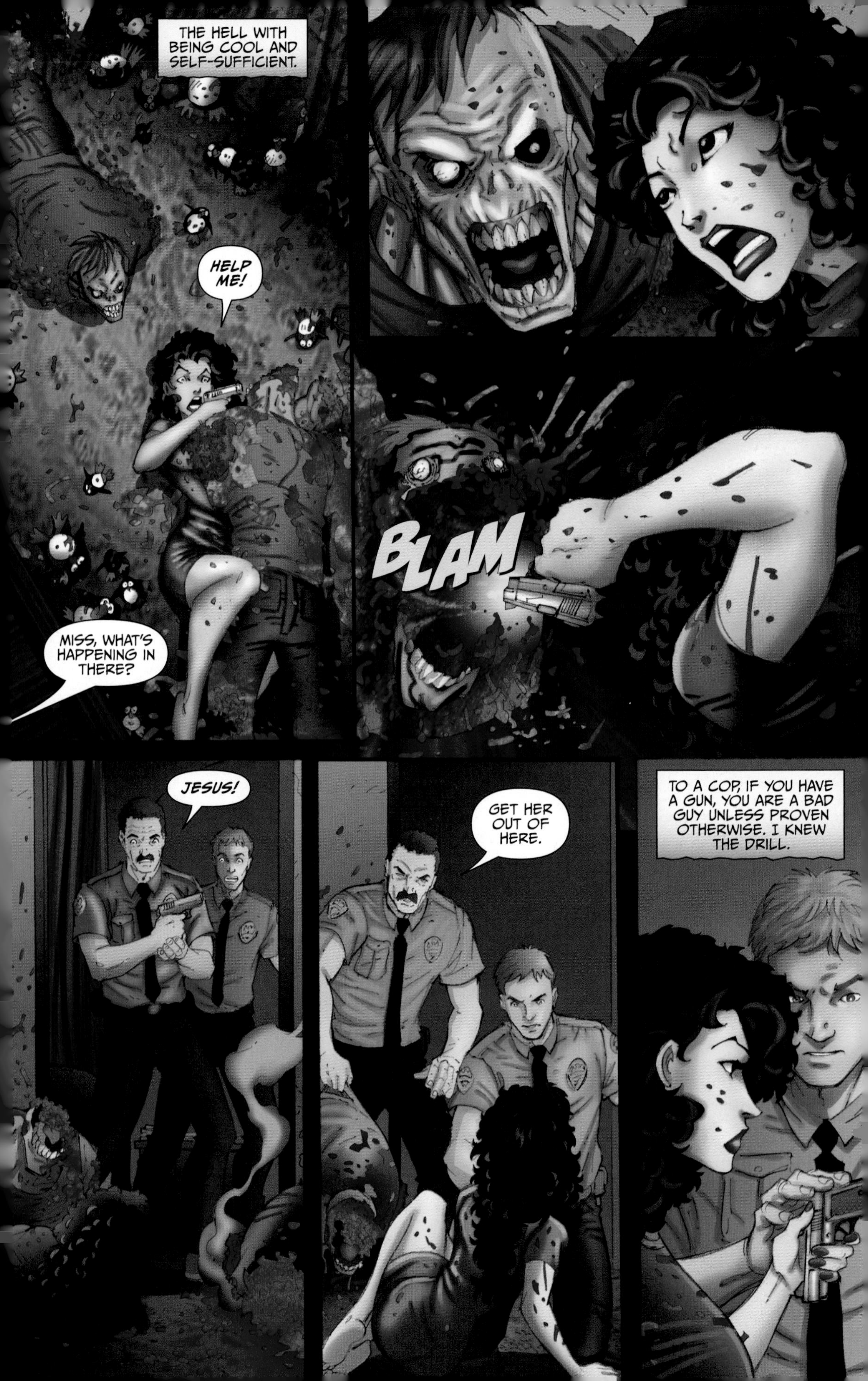
THE HELL WITH BEING COOL AND SELF-SUFFICIENT.
HELP ME!
MISS, WHAT'S HAPPENING IN THERE?
BLAM
JESUS!
GET HER OUT OF HERE.
TO A COP, IF YOU HAVE A GUN, YOU ARE A BAD GUY UNLESS PROVEN OTHERWISE. I KNEW THE DRILL.

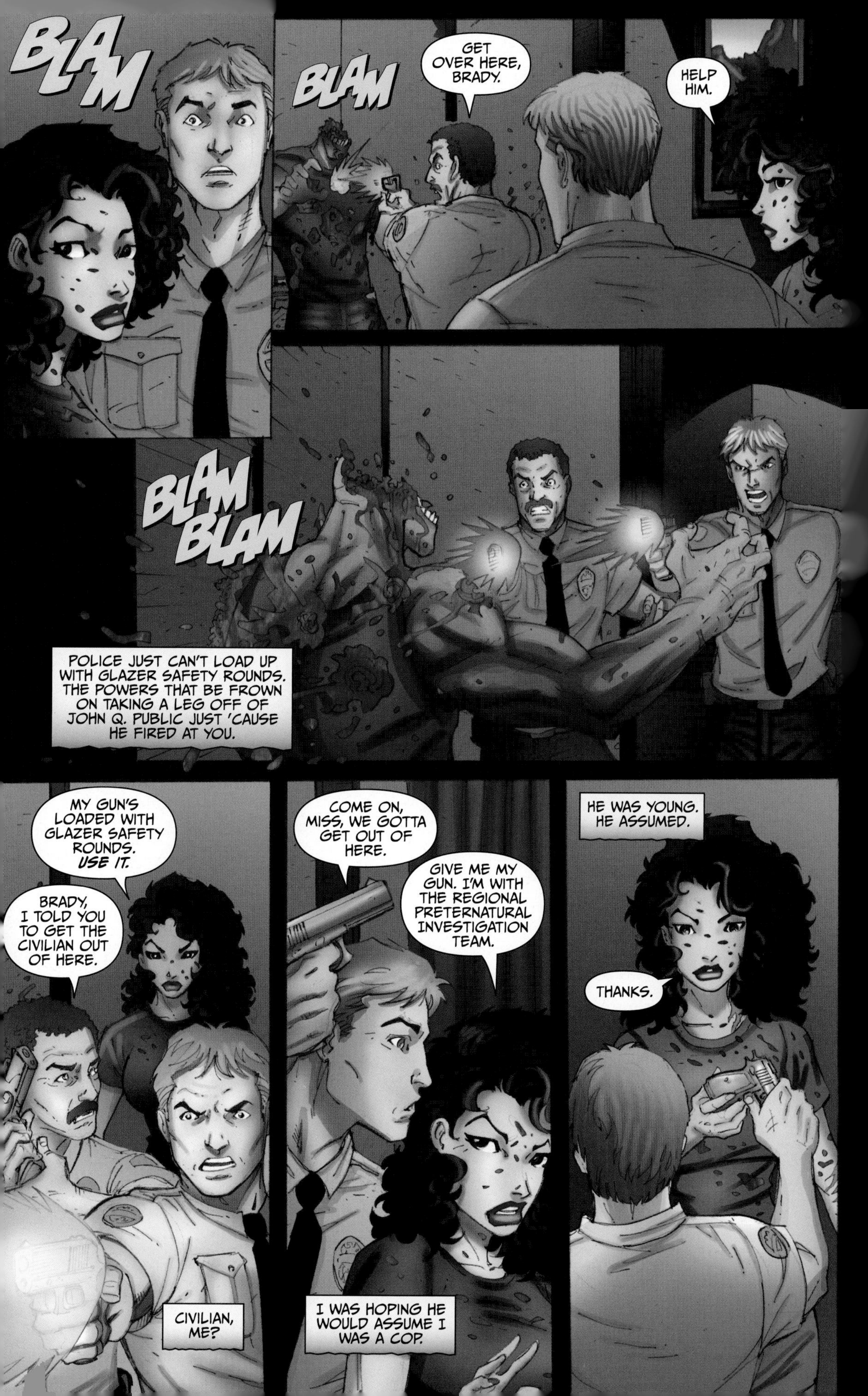
BLAM
BLAM
GET OVER HERE, BRADY.
HELP HIM.
BLAM BLAM
POLICE JUST CAN'T LOAD UP WITH GLAZER SAFETY ROUNDS. THE POWERS THAT BE FROWN ON TAKING A LEG OFF OF JOHN Q. PUBLIC JUST 'CAUSE HE FIRED AT YOU.
MY GUN'S LOADED WITH GLAZER SAFETY ROUNDS. USE IT.
BRADY, I TOLD YOU TO GET THE CIVILIAN OUT OF HERE.
CIVILIAN, ME?
COME ON, MISS, WE GOTTA GET OUT OF HERE.
GIVE ME MY GUN. I'M WITH THE REGIONAL PRETERNATURAL INVESTIGATION TEAM.
I WAS HOPING HE WOULD ASSUME I WAS A COP.
HE WAS YOUNG. HE ASSUMED.
THANKS.

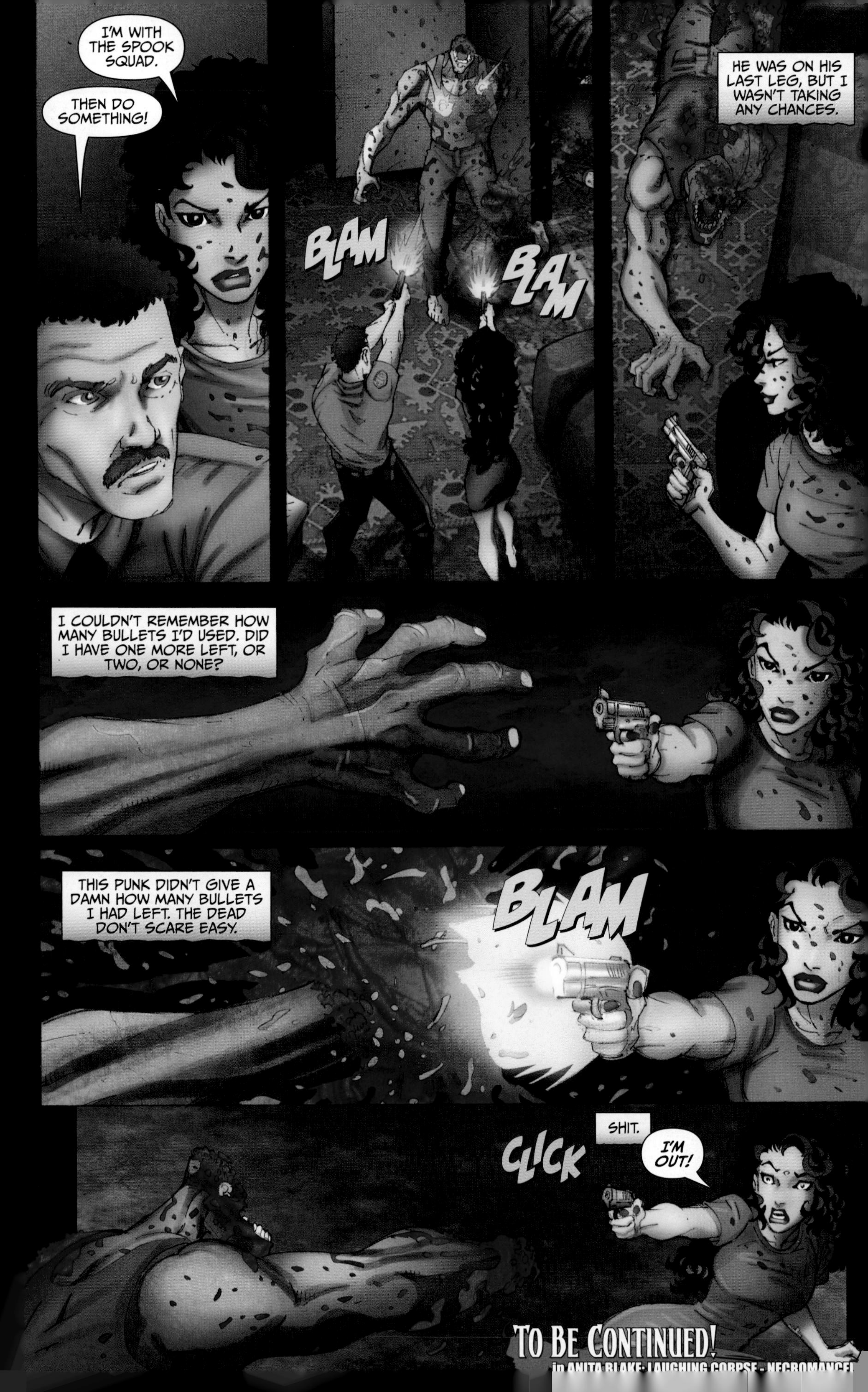
I'M WITH THE SPOOK SQUAD.
THEN DO SOMETHING!
BLAM
BLAM
HE WAS ON HIS LAST LEG, BUT I WASN'T TAKING ANY CHANCES.
I COULDN'T REMEMBER HOW MANY BULLETS I'D USED. DID I HAVE ONE MORE LEFT, OR TWO, OR NONE?
THIS PUNK DIDN'T GIVE A DAMN HOW MANY BULLETS I HAD LEFT. THE DEAD DON'T SCARE EASY.
BLAM
CLICK
SHIT.
I'M OUT!
TO BE CONTINUED!
in ANITA BLAKE: LAUGHING CORPSE - NECROMANCE

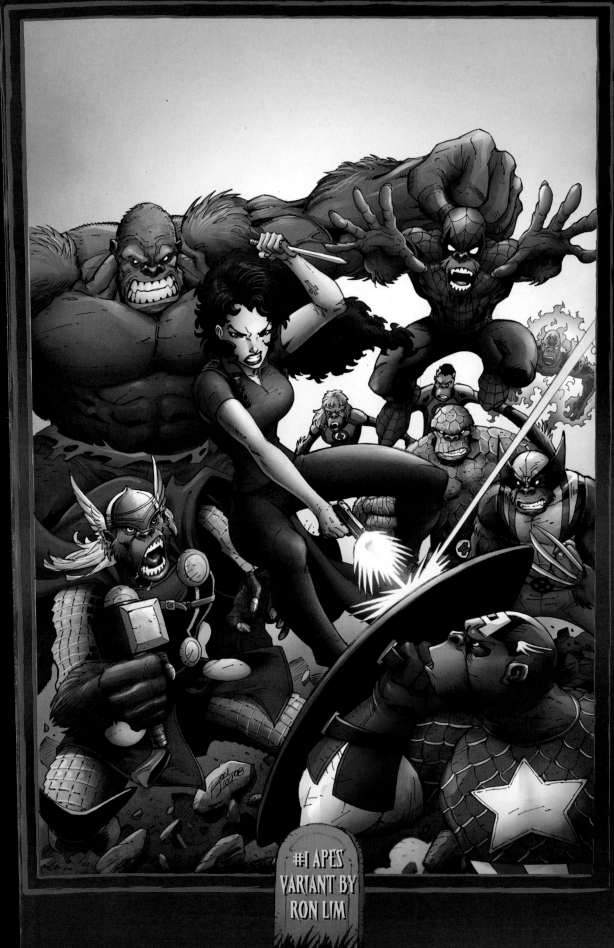

#1 APES
VARIANT BY
RON LIM